MOSCOW AND THE THIRD WORLD UNDER GORBACHEV

About the Book and Authors

Soviet policy toward the developing world has changed dramatically since Mikhail Gorbachev assumed power in 1985. This book explores the shape and scope of Moscow's "new thinking" in its Third World context—highlighted by the USSR's surprising withdrawal from Afghanistan in 1988. Other policies examined include putting pressure on allies such as Cuba and Vietnam to end their military involvement in Angola and Cambodia respectively; expanding relations with old adversaries such as China, South Korea, South Africa, and Israel; and pursuing closer ties to developed Third World countries while reducing support for weak states.

After reviewing the foreign policy record Gorbachev inherited, the authors assess his economic and strategic priorities in the diplomatic arena and their impact on specific regions. Each regional chapter reviews past Soviet policy, examines the rationale for Gorbachev's present initiatives, and weighs future trends—including implications for U.S.-Soviet relations.

Thoroughly updated through the winter of 1990, this book provides the most current analysis available of a vital and continuously evolving part of the world.

W. Raymond Duncan is Distinguished Teaching Professor at the State University of New York, Brockport. **Carolyn McGiffert Ekedahl** is a senior analyst with the Central Intelligence Agency.

MOSCOW AND THE THIRD WORLD UNDER GORBACHEV

W. Raymond Duncan
and Carolyn McGiffert Ekedahl

Westview Press
BOULDER, SAN FRANCISCO, & OXFORD

The views expressed herein are those of the authors and not those of the U.S. government.

Published in 1990 in the United States of America by Westview Press, Inc., 5500 Central Avenue, Boulder, Colorado 80301, and in the United Kingdom by Westview Press, Inc., 36 Lonsdale Road, Summertown, Oxford OX2 7EW

Library of Congress Cataloging-in-Publication Data
Duncan, W. Raymond (Walter Raymond), 1936–
Moscow and the Third World under Gorbachev / W. Raymond Duncan and Carolyn McGiffert Ekedahl.
p. cm.
Includes bibliographical references.
ISBN 0-8133-0518-7. ISBN 0-8133-1052-0 (pbk.)
1. Developing countries—Foreign relations—Soviet Union.
2. Soviet Union—Foreign relations—Developing countries. 3. Soviet Union—Foreign relations—1985- . 4. Gorbachev, Mikhail Sergeevich, 1931- . I. Ekedahl, Carolyn McGiffert, II. Title.
D888.S65D855 1990
327.4701724—dc20

89-78300
CIP

Printed and bound in the United States of America

The paper used in this publication meets the requirements of the American National Standard for Permanence of Paper for Printed Library Materials Z39.48-1984.

10 9 8 7 6 5 4 3 2

CONTENTS

TABLES AND MAPS

Tables

Maps

PREFACE AND ACKNOWLEDGMENTS

Understanding Soviet relations with the Third World has challenged Western students and policy-makers since Nikita Khrushchev first courted emerging nationalist leaders in the mid-1950s. With the rise to power of Mikhail Gorbachev thirty years later, the subject has generated renewed debate. Some observers see Soviet foreign policy as substantively changed under Gorbachev. From this perspective, the underlying assumptions, basic concepts, and policy perceptions guiding Soviet foreign policy since World War II have been scrapped. Writing in *Foreign Affairs* in 1989, Robert Legvold, Director of the W. Averell Harriman Institute of the Advanced Study of the Soviet Union, argues that:

> A revolution is underway in Soviet foreign policy greater than any in the postwar period, indeed greater than any since Lenin in the early years of his regime accepted the failure of the pan-European revolution and allowed the Soviet Union to join in the game of nations.[1]

That Soviet foreign policy may be undergoing change of revolutionary proportions is suggested by Gorbachev's claim in his historic speech to the United Nations in December 1988 that "the primacy of universal human values has been substituted for the battle between communism and democratic capitalism." Gorbachev has publicly expressed his view that class conflict, ideological confrontation, one-sided reliance on military power, and the use of force as an instrument of foreign policy are no longer viable and must be replaced by a reduction in East-West tension and an end to the Cold War. Many of those who hold the view that Gorbachev has forged a revolution in foreign policy tend to believe the West should cooperate with the Soviets to resolve key points of tension and thereby help Gorbachev with his reforms.

A second school of thought is more cautious in assessing Soviet foreign policy under Gorbachev, viewing it essentially as a continuation of previous decision-making imperatives, operating within a traditional conceptual framework. From this perspective, Gorbachev's Third World approach continues many of Moscow's older policies and strategic-military objectives, although new tactics have been adopted here and there—as in the Afghanistan pull-out. Alvin Z. Rubinstein, a top scholar in the field of Soviet foreign policy, writes:

> Soviet policy remains, in the main, unchanged. There has been essential continuity, with increments of intensity in a number of areas. Above all, there is no convincing evidence that Gorbachev is disposed to disengage from entrenched positions in the Third World because of a desire to focus on domestic problems or out of pessimism over the prospects of countries with a "socialist system" or out of a desire to improve relations with the United States.[2]

In support of this argument, Rubinstein cites Soviet efforts to maintain a presence in Afghanistan, continue close contacts with India ("the centerpiece of Soviet strategy in the Third World"), and retain solid relations with old clients, such as Syria, Libya, Algeria, and the People's Democratic Republic of Yemen (PDRY)—all of which still receive Soviet arms.[3]

A third school of thought remains even more suspicious of Soviet intentions,[4] arguing that, in the past, the Soviets have used "peace offensives" to gain time and advantage. Observers of this school believe that history is cyclical and that Moscow eventually will resume its aggressive policies. They support their thesis by arguing that Gorbachev's efforts to rejuvenate the Soviet system will fail. They tend to think that Western powers should not move quickly to provide support to Gorbachev and should be careful to protect their vital interests against the traditional Russian tendency to expand.

The view adopted here is very close to the first—that Gorbachev's policy initiatives do in fact represent a dramatic shift.[5] At the same time, we believe that the same fundamental forces shape current policy formation and execution as have shaped them in the past—and that these forces include pragmatism, realism, and power politics. The changes Gorbachev is orchestrating are designed to maximize his ability to secure vital Soviet interests—national security, economic development, and protection of political sovereignty. These changes constitute a substantive and fundamental reorientation of Moscow's approach, including that to the Third World.

What is striking about Gorbachev's stance is its heightened pragmatism and the downgrading of ideological formulas and perceptions. This shift raises a number of questions. Does Gorbachev's brand of Third World politics represent a fundamental change in Soviet views about the USSR's role and strategy toward the developing countries? Will this shift in emphasis survive after Gorbachev? How has Moscow redefined its Third World presence? What are the implications of these new Soviet policies for Western diplomacy? How does Moscow seek to advance its influence in the Third World under Gorbachev? What lessons, if any, have the Soviets learned from their expansionism of the 1970s, and what are the implications of those lessons for US-Soviet relations? Has ideology disappeared from Soviet decision-making? How, and in what ways, has Soviet behavior changed with respect to the local politics and economic performance of Third World countries? What is the nature of emerging Soviet-client relationships?

Developing cogent answers to these questions should help in understanding the complexity of Soviet–Third World relations and provide insight into how exposure to Third World behavior shapes Soviet decision-making. Soviet policy under Gorbachev, moreover, offers a valuable laboratory in which to probe underlying assumptions of US policy. What policies should the United States adopt in the 1990s to best serve its vital interests in view of shifting Soviet–Third World relations?

Among the many individuals contributing to this project, we would like especially to thank Professor Melvin A. Goodman of the National Defense University—who took extra time in reading the manuscript, making suggestions, and pointing out flaws in the argument—and Vicky Willis, of the Document Preparation Center, State University of New York, College at Brockport, who spent many hours typing and retyping the manuscript in preparation for its publication. We would also like to thank James B. McGiffert for his thoughtful editing, Wayne Limberg and Mark V. Kauppi for "brainstorming" on the Africa section, Dennis Andres for running down leads for the Latin American chapter, and Jorge F. Perez-Lopez for his insight on Cuba. The final version of the book—and responsibility for its contents—of course remain our own, and the views expressed are not necessarily those of the institutions for which we work. Finally, we greatly appreciate the moral support and encouragement extended by Susan L. McEachern of Westview Press.

W. Raymond Duncan
Carolyn McGiffert Ekedahl

NOTES

1. Robert Legvold, "The Revolution in Soviet Foreign Policy," *Foreign Affairs* "America and the World 1988/89," Council on Foreign Relations, Inc., Vol. 68, No. 1 (1989), pp. 82–98. For other views of fundamental change in Soviet relations with the Third World, see Jerry Hough, *The Struggle for the Third World: Soviet Debates and American Options* (Washington, DC: The Brookings Institution, 1986); Elizabeth Valkenier, "Revolutionary Change in the Third World: Recent Soviet Assessments," *World Politics* 38, No. 3 (April 1986), pp. 415–434; and Valkenier, "New Soviet Thinking About the Third World," *World Policy Journal* 4, No. 4 (Fall 1987), pp. 651–674. See also Jack Snyder, "The Gorbachev Revolution: A Waning of Soviet Expansionism?" *International Security* 12, No. 3 (Winter 1987–1988), pp. 93–131.

2. Alvin Z. Rubinstein, "The Future of Soviet Policy in the Third World," in Carol R. Saivetz, ed., *The Soviet Union in the Third World* (Boulder, CO: Westview Press, 1989), p. 197. Rubinstein's observations are drawn from his own book, *Moscow's Third World Strategy* (Princeton: Princeton University Press, 1988).

3. Rubinstein, "The Future of Soviet Policy in the Third World," pp. 198 ff. Other observers who see Moscow's approach to the Third World as essentially the same as in previous years include Daniel Papp, *Soviet Perceptions of the Developing*

Countries in the 1980's: The Ideological Basis (Lexington, MA: Lexington Books, 1985); Francis Fukuyama, *Moscow's Post-Brezhnev Reassessment of the Third World* R-3337-USDP (Santa Monica, CA: RAND Corporation, 1986); Fukuyama, "Gorbachev and the Third World," *Foreign Affairs* (Spring 1986), pp. 715–731; and Fukuyama, "Patterns of Soviet Third World Policy," *Problems of Communism* (September-October 1987), pp. 1–13.

4. See, for example, Robert M. Gates, "The Uneven Cycles of Kremlin Reform," *The Washington Post,* Outlook section, April 30, 1989.

5. For an insightful discussion of Gorbachev's views of the Third World as an amalgam of contending schools of thought among Soviet intellectuals regarding key trends in the developing countries and how Moscow should respond in foreign policy goals and techniques, see David E. Albright, "The USSR and the Third World in the 1980s," *Problems of Communism* (March-June 1989), pp. 50–70.

MOSCOW AND THE THIRD WORLD UNDER GORBACHEV

INTRODUCTION: GORBACHEV AND THE THIRD WORLD

By the time Mikhail Gorbachev came to power in March 1985 the Soviet Union had been deeply involved in the Third World for over three decades. Since 1954–1955, when Nikita S. Khrushchev first initiated a sustained drive to expand relations with the lesser developed countries, Moscow has used this part of the globe to break out of continental isolation, project power, and gain world class status as a superpower competitor with the United States. Third World countries, conversely, have taken advantage of Soviet attention to pursue their own foreign policy aims. How could Cuba, Vietnam, Syria, Ethiopia, Libya, and Angola have managed without the support and military assistance of the Soviet Union over the years? The impact of expanding Soviet-Third World relations—escalating East-West tensions, rising levels of world military spending, and protracted regional conflicts—make this a subject well worth examining.

Whether Moscow will be able to hold onto its expanded and costly Third World empire in the years ahead—as economic and political problems mount—remains an open question. But one thing is certain—Gorbachev's "New Thinking" in foreign policy is having a significant impact on Moscow's Third World relations as Soviet leaders seek to redefine the nature of their presence in Africa, Asia, the Middle East, and Latin America. While Moscow's military withdrawal from Afghanistan has been one of the most dramatic events since Gorbachev came to power in 1985, the new Soviet leader also urged Cuba to pull its 50,000 troops out of Angola and put pressure on Vietnam to withdraw from Cambodia. These moves illustrate Moscow's new emphasis on the political settlement of regional conflicts as it seeks to reduce East-West tension and ease the burden of sustaining economically weak allies beleaguered by costly civil wars.

Hoping to reduce Moscow's defense needs—and thus be able to shift investment from the military to the civilian economic sector—Gorbachev has tried to ease tensions with old adversaries, notably China. The May

1989 Sino-Soviet summit in Beijing was the first meeting between the communist giants after 30 years of intense hostility. Gorbachev has opened the door to improved relations with other countries previously treated as international pariahs, such as Israel, South Korea, and South Africa. And, Soviet officials have travelled throughout the Third World, outlining new diplomatic initiatives to endorse nuclear free zones, widen commercial ties, peacefully settle regional conflicts, and strengthen relations with moderate industrialized countries like Argentina, Brazil, India, and Mexico.

Gorbachev has advanced numerous diplomatic initiatives designed to ease military competition with the United States and strengthen international cooperation. His most dramatic efforts have been in the arms control field—and he has made effective use of public relations to advance his policies. In pressing his peace agenda with the United States, for example, Gorbachev sent Marshal Sergei F. Akhromeyev, former chief of the Soviet general staff and then Gorbachev's top military adviser, to the United States to make an unprecedented appearance as a witness before the House Armed Services Committee in late July 1989. Testifying before the House Committee, Akhromeyev said:

> I am personally convinced that neither the United States nor its allies intend today to unleash a warfare against the U.S.S.R. and its allies. . . . We are telling our people that the tensions in the world, and war danger, have diminished. And this has been the result of positive changes in the relations between the U.S.S.R. and U.S.[1]

Who could have imagined such a statement before members of the US Congress during the period of Soviet expansion in the mid-1970s or even in the early 1980s, when US President Ronald Reagan referred to the USSR as the "evil empire."

These initiatives by no means indicate a Soviet withdrawal from the Third World, a point made clear when Gorbachev visited Cuba in April 1989. Gorbachev refused to use the occasion to reprimand Fidel Castro for Havana's notorious economic inefficiency or to threaten reduced support. Despite its military withdrawal from Afghanistan, Moscow has continued its support for the Najibullah regime. And the Soviets continue to supply sophisticated weapons to radical clients around the world.

Although the Soviet Union has not withdrawn from the Third World, the distinctly new patterns established by Gorbachev suggest fundamental change in the thought and action guiding Soviet–Third World decision-making. Driven by economic and security imperatives, Gorbachev's "new political thinking" represents a basic shift in policy assumptions, objectives and techniques. Gorbachev has downgraded ideology, rejected military expansion, pursued closer relations with capitalist-oriented Third World states and cooperated with the United States in negotiating political settlements to Third World conflicts. These shifts have been tailored to support the high-priority goals of reduced East-West tension, physical security at lower costs, and, above all, the resurrection of the troubled Soviet economy.

In portraying Gorbachev's policy toward the Third World as a turning point or watershed, one must recognize that Soviet foreign policy is closely connected to the underlying assumptions guiding Soviet domestic relations. Soviet policy toward the Third World must be viewed in the context of *perestroika* and *glasnost*—the effort to reform the Soviet Union's political and economic structure. From this perspective, Soviet policy toward the Third World under Gorbachev is just one aspect of the fundamental change occurring in the Soviet Union.

The epochal events of 1989 alone illustrate this transformation of Soviet politics and foreign policy. Before Gorbachev, one could not have imagined the defeat of Party officials in legislative elections in the U.S.S.R., the Baltic states moving toward capitalist socialism, Hungary's ruling communist party changing its name and rejecting orthodox Marxism, and Poland's first non-Communist Prime Minister in 40 years.[2] Nevertheless, the question of Gorbachev's longevity and the durability of his policies remains open.

There certainly is disagreement within the Soviet leadership about many aspects of "new thinking"—including policies in the Third World. By 1989 it was not unusual, for example, to hear Soviets criticizing the high levels of economic aid being extended to countries such as Cuba and Vietnam. And as one student of Soviet-Third World relations has noted, Soviet policies toward the Third World are still in transition.[3] Karen Brutents, at the time a deputy director of the CPSU International Department, told a conference of the Ministry of Foreign Affairs in late July 1988 that "It is . . . only fair to say that the problems of developing countries have yet to be worked out in accordance with the concept of new thinking."[4] Nonetheless, in spite of the uncertainties and confusion, Gorbachev and "new thinking" were dominant in Soviet foreign policy making as Moscow moved into the 1990s.

METHOD OF APPROACH

Our study of Soviet policy in the Third World under Gorbachev examines the rationale for and implications of Moscow's behavior. Materials studied include policy statements by Soviet and Third World leaders, official communiques, and relevant press commentary. We have used official economic and military aid data, Soviet and Third World academic journal articles, and a variety of secondary sources. This material is used both to structure the argument chronologically by region and to analyze functional issues, such as the nature of key Soviet-Third World relationships, sources of continuing strains in relations, influence-seeking by both parties on each other, and the impact of the Soviet approach on third parties, such as the United States and China.

CHAPTER OUTLINES

The chapters that follow are arranged to facilitate understanding of Soviet–Third World relations under Gorbachev both chronologically and analytically. Chapter 1 provides guidelines for the study of Soviet foreign policy. It highlights the dynamics of Moscow's evolving approach to the Third World—its motivations, capabilities, the opportunities it has exploited, and the limits to its success.

Chapter 2 focuses on Moscow's perception of the Third World when Gorbachev came to power in March 1985. It presents a balance sheet of Soviet benefits and costs, examining trends up to the time of Gorbachev's assumption of power.

Chapter 3 examines Soviet domestic goals and shifting international trends in an effort to put Moscow's Third World policy into context. What economic and strategic priorities has Moscow been pursuing since Gorbachev came to power and why has Gorbachev tried to alter the international environment?

Chapter 4 focuses directly on Gorbachev's approach to the Third World—viewing it as a product of the economic and strategic priorities examined in Chapter 3. What is the connection between Moscow's "New Thinking" about domestic and international trends and its relations with the developing countries? Does Gorbachev's approach to the Third World represent substantive change in Soviet foreign policy objectives or merely a temporary shift in tactics designed to achieve old goals? What lessons have the Soviets drawn from the consequences of their actions during the mid-to-late 1970s when they sharply expanded their presence in Third World settings, and what have been the policy consequences?

Chapter 5 serves as an introduction to our regional case studies, addressing Moscow's withdrawal from Afghanistan. Here we probe the rationale for the withdrawal, the policy complications involved, and the implications of the withdrawal for the political settlement of other Third World regional conflicts. Certainly Afghanistan has been high on Gorbachev's agenda, and he has stated that untying the "Afghanistan knot" holds deep implications for resolving conflict elsewhere. Overall, where does Afghanistan fit into Gorbachev's broader Third World posture?

Chapter 6 focuses on the Middle East. As in each of the regional case studies, this chapter provides a brief historical overview of Soviet relations in the region, followed by a section which examines Soviet policy toward the Middle East peace process, the Iran-Iraq war, and specific client states. The purpose of these chapters is to assess the nature of regional political dynamics, their differences in terms of the opportunities and constraints operating on Soviet policy, and likely future trends. This chapter looks briefly at the nature of shifting relationships with special clients, e.g., Syria and Iraq, and, lastly, examines Soviet prospects in the area.

Chapter 7 examines Asia, where Gorbachev's May 1989 summit meeting with Chinese leaders symbolized the transformation of Sino-Soviet relations—just as Vietnam's withdrawal from Cambodia reflected the results of "new thinking" in Southeast Asia. These moves demonstrate how Gorbachev's July 1986 address in Vladivostok—a major speech in which Gorbachev insisted that the USSR was an Asian power with Asian responsibilities—has been translated into policy. Gorbachev has upgraded Soviet diplomacy in Asia, with special attention to China, Southeast Asia, and the Korean Peninsula. The Far East is important to Moscow because of its economic dynamism; while the USSR is a part of Asia, it is at an economic disadvantage compared to countries such as Japan, Taiwan, Singapore, Hong Kong, and South Korea. How have the Soviets reacted to the remarkable economic boom in these nations compared to the sluggish economies of Soviet allies such as Laos, Cambodia, and Vietnam?

Chapter 8 concentrates on Africa, where the USSR has had to contend with the rising costs of supporting beleaguered pro-Marxist allies in Angola, Ethiopia, and Mozambique. What new opportunities are available to Moscow given South Africa's political instability and the limited capabilities of the African National Congress (ANC) and South African Communist Party (SACP)? Do Soviet analysts currently look favorably upon economic and political development trends in Africa or are their assessments pessimistic? What is the nature of the Soviet-Cuban relationship regarding Moscow's ties in Africa?

Chapter 9 is a study of Latin America, a region under rapid change. How has Gorbachev reacted to the shift toward civilian regimes in South America, Cuba's rising needs and sagging economy, Central America's fragmented guerrilla movements, and US-backed Contra opposition to Nicaragua's Sandinistas? Has Moscow de-emphasized its relations in this part of the world or demonstrated rising interest. Have the Soviets stopped shipping arms to Nicaragua? What implications can be drawn regarding Soviet-US cooperation in this part of the world?

Chapter 10 provides a concluding assessment of Soviet–Third World relations under Gorbachev, with attention to the implications for US policy and alternate scenarios for the future. It stresses the need to avoid oversimplifying the rich complexity of Soviet relations with the Third World, to understand the limitations as well as the opportunities for expanding Soviet influence, and to base our own foreign policy on a rigorous analysis of local and regional settings. How, and in what ways, must we distinguish between different Third World regions in terms of Soviet assets and liabilities? Where and to what extent should we be concerned about the "Soviet threat"? Do emerging Soviet patterns of behavior in the Third World create an opportunity for Soviet-US cooperation?

NOTES

1. Akhromeyev's statement before the House Armed Services Committee, *The New York Times*, July 31, 1980.

2. Gorbachev moved quickly to establish cordial relations with the new Polish Prime Minister, Tadeusz Mazowiecki. Mazowiecki, a member of the Solidarity organization, reaffirmed his commitment to the Warsaw Pact. See Bill Keller, "Soviet Congratulations Sent to New Premier of Poland," *The New York Times*, August 25, 1989, p. A8.

3. See David Albright, "The USSR and the Third World in the 1980s," *Problems of Communism* (March-June 1989), pp. 50–70.

4. Karen Brutents, "Cooperation and Dialogue with Political Parties and Movements," *International Affairs* (November 1988), pp. 38–39, as quoted in Albright, "The USSR and the Third World in the 1980s," p. 58.

PART ONE

The Study of Soviet–Third World Politics

1

THE STUDY OF SOVIET–THIRD WORLD RELATIONS

In order to better understand this book's interpretation of the significance of Gorbachev's approach to the Third World, the reader should be aware of the assumptions which lie behind the analysis. These assumptions will not be explored at length here, as each concerns a subject which is itself worthy of extensive study and debate. But as all pervade our assessment of Soviet decision-making and policy, they should be addressed at least briefly.

On the surface, Soviet foreign policy appears easier to understand than the policies of seemingly more complex Western societies. Marxist-Leninist formulations appear prescriptive; the Soviet Union is ruled by a single party and theoretically should have a less complicated decision-making process. In addition, Moscow appears to have pursued a reasonably straight forward effort to expand its presence and build influence in the Third World in recent years. In contrast, the industrialized societies of the West have contending party systems, numerous ideological currents, competing interest groups, electoral politics, debate-oriented media, and rather ambivalent approaches to Third World countries and situations.

But the formation of Soviet foreign policy is more complex than it may seem, and is the product of numerous interacting domestic, regional, and international forces. On the domestic front, key factors include geography, historic legacy, ideology, nationalism, leadership personalities, political and economic priorities.[1] Geography and history, most notably the lack of natural barriers and repeated foreign invasions, have produced a nation preoccupied with security, outside threats, and a perceived need to project outward in order to safeguard the motherland (*Rodina*).[2] Marxist-Leninist ideology, with its messianic message of inevitable revolution, has reenforced the inclination to look outward to face perceived foreign threats. The predominance of Russian nationalism in Soviet life—with its singular psychology of inferiority and pride—has had its own impact on foreign policy. Soviet decision-making has been shaped by a Russian-oriented perception of domestic and foreign threats, a fusion of nationalism and Marxist-Leninist ideology that has linked Russian insularity with a fervent ideology—complicated by the co-existence of nationality groups with non-Russian traditions.

Non-Russian national groups inside the USSR and along the Soviet border in East Europe have become increasingly important factors in Soviet policy since Gorbachev's emergence as top decision-maker. In pursuing his policy of internal and external openness (*glasnost*), designed to generate creative and dynamic decision-making and alter external perceptions of the USSR, Gorbachev has unleashed nationality problems within it. Non-Russian nationalism—from Armenian *versus* Azerbaijan national conflict, to Baltic nationalism in Estonia, Latvia, and Lithuania (including Estonia's startling declaration of independence from the USSR in 1988) and Islamic unrest in Central Asia—could undermine Gorbachev's agenda.[3] Heavy-handed repression of internal nationalism could seriously damage his image abroad. Perceived as flexible and adaptable, Gorbachev gains credibility; seen as repressive, he might lose his appeal in the West. The tragic end to the student protests in China in June 1989 and the consequences of the Chinese crackdown will serve as a warning to Gorbachev of the difficulty in maintaining order while encouraging openness.

Soviet decision-making is a complicated procedure—far from the strong-man rule of the days of Joseph Stalin. It features contending interest groups, factionalism, and bureaucratic politics. Foreign policy-making is influenced by increasing pluralism and bureaucratic infighting by elites that espouse a variety of views and compete for scarce resources—as demonstrated by Gorbachev's efforts to reform the Soviet economy (*perestroika*). Seeking to strengthen his position, Gorbachev has made numerous personnel changes at the highest levels of the Party and government.[4] The differing personalities and leadership styles of Soviet General Secretaries also have an impact on the content of foreign policy—a point underscored by Gorbachev's dynamic and creative approach compared to Leonid Brezhnev's conservative, consensus-oriented style.[5]

Finally, Soviet foreign policy, like the foreign policies of other states, is conditioned by domestic problems and priorities. The decline in economic productivity, hard currency earnings, and oil production all affect Moscow's foreign policy objectives and generate diverging views of policy priorities. Economic problems and the uncertainties of reform make predictability in the foreign policy arena even more essential. Whether Gorbachev can succeed in his domestic policy innovations—against entrenched Stalinist forces and conservative opposition—may depend to a considerable extent on his success in the realm of foreign policy.

Regional politics in the Third World shape Soviet foreign policy perceptions and actions, offering opportunities and imposing constraints. The environment in which Moscow is operating is as important as Soviet intentions and capabilities. Regional political and economic dynamics—nationalism, ethnic and regional conflicts, culture, religion, power aspirations, natural resources, personalities, and geopolitics—create Soviet policy options. In the Middle East for example, Moscow's ambitions must be adapted to an environment shaped by Arab-Israeli tensions, Islamic fundamentalism, Iranian-Iraqi and Syrian-Iraqi hostility, Palestine Liberation Organization (PLO) factionalism, and independent leaders like Hafiz al-Assad.[6] These forces create opportunities for Soviet involvement; at the same time they obstruct and limit Moscow's influence.

Soviet relationships with its Third World clients are diverse. As the United States has discovered, even a superpower cannot control its clients, and the more distant the client, the more difficult to influence. Studies of Soviet-Cuban relations suggest, for example, that the Soviets have limited ability to influence Fidel Castro and, in some cases, may be influenced by Cuba instead.[7] The same can be said of Soviet ties with independent-minded Vietnam.[8] And Moscow's difficulties with strong-willed leaders in Middle East states, like Libya's Muammar Qadhafi and Syria's Hafiz al-Assad, are chronic.[9]

Soviet ties with regional clients have become increasingly complex in the 1980s. Having established close patron-client links with pre-industrial and economically weak states, such as Angola, Ethiopia, and Nicaragua during the 1970s, Moscow has been holding onto these gains without committing additional resources to meet their rising demands.[10] In addition, many of these clients are politically unstable, threatened by leadership factionalism, and facing viable insurgencies seeking their overthrow. They do not provide appealing models of socialist development for other Third World countries. Finally, Soviet foreign policy complexities arise from regional conflicts, such as the Iran-Iraq war, Ethiopian-Somali tensions, Libya's adventures in Chad, and Vietnam's occupation of Cambodia. The difficulties of handling two clients at odds with each other became particularly pronounced for the USSR in the 1970s and 1980s as Ethiopia went to war with Somalia, Iraq attacked Iran, and, more recently, Syria and Iraq faced off in Lebanon.

International politics on a broader scale further complicate Soviet–Third World relations—both for Gorbachev and for those who wish to understand his policies. The bi-polar power configuration, which characterized the immediate post–World War II period, has eroded and been replaced by an international system with various centers of power, including Western Europe and Japan. A world of rapid economic, scientific, and technological change threatens to leave the USSR behind—not only in civilian high-technology production (e.g., computerized communications, information processing, advanced technological processes, and integrated systems of machines and equipment), but also, ultimately, in military technology.

The international system, moreover, has become highly interdependent. Environmental problems, food supply and demand, vital raw materials and natural resources, trade, and security cannot be dealt with by countries acting alone.[11] Gorbachev is acutely aware of these trends—from the threat of nuclear war to global environmental pollution—and is equally concerned that Moscow's non-participant status in global economic institutions like the World Bank, the International Monetary Fund (IMF), and the General Agreement on Tariffs and Trade (GATT) makes the USSR a less effective player in international economic affairs.[12]

Various US policies have added to the costs of Soviet foreign policy during the 1980s. Rising US military weapons expenditures and modernization, a commitment to support anti-Soviet insurgencies in the Third World, and an apparent determination to press for the Strategic Defense Initiative (SDI) put pressure on Moscow.[13] US defense expenditures, for example, measured in constant 1982 dollars, rose from a yearly average of $158.1 billion during the years of Jimmy Carter's Presidency (1977–1980) to an annual average of $216.9 billion during President Ronald Reagan's tenure (1981–1988).[14] Despite the demise of the bipolar world system and the rise of global interdependence, relations with the United States in many ways remain central to Soviet foreign policy decision-making, for it is only here, by reducing the arms race and military expenditures, that resources can be found to underwrite Soviet economic restructuring and growth. By the end of Brezhnev's rule, it had become clear to Soviet analysts that militant pursuit of Moscow's interests in highly unstable Third World settings where US and Soviet clients were in competition was undermining Soviet efforts to reduce East-West tensions.[15]

INNOVATIVE CHANGE UNDER GORBACHEV

All of these complexities have been further compounded by the extraordinary pace of change introduced by Mikhail Gorbachev. Soon after assuming power, Gorbachev undertook a major shake-up of the top ranks of the Soviet leadership, initiated a drive for economic reform, and launched a barrage of arms control proposals that left the West and the United States racing to catch up. Departing from traditional Soviet secrecy, he called for increased openness, expanded liberties, and greater democratization of decision-making—all designed to make the USSR more efficient and powerful by encouraging the initiative and creativity of the Soviet masses.

Gorbachev's amazingly rapid changes in turn have produced complicated problems of management with no guarantee of success. The Gorbachev years have stimulated considerable criticism and reassessment of Soviet economic policies, denunciations of the slow pace of economic progress, public criticism of the rapid de-Stalinizing of the Soviet system, and outright opposition to political reform. After over four years of reform the Soviet consumer could see little improvement in the standard of living, defense spending had not decreased significantly, and the continuing poor performance of the economy threatened to produce increased internal tensions. Not least among Gorbachev's critics was Soviet Nobel Prize–winning human rights advocate Andrei Sakharov, who warned that political reforms might give Gorbachev a dangerous monopoly of power.[16] But then no one said

Gorbachev's program for change would be easy, especially in a system as entrenched and inflexible as the Stalinist bureaucracy he inherited.

TRADITIONAL ASSUMPTIONS DRIVING SOVIET POLICY IN THE THIRD WORLD

Soviet relations with the Third World since Gorbachev's assumption of power must be viewed against the background of traditional perceptions and expectations shaping Moscow's approach to developing countries. Examining the legacy of the past will set the framework for our assessment of how Soviet–Third World relations are changing under Gorbachev, the mix of continuity and change, and the nature of shifting Soviet–Third World relationships. These operative factors, inherited by Gorbachev, address:

Factors Driving Soviet Foreign Policy

1. the quest for security,
2. the predominance of realism,
3. the role of ideology,
4. the focus on military strength, and
5. the avoidance of conflict.

The Complexity of Soviet–Third World Relationships

6. presence and influence,
7. benefits versus costs, and
8. opportunities and constraints.

The Dynamics of Soviet Policy Toward the Third World

9. lessons from the past, and
10. operating rules of Soviet foreign policy behavior.

FACTORS DRIVING SOVIET FOREIGN POLICY

1. The Quest for Security

The need to protect the Rodina is the single most important factor behind Soviet foreign policy. The absence of natural barriers and repeated invasions from both East and West have imbued the Soviets with an almost pathological sense of insecurity and have fostered a conviction that expansion provides the best defense. The need to build (and overbuild) military strength to provide adequate strength for the Rodina is an inheritance of the past.[17]

Russian nationalism reinforces this identification with past vulnerabilities, the need to protect Russian culture, a wariness of Asian minorities and numbers, and a long-lived love-hate relationship with the West.[18] These forces merge with Marxist-Leninist prescriptions for treating the West as a natural adversary, but they have their own separate roots in Soviet thinking, and they accentuate the need for tactical readjustments to protect the homeland in a hostile environment.[19] The Russian legacy thus feeds a perception of foreign relations as a permanent test of wills, a continuum of conflict and crisis in which events must be adroitly manipulated to reduce risk and enhance power—in order to safeguard the Rodina.

2. The Predominance of Realism

The conduct of Soviet foreign policy is highly pragmatic. By this we mean that Soviet leaders typically calculate how to advance state interests through the judicious use of power in international relations.[20] Political realism—focusing on how, when, and where to use power in world politics—is strongly ingrained in the Russian national tradition. Like the practitioners of power politics elsewhere, Soviet leaders continue to emphasize causal relationships between the volatile international system and the state's foreign policy. Conditioned by geography, history, and ideology to believe that international politics is largely a struggle for power, they have time and again opted for policies that center on power balances and power equations to advance national security, even if it meant the temporary abandonment of Marxist-Leninist principles, the postponement of the spread of communism, or the sacrifice of a local communist party in some distant land.

From the early days of Soviet history, Moscow's leaders have pursued power politics, not idealistic objectives, in dealing with the outside world.[21] This approach to foreign policy—accommodating Soviet interests to external realities and pursuing opportunities to expand power—contrasts sharply with that of the United States, which, by virtue of its geographic security and historic legacy, long avoided entanglement in the affairs of far-off regions.[22] Not until 1947, when it embarked upon the policy of containing the USSR through the creation of "permanent alliances" did the United States become systematically involved in projecting its power abroad.[23] Russians have been doing this for centuries.

Kremlin leaders have demonstrated a repeated capacity to seize or create opportunities in pursuit of Soviet interests. This process began with the 1918 Treaty of Brest-Litovsk, when, in an effort to protect their national security by stopping the Central Powers' advance, the Soviets signed a peace settlement in which they lost one third of Russia's industry, land, and people.[24] After World War II, some scholars argue that Joseph Stalin pursued a policy of pragmatic exploitation to move into power vacuums in East Europe.[25] This opportunistic approach to foreign policy remains pronounced in Soviet foreign policy today.

While maintaining physical security is the primary goal of Soviet foreign policy, Moscow in fact pursues a range of objectives that vary in significance depending upon their contribution to its vital concerns.[26] These interests, like those of other countries, can be classified in the categories of physical security, economic security, and political security. Within these categories, some interests rank higher in importance (saliency) than others. Protecting the homeland, guaranteeing access to raw materials abroad, and maintaining superpower status all rank higher, for example, than protecting foreign communist parties and spreading communism throughout the world.[27] These various interests are connected to issues—the actions and events through which interests are pursued; building a strong military force (issue) is keyed to protecting the homeland (salient interest). Interests and issues must be studied, from the perspective of both the USSR and the Third World country, in order to understand the nature of their relationship and the motivations on both sides. It would be inaccurate to assume that Moscow's leaders pursue opportunities to advance only one goal, such as the expansion of Marxism-Leninism, as one might think is implied by the guiding ideology of the USSR.[28]

3. The Role of Ideology

Marxist-Leninist ideology has provided the context and framework for Soviet policy—but has not itself been a primary determinant of policy. Marxism-Leninism has served both as a guide for analyzing the nature of the international system and a yardstick for measuring the progress of the USSR within that system.[29] Inherent in the ideology is the promise that patience will pay off in the long-run—that progress is inevitable and that setbacks, therefore, will prove transient.

Second, Marxism-Leninism focuses on competition between the two dominant world systems—socialism/communism and capitalism/imperialism—and the importance of power in this competition.[30] As a view of a sharply competitive world, it has complemented the Russian legacy and psychology. This competitive thrust is unlikely to completely disappear (although Gorbachev is attempting to redefine and rechannel it). Third, Marxism-Leninism has provided a source of legitimacy for the Soviets, who use ideology to justify and substantiate their positions on moral grounds.

Fourth, Marxism-Leninism, with its dialectic approach, has justified the Soviets in pursuing what has been essentially a two track foreign policy; on the one hand, they have cultivated state-to-state relations; on the other, they have supported local communist parties and leftist groups seeking to undermine those same states. These seemingly contradictory strands of foreign policy are not unique to the Soviet Union, but the ideological rationale provides a stronger justification and framework for implementation than is the case elsewhere.

4. The Focus on Military Strength

The Soviets have introduced the complex concept of "correlation of forces" as a measure of the relative strengths of capitalism and socialism. While the term incorporates a broad array of factors (including economic strength, ideological commitment, allies), the most important component of this power equation is military strength. Like political realists everywhere, the Soviets believe that military power—backed by a healthy economic base—is the key to security and superpower influence in world affairs.

Over the years the Soviets have demonstrated a tendency to give high priority to augmenting their military capability even if it meant sacrifice elsewhere. This occurred under Joseph Stalin, with his heavy investment in the military sector; under Khrushchev, with his emphasis on strategic rocket forces; and under Brezhnev, with his renewed commitment to build conventional forces and an increased capability to project power into Third World areas.[31]

Moscow's preoccupation with security and the development of its military power has produced significant improvement in its capabilities over the years. By the early 1970s, the Soviets had achieved nuclear parity with the United States, developed an enormous conventional military arsenal, and expanded their resources for power projection abroad. In addition, their military assistance programs were tailored to serve the security needs of Third World leaders facing internal and external opposition.

Consider the world the Russians have looked out upon over the centuries: no natural frontiers as barriers to successive invasions and interventions (at least 160 foreign invasions between 1228–1462, 10 great wars with Sweden and Poland during the 17th and 18th centuries, the Napoleonic War, the Crimean War, the Russo-Turkish Wars, the humiliating Russo-Japanese War, and World War I). In the Soviet period, the intervention of the West during the Civil War and the deeply traumatic loss of over 20 million people during World War II continued to shape Moscow's perceptions.[32]

5. The Avoidance of Conflict

While they have sought to improve their relative military position, the Soviets have proceeded cautiously in areas where they foresee potential superpower confrontation. They certainly view the world as a competitive arena—from the perspectives both of ideology and of power politics—and are prepared to compete aggressively; but they retain as their highest priority safeguarding the security of the homeland. This means avoiding war. Time and again the Soviets have backed away from direct confrontation with the United States. An apparent exception (and then the proof) was the Cuban missile crisis of 1962. This "adventurism," however, was one of the major charges made in the overthrow of Nikita Khrushchev two years later.

THE COMPLEXITY OF SOVIET–THIRD WORLD RELATIONSHIPS

6. Presence and Influence

Moscow's presence in the Third World does not translate into a corresponding ability to influence events.[33] Any assumption that it does would oversimplify the dynamics of the international system—missing the impact Third World countries themselves have on Soviet foreign policy, the effects local politics have on Soviet behavior, and the complexity of regional politics. Influence—by which is meant how, and in what ways, one country shapes the behavior of another—is a complicated process. Influence in relationships between the Soviets and a Third World state may be short term, is subject to change, and is conditioned by the behavior of third party actors, such as other regional countries or the United States.

Nor is influence comprehensive. Moscow's close ties with a Third World state do not guarantee it influence in all areas of that state's domestic and international behavior. Angola may look to the Soviets for military and security support, for example, but look to the West for economic assistance. The Soviets may convince Cuba to tolerate a substantial presence on the island, but have little success persuading the Cubans to alter the management of their economy.[34] Separating presence from influence and focusing closely on where the Soviets have influence and what its nature and limits are will help clarify the importance of various Soviet–Third World relationships. This may be a particularly useful exercise in assessing the Soviet approach and record under Gorbachev as the Soviets move to hold onto old clients while reducing the costs of these relationships and expanding their ties to newly industrializing and frequently moderate Third World countries.

7. Benefits Versus Costs

The Soviets are seeking to maximize benefits and minimize costs in relations with Third World states—and the latter are doing the same. Highlighting benefits and costs for each side demonstrates the rich diversity of Soviet–Third World relationships, the range of interests at stake for each side, and the ways in which each tries to get as much as possible out of the relationship. A key task is to assess the susceptibility of each side to the pressures of the other—and to possible overtures by third parties outside the relationship.

Soviet-Cuban relations are a case in point. Cuba has benefited from its Soviet ties in terms of economic and military aid, backing for Havana's foreign adventures, defense against the United States, and preservation of Castro's revolution at home.[35] In return, the Soviets have gained military access and presence in a key geostrategic location, a base of operation from which to expand their presence in the Third World and capability to gather intelligence information against the United States.[36] Each side has been able to advance its interests by cooperating with the other.

Still, both sides have incurred costs, and the two have contradictory policy priorities. The Soviets have put $4–5 billion annually into Cuba—a significant drain on the Soviet economy with its shrinking resources and productivity problems. Moscow is frustrated by Cuba's lacklustre economic performance and refusal to follow Soviet advice. For the Cubans, the Soviet inattention to the Third World at the 27th Party Congress of February-March 1986, earlier tepid backing of Maurice Bishop in his struggle for power in Grenada, and low-key reaction to the US intervention there have been sources of friction.[37] Strains also have arisen over difference in approach to East-West (Moscow's priority) and North-South (Havana's priority) issues, support for national liberation movements, and treatment of regional conflicts. Each Soviet–Third World relationship has its own set of cost/benefit issues; their importance fluctuates over time as do the nature and extent of influence/susceptibility factors—thus creating a dynamic interaction in relations.

8. Opportunities and Constraints

The Soviets constantly seek to identify and exploit opportunities to advance their position in the Third World. Opportunities vary from country to country and region to region and often result from unpredictable events and conflicts.

Moscow's greatest opportunities have been created by regional tensions that produce regimes in need of military assistance. Over the years, these openings have enabled Moscow to provide military/security assistance—its most important instrument of policy in the Third World. Soviet military aid has been instrumental in the consolidation and sustenance of pro-Soviet regimes in Cuba, Vietnam, Angola, Ethiopia, and Afghanistan. Other opportunities have been created by the regional power aspirations of countries like Syria and Iraq, where Soviet military support has proved crucial. Still another kind of opportunity stems from the desire of Third World countries to use the USSR for their own geopolitical purposes—as in Mexico's efforts to distance itself from the United States or in India's desire to counter Chinese pressures. The USSR's ties to legal communist parties in civilian ruled countries (Argentina, Brazil) and its role as protector to small state commercial interests, as in the flagging of Kuwaiti oil tankers, illustrate the diversity of possible openings.

These opportunities are offset by constraints, which also come in a variety of forms. They include religion (anti-atheistic Islam has undermined Soviet efforts to gain influence in the Middle East, and Hispano-Catholic sentiments work against Soviet inroads in Latin America) and nationalism (or ethnicism) which appears to be a more dominant and permanent force than communism. During the 1980s Moscow faced a growing inability to deal with ethnic national movements (some communist in orientation) in the Third World. Outside of military aid, what do the Soviets have to offer Angola's MPLA leaders who have faced an opposing national movement in the UNITA forces? To what extent will the Soviets support Ethiopia's Mengistu, who faces opposing nationalists in the Tigrean and Eritrean national liberation movements? In a sense, the tenacious loyalty inspired by ethnic nationalism inside the USSR itself is replicated throughout the Third World.

Among the constraints that inhibit Soviet expansion are local politics and the needs of local political leaders for economic aid. Political parties are notoriously fragmented, for example, in Latin America where political unity is challenged by dominant personalist followings. Coalitions are fragile and presumed partners may prove short-lived.[38]

The Soviet Union has not been in a position to provide the amount of economic aid requested by local leaders. And when they receive substantial economic aid, as in Cuba, pro-Marxist regimes have not been able to use it to create viable economies. This experience has undermined Soviet leaders' inclinations to create "other Cubas" even if they could. Nicaragua is a classic case in point. Despite meeting Managua's oil needs, Moscow has provided inadequate aid to this Central American client. Managua's economic conditions worsened dramatically during the late 1980s, as demonstrated by high unemployment, starvation, children begging in the streets, robberies of food, teachers deserting the classrooms, and professionals leaving the country—and Moscow gave no indication that it would increase its aid.[39]

THE DYNAMICS OF SOVIET POLICY TOWARD THE THIRD WORLD

9. Lessons from the Past

With over thirty years experience in Third World activities, Moscow's leaders have been accumulating increasing knowledge about these regions and about their own capabilities. One sees evidence of widening insight in the rise of Soviet academic institutes studying Third World regions, in the closer interaction between foreign policy analysts and government officials, and in the greater sophistication of Soviet analysis of the Third World.

Moscow's increased professionalism and understanding of Third World dynamics have given it the capacity to differentiate among Third World countries and to assess the latter's prospects both for economic development and political survival. Sharper assessments of political leaderships, economic development, and cultural realities have reduced the tendency to expect the sudden shifts in favor of socialism which seemed to have led Khrushchev astray in the late 1950s and early 1960s. Soviet leaders, additionally, have become more adept at diplomacy, more skilled in packaging their policy, and more imaginative in their diplomacy. When Soviet Ambassador to Nicaragua Valeriy Nikolayenko took up his post in October 1988, for example, he brought with him a new expertise in Latin American affairs. He spoke fluent Spanish and English, was willing to give open interviews to western press representatives, and was openly frank about Nicaragua's development difficulties.[40]

10. Operating Rules of Soviet–Third World Behavior

Close examination of Soviet behavior in the Third World suggests that Moscow has had several operating rules. The following list is by no means exhaustive but suggests the kinds of patterns we are looking for in

Soviet foreign policy behavior. First, the Soviets, as mentioned earlier, have been committed to avoiding direct confrontation with the United States over Third World regional issues and have avoided actions which they believed might precipitate a strong US reaction.

Second has been a continuing determination to maintain superpower equality with the United States through widened access to Third World regions using a variety of policy instruments—economic aid, military and security assistance, exploitation of anti-colonial and anti-imperialist sentiments, cultural exchanges, student scholarships, active measures, and the use of surrogates. Traditional diplomacy has been accompanied by a second track of support for national liberation movements, aid to local communist parties, and active measures. These have entailed forgery, disinformation, manipulation of foreign media, agents of influence, false rumors, use of clandestine radio stations, blackmail, bribery, and support for front groups, such as the World Peace Movement.

Third, in pursuit of superpower equality, Soviet leaders have taken advantage of opportunities to undercut and supplant US power and, generally, to compete more effectively with the United States on a global scale. This goal frequently has led the Soviets to exploit regional tensions by providing assistance to a participant in a local conflict, by supporting a country that considers itself the target of US interference, or by exacerbating regional tensions (as in Lebanon in 1983).

CONCLUSION

To the extent we have explained the assumptions underlying our approach to Soviet foreign policy, we will have provided the reader with a framework in which to set our subsequent analysis. Objectivity and balanced assessments are difficult, but not impossible, to achieve in the study of Soviet–Third World relations. Certainly the temptation to fall into simplistic explanations of Soviet behavior is strong. The Soviet threat is powerfully ingrained in the American psyche after four decades of Cold War and Containment policy. The Soviet presence in Cuba and Moscow's expansion during the mid to late 1970s reinforced old stereotypes of a Soviet Union intent on exporting communism around the world—unless countered by US power.

But a closer look demonstrates that reality is far more complicated. By the early 1960s dreams of a communist empire had already unravelled with the Sino-Soviet split, Yugoslavia's defiance of Soviet control, and Rumania's pursuit of an independent policy. Subsequently, Third World countries successfully courted by the USSR would move away (Egypt, Somalia, Guinea, Ghana, and Mali). Many times over the years the Soviets have attained influence in a Third World country only to lose it later—as dramatically illustrated by Anwar Sadat's demand that the Soviets leave Egypt in 1972. Most Soviet–Third World relationships, moreover, are marked as much by their strains as by their strengths, as in Cuba, Syria, Libya, and Vietnam.

As we approach the 21st century, it is important to understand the nature and significance of Soviet–Third World relations. This is so because Third World economic and political instability promises to be high, regional conflicts will tempt both the USSR and United States to take sides, and direct conflict between Soviets and Americans in a Third World setting remains a possibility. Clarity in understanding the basic nature of the Soviet threat in the Third World will contribute to our ability to adopt rational and appropriate policies toward the USSR and toward regional states and situations.

NOTES

1. For background reading, see Joseph L. Nogee and Robert H. Donaldson, *Soviet Foreign Policy Since World War II* (New York: Pergamon Press, 1988); Robbin F. Laird and Erik P. Hoffman, *Soviet Foreign Policy in a Changing World* (New York: Aldine Publishing Co., 1986); Morton Schwartz, *The Foreign Policy of the USSR: Domestic Factors* (Encino, CA: Dickenson Publishing Co., 1975); Seweryn Bialer, *The Soviet Paradox: External Expansion, Internal Decline* (New York: Vintage Books, 1987); and Curtis Keeble, "The Roots of Soviet Foreign Policy," *International Affairs* 60, No. 10 (Autumn 1984), pp. 561–578.

2. See Alvin Z. Rubinstein, *Soviet Foreign Policy Since World War II: Imperial and Global* (Boston: Little, Brown and Co., 1985); Jiri Valenta and William Potter, *Soviet Decision-Making for National Security* (London: George Allen & Unwin, 1984); Robert F. Byrnes, ed., *Sources of Soviet Conduct in the 1980s After Brezhnev* (Bloomington: Indiana University Press, 1983); and Seweryn Bialer, *The Domestic Context of Soviet Foreign Policy* (Boulder, CO: Westview Press, 1980).

3. Armenian-Azerbaijani ethnic national conflict erupted in Nagorno-Karabakh, a predominantly Armenian area now controlled by the Azerbaijan republic, in early 1988, leading to the death of 32 people killed in anti-Armenian riots in the Azerbaijani city of Sumgait in late February. Later disturbances in November 1988 led to 28 deaths, with large numbers of Armenians fleeing the countryside for their lives and Soviet military forces sent into the region in an attempt to maintain order. See *The Washington Post*, December 2, 1988. Armenians, mainly Christian, perceive Azerbaijanis, mostly Moslem, as genocidal Islamic neighbors. In addition, Armenians fear Islamic Turks, who massacred Armenians in 1915. See *The New York Times*, September 25, 1988, and *The Washington Post*, March 5, 1988. Islamic-based nationalism is especially troublesome for Russian leaders, because the USSR is comprised of 45 million Moslems, 16 percent of the total Soviet population. Having little cultural links with Russia, they have the least to lose in combating Soviet control; Islamic discontent frequently takes anti-Russian and anti-Soviet forms. Islamic peoples concentrate in six southern republics: Kazakhstan, Uzbekistan, Turkmenistan, Tadzhikistan, Kirghizia and Azerbaijan. They are multiplying at two to three times the rate of Slavic and European populations in the USSR. Estonians, who identify more with Finland and Sweden than the USSR, were urging new freedoms for Estonia in late 1988, along with Latvia and Lithuania; and Estonia asserted control of its own affairs in November 1988—a move rejected by Soviet

authorities. See *The Philadelphia Inquirer,* November 17, 1988; and *The New York Times,* October 28, 1988, and November 10, 1988.

4. *The New York Times,* October 1 and 2, 1988.

5. See Timothy J. Colton, *The Dilemma of Reform in the Soviet Union* (New York: Council on Foreign Relations, 1986), Chs. 1–2; and Harry Gelman, *The Brezhnev Politburo and the Decline of Détente* (Ithaca: Cornell University Press, 1984).

6. Adeed Dawisha and Karen Dawisha, eds., *The Soviet Union and the Middle East* (London: Holmes and Meier Publishers, for the Royal Institute of International Affairs, 1982); Robert O. Freedman, *Soviet Policy Toward the Middle East Since 1970* (New York: Praeger, 1982); and Mark Kauppi and R. Craig Nation, eds., *The Soviet Union and the Middle East in the 1980s* (Lexington, MA: D. C. Heath, 1983).

7. Edward Gonzalez, "Cuba, the Third World and the Soviet Union," in Andrzej Korbonski and Francis Fukuyama, eds., *The Soviet Union and the Third World: The Last Three Decades* (Ithaca and London: Cornell University Press, 1987), pp. 123–47; W. Raymond Duncan, *The Soviet Union and Cuba: Interests and Influence* (New York: Praeger, 1987); Cole Blasier, *The Giant's Rival* (Pittsburgh: University of Pittsburgh Press, 1983); and Cole Blasier and Carmelo Mesa-Lago, eds., *Cuba in the World* (Pittsburgh: University of Pittsburgh Press, 1979).

8. On Soviet-Vietnamese relations as a marriage of convenience, see Douglas Pike, *Vietnam and the Soviet Union: Anatomy of an Alliance* (Boulder, CO: Westview Press, 1987); and on Vietnamese desire to diminish their dependence on the USSR, see Robert Shaplen, *Bitter Victory* (New York: Harper and Row, 1986).

9. Galia Golan, "Gorbachev's Middle East Strategy," *Foreign Affairs* 66, No. 1 (Fall 1987), pp. 41–57; and Robert G. Neumann, "Assad and the Middle East," *Foreign Affairs* 62, No. 2 (Winter 1983–84), pp. 237–56.

10. See Francis Fukuyama, "Gorbachev and the Third World," *Foreign Affairs* 64, No. 4 (Spring 1986), pp. 715–31; and Joseph Whelan and James Dixon, *The Soviet Union and the Third World, 1980–85* (Washington, DC: Pergamon-Brassy, 1986).

11. James Lee Ray, *Global Politics* (Boston: Houghton Mifflin Company, 1987), Parts 4–6; and Walter S. Jones, *The Logic of International Relations* (Boston: Little, Brown & Co., 1985, fifth edition), Ch. 15.

12. On Gorbachev's concern with increasing environmental interdependence, see his Political Report of the CPSU Central Committee to the 27th CPSU Congress, February 26, 1986, Foreign Broadcast Information Service (FBIS), Soviet Union (March 28, 1986), Vol. III, No. 060, Supplement 066.

13. On the Reagan defense build-up, amounting to over $536 billion in added funding, beyond inflation, during 1981–1987, see Joseph Kruzel, ed., *American Defense Annual* (Lexington, MA: D. C. Heath and Co., 1987).

14. See *The New York Times,* November 27, 1988.

15. See Jerry F. Hough, *The Struggle for the Third World* (Washington, D.C.: The Brookings Institution, 1986), Chs. 7–8.

16. *The New York Times,* November 2, 1988.

17. For a study of recent evolution of Soviet military thinking, see Michael MccGwire, *Military Objectives in Soviet Foreign Policy* (Washington, D.C.: The Brookings Institution, 1987).

18. See Seweryn Bialer, "The Political System," in Byrnes, ed., *Sources of Soviet Conduct in the 1980s After Brezhnev,* Ch. 1.

19. *Ibid.*

20. For an analysis of the "realist" interpretation of Soviet foreign policy, see Richard K. Herrmann, *Perceptions and Behavior in Soviet Foreign Policy* (Pittsburgh, PA: University of Pittsburgh Press, 1985).

21. Rubinstein, *Soviet Foreign Policy Since World War II: Imperial and Global,* Ch. 1.

22. George F. Kennan, *American Diplomacy* (Chicago: The University of Chicago Press, 1984).

23. John Spanier, *Foreign Policy Since World War II* (New York: Holt, Rinehart and Winston, 1985).

24. See, for example, Rubinstein, *Soviet Foreign Policy Since World War II*

25. See Louis J. Halle, *The Cold War as History* (New York and London: Harper and Row, 1967).

26. See Duncan, *The Soviet Union and Cuba: Interests and Influence.*

27. See Robert H. Donaldson, ed., *The Soviet Union in the Third World: Successes and Failures* (Boulder, CO: Westview Press, 1980).

28. On communism's many roles and adaptability to different political cultures, see Tony Smith, *Thinking Like a Communist: State and Legitimacy in the Soviet Union, China, and Cuba* (New York: W. W. Norton and Co., 1987).

29. *Ibid.*

30. *Ibid.*

31. Background reading on these points is found in Adam Ulam, *Expansion and Coexistence: The History of Soviet Foreign Policy 1917–67* (New York: Frederick A. Praeger, 1968); and Ulam, *Dangerous Relations: The Soviet Union in World Politics, 1970–1982* (New York: Oxford University Press, 1983).

32. Soviet losses over the years are cited in Ruth Leger Sivard, *World Military and Social Expenditures* (Washington, D.C.: World Priorities, 1987), p. 30.

33. On the question of presence *versus* influence, see Alvin Z. Rubinstein, *Soviet and Chinese Influence in the Third World* (New York: Praeger, 1975), Ch. 1; and Duncan, *The Soviet Union and Cuba: Interests and Influence,* Ch. 1.

34. See *Cuba—Quarterly Situation Report: First Quarter 1988* (Washington, D.C.: United States Information Agency, Radio Marti Program, 1988).

35. W. Raymond Duncan, "Castro and Gorbachev," *Problems of Communism* 35, No. 2 (March–April 1986), pp. 45–57.

36. *Ibid.*

37. *Ibid.*

38. See Gary W. Wynia, *The Politics of Latin American Development* (Cambridge: Cambridge University Press, 1985); also Richard N. Adams *et al., Social Change in Latin America Today* (New York: Vintage Books, 1960), especially essay by John P. Gillin, "Some Signposts for Policy," pp. 14–62.

39. *The New York Times,* October 16, 1988.

40. *The Washington Post,* November 6, 1988.

PART TWO

Soviet Policy Toward the Third World: Gorbachev's New Directions

2

MOSCOW AND THE THIRD WORLD: THE RECORD

As the Gorbachev regime addressed its domestic and foreign policy priorities in early 1985, it must also have reviewed the role and importance of the Third World for its broader objectives. It may have constructed, at least intuitively, a balance sheet contrasting successes and failures, benefits and costs, positive and negative trends. It may also have reevaluated its objectives and its instruments of policy to determine where changes might be made that would better serve Soviet interests. This chapter will provide a brief assessment of the USSR's Third World position and prospects as the new regime might have viewed them.

MOTIVATIONS AND OBJECTIVES

For over 30 years the Soviets considered the Third World a relatively safe arena for competition with the West. It first attracted serious Soviet attention in the mid-1950s, when Nikita Khrushchev assumed power, and it subsequently became a central target in Moscow's efforts to expand its strategic position at Western expense and to gain recognition as a global power.

Motivated by both an historic Russian sense of insecurity and the Marxist-Leninist world view of socialism's inherent antagonism with the "imperialist" West, the Soviet Union tried to match and ultimately exceed the US global reach by enhancing its own power in the Third World. The dynamic components of nationalism and ideology fed a Soviet quest not merely to maintain a traditional balance of power but to continually strengthen Soviet influence at the expense of the West.[1]

In order to enhance their power, bolster their ability to project that power, and generally strengthen their own position at the expense of the United States, the Soviets pursued policies aimed at:

- Improving their position, first, in geographically contiguous or proximate areas such as the Middle East, South Asia, and East Asia; then in geopolitically important Third World countries, such as Cuba and Vietnam; then in the Third World generally.
- Establishing close ties with key regional states and developing access to naval, air, and intelligence gathering facilities.
- Strengthening left-wing forces wherever possible, with special attention to pro-Soviet Marxist regimes, as in Angola, Ethiopia, and South Yemen.
- Promoting the USSR's status as a global power through inclusion in regional negotiations and international organizations and support for pro-Soviet clients whose foreign policies advanced Soviet interests.
- Achieving sufficient success to demonstrate the vitality of Marxist-Leninist ideology and the credibility of the USSR's claims to be a revolutionary power.[2]

A WORLD OF OPPORTUNITIES

Post–World War II developments in the Third World provided the Soviets numerous opportunities to expand their presence and influence at Western expense. Of greatest importance was the demise of imperialism and the break-down in Western-dominated order. The British withdrew from the Middle East and India, the French from Africa and Southeast Asia, and the Dutch from Indonesia. The withdrawals were accomplished with varying degrees of difficulty, created numerous political anomalies, and left a residue of bitterness and anti-Western sentiment. The emerging movements and governments tended to be intensely nationalistic and frequently willing to develop friendly relations with the USSR, which they perceived as the natural antagonist of the imperial powers. The new governments were looking for economic and military assistance as well as for political backing against the West and against emerging regional antagonists.

In the Middle East, the creation of Israel and the resulting Arab-Israeli conflict provided an opening for Moscow in its efforts to court emerging radical Arab states. Similarly, opportunities were created in South Asia, by Sino-Indian and Indo-Pakistani tensions, and in Southeast Asia, by Hanoi's war against the US-backed south and its traditional antipathy for China. In southern Africa, the racial issue provided a natural focal point for Moscow as it moved to expand its relations with Black African states.

The chronic instability that plagued the Third World and produced numerous coups and revolutions provided ample openings for Soviet exploitation. Existing governments, typically autocratic and repressive, and frequently linked politically and economically to the West, were replaced by radical, often military, and ostensibly more popular regimes. Such regimes, in rejecting the policies and ties of their predecessors, often looked to the socialist East for assistance.

During the 1970s, further opportunities arose. The United States experienced setbacks in its own position, most dramatically highlighted by its defeat in Vietnam and the overthrow of the Shah in Iran. The collapse of the Portuguese empire in Africa provided additional emerging states for Moscow to cultivate.

INSTRUMENTS OF SOVIET POLICY

Over the years, the Soviets developed a wide range of policy instruments to advance their objectives in the Third World. Most effective, by far, was their arms transfer program. Since the mid-1950s, equipment deliveries have totaled over $85 billion and since the mid-1970s have earned Moscow up to $10 billion annually in hard currency. Only sales of oil have earned more hard currency for the Soviets. The program has had other benefits for Moscow. It has created dependence on the part of many recipients based on the need for resupply, maintenance, modernization, and training. And it has led to the stationing of large numbers of Soviet military personnel and advisers in the Third World as well as to extensive training programs for Third World personnel.

The Soviets successfully exploited regional conflicts, usually offering support to nations or groups opposing US-backed states. This approach enabled them to gain entry to Third World states and then to use their arms aid program to establish close relationships.

In addition, the Soviets:

- Extended economic assistance, including credits and technical assistance, which gave them a sizable physical presence and helped expand their commercial relationships with Third World states.
- Used East European and Cuban intermediaries to train Third World intelligence services, provide technical support, or furnish combat troops in defense of other clients.
- Supported "national liberation" movements with the objective of changing the existing order and gaining clients.
- Used unconventional means—active measures, including misinformation and covert operations—as well as more conventional policies, to strengthen their influence, promote leftist causes, and undermine their adversaries, both the West and China.
- Exploited various forms of Third World anti-colonialism and anti-Western sentiment through conferences, the media, front organizations, and international institutions such as the United Nations.
- Used ideological flexibility in dealing with Marxist and non-Marxist government and opposition groups.

Ideology and Nationalism: Factors in the Third World Response

The appeal of communism to emerging Third World leaders appears, in hindsight, to have been inevitable. Numerous leaders had increasingly used ideology (fascism, communism, socialism) in the nineteenth and early twentieth centuries because these ideologies performed functions vital to their acquisition and consolidation of political power. An appealing ideology could arouse intellectuals and the public to political action and could be adapted to local situations.

Third World intellectuals, rising to prominence after World War II, as colonialism faded, also turned to ideology to mobilize the masses, promote change in the status quo, and legitimize their political rule. Various non-communist ideologies emerged, including the nationalist movements of Latin America, regional movements such as Nasser's pan-Arabism; and, more recently, the Islamic fundamentalism of Iran's Ayatollah Khomeini.

Communism held a special ideological appeal because its anti-colonial and anti-imperialist concepts fit the experiences and cultures of Third World countries.[3] It provided a comprehensive view of the world, promising self-sufficiency and security to new leaders and their followers—and it could be adapted relatively easily to the unique cultures and historic legacies of different Third World regions.[4] With a moral tone and "scientific" claim to effective resolution of complex issues, communism promised an up-to-date plan for human progress and inevitable modernization.[5] Soviet, Chinese, and Cuban brands of communism illustrate communism's many faces and its adaptability to the diverse needs of political leaders operating in *sui generis* national and political settings.[6] No two kinds of Marxism-Leninism are exactly alike; rather each carries the imprint of distinct nationalism and personal leadership not only between countries, but within countries—from Lenin to Gorbachev, Mao Zedung to Deng Xiaoping, Ho Chi Minh to Phan Van Dong or Do Muoi. Competing Marxist-Leninist factions in Third World states today—within Nicaragua's National Directorate, among El Salvador's leftist guerrilla leaders, or between Ethiopia's Mengistu Haile Mariam and the Eritrean National Liberation Movement—illustrate Marxism-Leninism's remarkable flexibility.

Third World revolutionaries have used Communist ideology for their own purposes, creatively adapting it in an effort to translate nationalist sentiments into a unifying ethos for development and mobilized change.[7] Communism has demonstrated a strong capacity to:

- Appeal to Third World nationalists seeking radical change.
- Support nationalist ambitions while leaving the reins of power in the hands of strong leaders.
- Provide outlets for new forms of national communism that remain within the family of socialist countries helped by the USSR.

- Infuse Third World leaders and followers with the idea of progress, modernization and confidence in attaining economic growth, thereby expanding the participation base.
- Define the country's national interest in terms of socialist and capitalist reference points, enemies, and friends—paralleling "we-they" aspects of nationalism.
- Express Third World nationalism's desire to be free of foreign rulers and have one's own self-government.
- Serve as an official rationale for and give direction to national policies.
- Forge a system of total rule and provide legitimacy to nationalist leaders.
- Unify fragmented sources of discontent inherent in the country's class and ethnic base by offering a coherent explanation of Third World poverty and underdevelopment.
- Serve as a higher rationalization of more basic objectives sought by nationalist leaders, such as improved living conditions and social amenities.
- Legitimize national objectives and facilitate communication between national leaders and the led.

HOW THIRD WORLD COUNTRIES USE THE SOVIETS

It would be inaccurate to depict Third World countries as compliant supplicants. Moscow's relations with Third World leaders have been a two-way street, with power-seeking flowing in both directions as each side has attempted to advance its own interests. Like the USSR's policy-makers, Third World leaders have pursued their own objectives—vital interests that fall into the category of physical security, economic well-being, and protection of political sovereignty. They have particularly sought access to Soviet weapons and training to enhance their physical security.

Both the USSR and its Third World clients have benefitted from these relationships, just as each has experienced costs in doing business with the other. They have continued to associate with one another so long as mutual interests are served, benefits outweigh costs, and the relationship is managed to each side's satisfaction. When these conditions are not met, the Soviets have been asked to leave—as Egypt's Anwar Sadat ejected them in 1972 and Somalia's Mohammed Siad Barre broke with them in 1977. Third World heads of state time and again have demonstrated their unwillingness to exchange one colonial master for another—a distinct limitation to Soviet influence. It should be remembered that Third World leaders like Fidel Castro, Siad Barre, Hafiz al-Assad, Mengistu Haile Mariam and many others are tough leaders who came up the hard way—and without Soviet assistance. They do not cave in easily to outside pressure. Most are less interested in Marxism-Leninism *per se* than in pursuit of their own personal and national interests.

Third World leaders have used the Soviet Union for a wide range of personal and national goals:

- *security assistance*: military equipment, training and spare parts; intelligence training in tactics and strategy; police and internal security assistance against insurgencies and other threats; and additional types of aid to keep Third World leaders like Castro, Assad, Nicaragua's Sandinistas, and Angola's Movement for the Popular Liberation of Angola (MPLA) in power.
- *economic development aid*: credits for purchase of Soviet goods; subsidized oil deliveries; technical assistance in agriculture, irrigation, dairy farming, and port construction—as in Nicaragua—hydroelectric power projects, and housing; and often conspicuous aid, such as Egypt's Aswan Dam; aid of this type has kept some Third World economies from total collapse as in the cases of Cuba and Vietnam.
- *diplomatic support*: political backing for domestic, regional, and international policies pursued by Third World leaders, as in Vietnam's invasion of Kampuchea, India's friction with Pakistan, and Nicaragua's problems with US-backed contras; buttressing in public forums like the United Nations; bolstering through radio and television broadcasting to specific Third World regions where clients have image and interests at stake.

In using the USSR to their advantage, Third World leaders have pursued numerous policy techniques. A check list would include the following:

- Providing the USSR opportunities for a physical presence—including air and/or port facilities—in geostrategically key areas of the world that allow Moscow to project power and gain regional influence; Angola, Egypt, Ethiopia, Libya, Somalia, Syria, Vietnam, Cuba, and Nicaragua illustrate the point.
- Making available construction of Soviet-controlled intelligence-gathering installations as in Cuba and Vietnam.
- Trading goods necessary for Soviet economic well-being (Argentina's grain, Brazil's foodstuffs, or Morocco's phosphates); holding out the promise of more lucrative trade in the future.
- Pursuing strong diplomatic relations, allowing Moscow to counter third party influence in the region (India's ties are one means for the USSR to counter Chinese and American influence in Southeast Asia; Vietnam and Nicaragua have followed a similar pattern); using diplomacy to open doors for Moscow to become a legitimate arbiter of regional disputes (as ties with Nicaragua enhance Moscow's status in Central America).
- Making available ground forces whose efforts advance Soviet interests, as Castro has done over the years; in return Cuba has received generous Soviet support that has advanced its foreign policy goals.

- Adopting Marxist-Leninist ideological precepts and even instituting a pro-Soviet Communist party, as in Cuba, Nicaragua, Vietnam, Angola, Ethiopia, and South Yemen—thereby giving credibility to Soviet global status and power.
- Using their own regional and international status as influence-seeking assets in dealing with Moscow, as demonstrated by Syria's Assad, Egypt's Sadat, Cuba's Castro, and India's Rajiv Gandhi.

While these policy techniques by no means exhaust the many ways Third World leaders have used available assets in seeking influence with Soviet decision-makers, they illustrate that small developing countries are not without resources in dealing with Moscow. Such valued resources come in objective and subjective forms—from assets like strategic location and fighting skills to intangibles such as the prestige of a Third World leader, reputation as a revolutionary model, skill in diplomacy, quality of the country's work ethic and unifying force of anti-colonial/anti-imperialist radical brands of nationalism. The value of a Third World country's assets varies from state to state, but the essential point is that leaders of small Third World states have their own leverage to use with Moscow.

A RECORD OF SUCCESS

Gorbachev and his colleagues undoubtedly recognized that Moscow had made dramatic gains in its global position since the 1950s and had legitimized its claims to global status. From a country with little role to play in the Third World, the USSR had established a physical presence in virtually every region of the world and had become a factor in every significant regional dispute. It had working relationships with almost all Third World countries;[8] had established a military presence and thus an enhanced capability to project power in all Third World regions; and had close political and security ties to strategically located allies in all Third World areas.

The number of pro-Soviet regimes in the Third World had increased dramatically since 1955. The Soviets had gained allies (Cuba, Vietnam, Syria, Ethiopia, Angola) in key regions of the world, and they had signed Friendship and Cooperation Treaties with 13 Third World states.[9] Most of the Soviet Union's closest allies in the Third World (Cuba, Vietnam, Ethiopia, Nicaragua) had come to power on their own, without Soviet support but with a commitment to a Marxist view of the world. The Soviets had built on this political affinity with the provision of economic and military aid.

Extensive arms supply relationships enabled the Soviets to enhance their Third World physical presence. They had thousands of military advisers and technicians stationed in a wide variety of Third World states, often serving as an integral part of the other state's military infrastructure. They had helped key clients (such as Cuba, Vietnam, Syria, and Ethiopia) upgrade their armed forces, enabling them in turn to pursue more active regional policies that complemented Soviet interests.

The Soviets had significantly enhanced their power projection and intelligence gathering capabilities in the Third World, gaining access to air and naval facilities in a number of countries. They could sustain their fleet outside home waters for longer periods of time through access to naval ports of call. And they had increased their deployment of naval aircraft outside the country; as of 1985, reconnaissance planes were flying routinely out of Cuba, Vietnam, Angola, South Yemen, Ethiopia, Syria, and Libya. The Soviets had intelligence collection facilities in strategic locations, and their military transport could provide resupply to most regions of the world.[10]

Moscow also had expanded its economic base in the Third World, establishing extensive trade relationships with many states, based largely on arms sales. Soviet access to Third World resources had helped to strengthen the USSR's economic base. The raw materials it imported facilitated its industrial development and also gave it flexibility. Imports of oil and natural gas, for example, could be re-exported to Third World clients, sold for hard currency in the West, allocated to East European clients, or used domestically. Agricultural imports offset the USSR's harvest shortfalls and improved the quality of consumer goods in the Soviet Union. Expanded fishing opportunities also served important food needs. At the same time, the Soviets gained new markets for their own goods, particularly in the fields of metallurgy and energy.[11]

Moscow's hard currency earnings from the Third World came primarily from arms sales and were vital in improving its balance of payments position and allowing it to import Western technology. As depicted in Table 2.1, Soviet military deliveries to the Third World increased dramatically after 1978. The average annual value of arms agreements was $500 million a year in the decade from 1955–1965, rose to $5 billion a year in the decade from 1965–1975, and, by the late 1970s and early 1980s, exceeded $10 billion a year. These earnings made possible the extension of economic and military assistance through favorable credit and repayment terms, which in turn established the base for much subsequent trade with Third World countries.[12]

Moscow's enhanced ability to extend economic and military assistance also reinforced its general capabilities in important regions, enabling it to support key clients (e.g., Cuba, Vietnam), strengthen ties to strategically located states, help pro-Soviet regimes consolidate their positions, and make inroads with countries basically Western in orientation. Table 2.2 depicts communist economic aid to less developed countries in terms of extensions and drawings. Table 2.3 illustrates Soviet economic aid extended to less developed countries through 1988; note the concentration of aid in the Middle East and South Asia over the years.[13] In the process of extending economic aid, the Soviets established a significant presence of economic technicians in the Third World. Table 2.4 shows East European economic aid extended to the less-developed countries (LDCs), by recipient.

TABLE 2.1 Communist Countries: Arms Transfers to Less Developed Countries, Agreements and Deliveries* (in million US $)

	Total Deliveries	*USSR Deliveries*	*Eastern Europe*		*China*	
			Agreements	*Deliveries*	*Agreements*	*Deliveries*
Total	243,335	207,290	22,270	20,265	20,140	15,780
1954–77	41,795	36,400	3,650	2,430	3,105	2,965
1978	10,315	9,600	560	550	235	165
1979	16,085	15,300	750	645	215	140
1980	14,835	13,900	905	670	885	265
1981	16,070	14,200	2,665	1,455	3,035	415
1982	19,035	15,950	1,960	2,025	1,830	1,060
1983	20,255	17,100	1,755	1,535	865	1,620
1984	20,765	16,475	1,800	2,255	380	2,035
1985	17,135	13,855	3,050	2,610	1,410	670
1986	19,095	15,955	2,175	1,820	1,785	1,320
1987	23,460	19,240	2,000	2,140	4,610	2,080
1988	24,490	19,315	1,000	2,130	1,785	3,045

*Data rounded to the nearest $5 million. Data for the Less Developed Countries include Cuba.

Source: Handbook of Economic Statistics: A Reference Aid (Washington, DC: Central Intelligence Agency, 1989), p. 174.

TABLE 2.2 Communist Countries: Economic Aid to Less Developed Countries, Extensions and Drawings* (in million US dollars)

	Total		*USSR*		*Eastern Europe*		*China*	
	Extended	*Drawn*	*Extended*	*Drawn*	*Extended*	*Drawn*	*Extended*	*Drawn*
Total	74,900	36,255	47,405	20,675	18,010	9,395	9,490	6,185
1954–78	31,205	14,245	16,610	7,915	9,565	3,530	5,030	2,800
1979	4,625	1,175	3,805	620	645	310	175	245
1980	4,455	1,565	2,605	955	1,330	335	520	275
1981	1,835	1,750	855	925	895	515	85	310
1982	2,155	2,400	1,395	1,300	725	690	35	410
1983	3,895	2,780	3,185	1,645	410	725	300	410
1984	6,240	2,620	3,205	1,510	2,125	760	910	350
1985	4,140	2,465	3,085	1,460	765	635	290	370
1986	4,270	2,375	3,160	1,310	870	685	240	380
1987	4,310	2,425	2,240	1,475	500	640	1,570	310
1988	7,770	2,455	7,255	1,560	180	570	335	325

*Data rounded to the nearest $5 million.

Source: Handbook of Economic Statistics: A Reference Aid (Washington, DC: Central Intelligence Agency, 1989), p. 174.

The USSR experienced the greatest expansion of its position in the Third World in the mid to late 1970s, when pro-Soviet regimes came to power in Angola, Ethiopia, Grenada, Nicaragua, and Afghanistan; its ally, Vietnam, extended its domain in Southeast Asia as Laos and Cambodia became Peoples Republics. The US setbacks in Vietnam and Iran, the

TABLE 2.3 USSR: Economic Aid Extended to Less Developed Countries (in million US $)

	1954–88	*1987*	*1988*		*1954–88*	*1987*	*1988*
Total	47,407	2,240	7,255	Other	354	4	29
Africa	10,261	242	186	East Asia	261	0	NEGL
Algeria	1,937	0	0	Indonesia	214	0	0
Angola	1,037	16	0	Other	47	0	NEGL
Burkina	6	0	NEGL	Europe	440	0	0
Cameroon	8	NEGL	0	Latin America	4,812	39	1,497
Central African Republic	3	0	0	Argentina	455	NEGL	0
Congo	74	0	0	Bolivia	204	0	0
Equatorial Guinea	4	0	0	Brazil	728	20	250
Ethiopia	1,462	158	6	Nicaragua	2,535	19	1,247
Ghana	110	0	0	Other	890	0	0
Guinea	454	18	10	Middle East and South Asia	31,633	1,959	5,572
Madagascar	309	0	23	Afghanistan	4,574	396	776
Mauritania	34	0	NEGL	Bangladesh	600	85	0
Morocco	2,098	0	0	Egypt	1,723	284	0
Mozambique	497	34	118	India	11,624	1,117	3,960
Nigeria	1,357	0	0	Iran	1,164	0	0
Senegal	8	0	0	Iraq	2,726	0	0
Sierra Leone	35	0	0	North Yemen	197	0	0
Somalia	164	0	0	Pakistan	1,210	0	0
Sudan	75	10	0	Sri Lanka	178	77	0
Tanzania	45	0	0	Syria	1,916	0	0
Tunisia	123	0	0	Turkey	3,399	0	0
Uganda	35	0	0	Other	2,322	0	836
Zambia	32	2	0				

Source: Handbook of Economic Statistics: A Reference Aid (Washington, DC: Central Intelligence Agency, 1989), p. 175.

TABLE 2.4 Eastern Europe: Economic Aid Extended to Less Developed Countries, by Recipient (in million US $)

	1954–88	*1987*	*1988*
Total	18,008	501	181
Africa	5,044	210	49
Algeria	974	0	0
Ethiopia	564	3	NEGL
Ghana	149	0	0
Guinea	130	0	0
Morocco	234	0	0
Nigeria	888	203	12
Somalia	41	0	0
Sudan	386	0	0
Tanzania	100	0	12
Tunisia	284	0	0
Zambia	166	0	0
Other	1,128	4	25
East Asia	682	0	0
Burma	213	0	0
Indonesia	367	0	0
Philippines	80	0	0
Other	22	0	0
Latin America	3,210	91	132
Argentina	298	0	0
Bolivia	124	0	25
Brazil	781	0	0
Colombia	141	0	30
Ecuador	27	0	0
Nicaragua	756	91	77
Peru	265	0	0
Uruguay	31	0	0
Venezuela	10	0	0
Other	777	0	0
Middle East and South Asia	9,072	200	0
Afghanistan	214	0	0
Bangladesh	718	0	0
Egypt	2,078	200	0
India	432	0	0
Iran	786	0	0
Iraq	493	0	0
Lebanon	9	0	0
North Yemen	38	0	0
Pakistan	724	0	0
South Yemen	204	0	0
Sri Lanka	93	0	0
Syria	1,759	0	0
Turkey	1,522	0	0
Other	2	0	0

Source: Handbook of Economic Statistics: A Reference Aid (Washington, DC: Central Intelligence Agency, 1989), p. 176.

establishment of a sizable Soviet military presence in Cam Ranh Bay in Vietnam, and the dramatic invasion of Afghanistan in 1979 added to the impression that the "correlation of forces" in the world had indeed shifted in Moscow's favor—as the Soviets were then claiming.[14]

SETBACKS AND COSTS

Moscow's gains were not made without setbacks and costs, and, over the years, there was increasing Soviet recognition of the obstacles to further progress. The endemic problems of economic development in backward Third World nations were an ongoing source of concern, and Soviet client states were a drain on Soviet resources. The reduction of Western influence was not always accompanied by a corresponding increase in Soviet influence. Important Third World leaders accepted Soviet aid and used Soviet leverage for their own purposes, but often pursued regional policies contrary to Soviet interests.

Seemingly promising situations proved disappointing. A number of major recipients of Soviet aid were overthrown or died,[15] and the policies they had pursued proved reversible. Following an unsuccessful Communist-led coup attempt in the Sudan in 1971, the Soviets were expelled from that country. The Marxist regime of Salvador Allende was unable to maintain power in Chile. In their greatest Third World loss (until Afghanistan), the Soviets were expelled from Egypt by Sadat in 1972.[16] The Soviets also were expelled from Somalia and the facilities at Berbera following their conclusion of an arms deal with Ethiopia in 1977.[17] In Africa, the pro-Soviet government of Mozambique entered into negotiations with South Africa, apparently without giving Moscow any forewarning.

Economically, the Soviets also faced disappointments. If arms sales were excluded, the Soviets actually had a negative trade balance with Third World countries. Soviet civilian machinery and equipment was reputed to be low in quality—with the exception of energy-related products. A large portion of Soviet credits extended for trade was never drawn by Third World states. Grant aid was declining because of the USSR's own declining economic growth rates. Heavy commitments to Cuba and Vietnam were a significant drain on Soviet resources (about $6 billion a year by 1985).[18] The total costs of Moscow's empire rose from an estimated $13-22 billion in 1971 to an estimated $36-47 billion in 1980—and rising.[19] Finally, the growing debt of Third World countries to the USSR had reached $18 billion by 1983—and much of that debt clearly would never be repaid.

From the point of view of ideological trends in the Third World, communism did not seem to be on the upswing. Communism as an ideology had failed to attract many adherents among either new leaders or the masses. Promised dreams often had proved ephemeral. Having been drawn to Marxism-Leninism as a natural outlet for translating nationalist sentiments into a plan of action for economic growth, political rule, and social progress, Third World leaders had not found it a reliable model for economic and political development. Countries as diverse as Angola, Cuba, Ethiopia, Mozambique, Nicaragua, South Yemen, and Vietnam were unable to separate totalitarian implications and consequences from communism's development-technical aspects, i.e., state planning and centralized decision-making.[20] They found themselves with over-bureaucratized, frequently corrupt, sagging economies; many were beleaguered by internal opposition groups—often ethnic national in nature—seeking access to political power sharing. Economic stagnation and political turmoil resulted in the declining appeal of communism as a model for change in what had become an interdependent world.

THE 1980s—A DECADE OF STAGNATION

Ironically, the invasion of Afghanistan marked the end of Moscow's era of greatest expansion. On the one hand, the invasion seemed a benchmark of Moscow's dynamic forward movement, positioning it for further adventures in South Asia and a possible drive toward the Persian Gulf. On the other, by demonstrating the need to invade in order to maintain a Marxist-Leninist government in power, it revealed the frailty of the Communist model and set the tone for the 1980s—a decade in which Moscow struggled to maintain its established positions.

The USSR's subsequent inability to quell the insurgency and establish the authority of the government within Afghanistan and in the international community was symbolic of the general sluggishness of the Soviet performance in the Third World during the 1980s. While Moscow had not lost ground, its failure to maintain the momentum of the previous decade suggested a loss of dynamism attributable to the absence of opportunities, the complexities of the international situation, and the difficulty of simply maintaining positions already established.

Between 1979 and 1985, there were no Soviet "successes" in the Third World. No new Marxist states had been created and prospects for the creation of such states seemed limited. Many of the nations which had moved into the "socialist-oriented" camp were under pressure from internal insurgencies. Many others were looking to the West for economic assistance.

CONSTRAINTS TO PROGRESS

A number of factors limited Moscow's efforts to expand its position in the Third World during the 1980s.

- There were few opportunities comparable to those of the post-war years and the 1970s.
- Much of Moscow's energy during the 1980s was devoted to maintaining positions already gained; many of its clients (Angola, Afghanistan, Ethiopia, Nicaragua, Mozambique) were having difficulty combatting effective insurgencies.

- The USSR was no longer primarily a supporter of "national liberation" movements. Rather it had become a "counter-insurgency" power. The only "national liberation" movements the Soviets directly supported (Palestinian and southern African groups) were targeted against states with which Moscow had no diplomatic relations (Israel and South Africa).
- Most Soviet client states faced serious economic problems and were having no more (and often less) success dealing with them than were other Third World states.
- The Soviet Union's own economic difficulties made it reluctant to furnish vital economic assistance, even to such close allies as Ethiopia. Its exclusion from international lending agencies also undermined its ability to play an active economic role internationally.
- Many Third World leaders were suspicious of Soviet intentions and viewed their own indigenous communist parties as potential threats. Soviet support for such parties often proved counterproductive (Egypt, Iraq, Sudan, Iran).
- With an expanded presence had come contradictions and complications. Two clients or potential clients might be in conflict (Syria-Iraq, Syria-PLO, Algeria-Morocco, Iran-Iraq, Somalia-Ethiopia), forcing difficult and often unsatisfactory policy choices. Moscow's clients might create broader regional difficulties for the USSR, as in the case of ASEAN's negative reactions to Vietnam's invasion of Cambodia.
- Problems with clients were chronic, stemming from differences over the extent of economic or military aid or differences over policy (such as the occupation of Afghanistan).
- Moscow did not have the key to the solutions to the most important regional disputes (e.g., the Arab-Israeli conflict or the problems in southern Africa).
- The Soviets generally had been unsuccessful in their efforts to convert their physical presence and their military supply relationships into political influence. Though dependent on Moscow in various ways, most clients continued to make their own policy decisions on matters of importance to them and to resist Soviet pressure. Moscow's chronic inability to influence Syrian decision making with respect to Lebanon was a clear example.
- The renewed US effort to oppose further Soviet and pro-Soviet advances in the Third World and the inability of the USSR to match the much greater power projection capabilities of the United States further reinforced the impression that the Soviet Union had lost its dynamism in the Third World.

In a way, the slowing of Moscow's Third World advance reflected its arrival as a world power. It now had equities to protect as well as accumulated liabilities. It was learning the limitations of military power and had its own economic problems. In addition, Third World leaders increasingly were realizing that they were no longer engaged in battles with Western "imperialism" but rather faced complex internal political and economic problems for which neither capitalism nor Marxism-Leninism offered a quick fix. The Soviet model had lost much of its appeal both because the Soviet Union itself was seen to be having economic difficulties and because Moscow's closest allies were having as many difficulties as other Third World states. Even the single party model of government had proved vulnerable; the factional and tribal infighting in South Yemen in early 1986 demonstrated that the Marxist-Leninist model provided no cure for internal instability.

The Perils of Empire: Afghanistan and Vietnam

Afghanistan and Vietnam illustrated the perils of the extended empire inherited by Gorbachev. Afghan rebels, mujahedin, fiercely resisted Soviet occupation, waging ceaseless warfare against Soviet forces after the invasion of December 1979. Using US-provided "stinger" missiles, the mujahedin were shooting down increasing numbers of Soviet helicopter gunships, raising the costs of Soviet intervention. Lost Soviet lives, demoralized and beleaguered troops, sagging enthusiasm, rising financial costs, declining prestige for the mighty Soviet army, Middle East opposition to the violation of an Islamic country, and increasing worldwide criticism of Moscow's actions turned Afghanistan into the Soviet Union's Vietnam.

In Vietnam, the Soviets gained numerous benefits as a result of having supplied Hanoi with arms and economic aid to fight against the United States. Soviet national security concerns in Asia and the Pacific made the military facilities provided by Cam Ranh Bay—Moscow's largest naval deployment base outside of the USSR—a key asset for Soviet power projection. But the costs of Soviet ties with Vietnam were high. Vietnam's economy, with little heavy industry and only a limited light industry with which to produce trade goods, was a drain on Soviet resources. With one of the worst trade deficits in the world, Vietnam required massive assistance far beyond what the Soviets or Eastern Bloc countries were willing or able to provide.[21] Since at least as early as 1980, Moscow had been deeply concerned with the state of Vietnam's economy and had sent delegations to assess Vietnamese use of Soviet aid. In the spring of 1982, the head of one such delegation, Mikhail Gorbachev—Politburo member in charge of agriculture—bluntly criticized Vietnam's waste of Soviet economic aid.[22]

SOVIET DEBATE OVER THIRD WORLD TRENDS

The growing complexity of the Third World environment and of Moscow's involvement in it fostered an internal Soviet discussion of the situation long before Gorbachev's ascension to power. Ongoing commentary by Soviet analysts during the 1970s and early 1980s reflected far more pessimistic assessments of Moscow's prospects than those expressed twenty or thirty years earlier, when the Soviet Union was embarking optimistically on its Third World ventures. A lively debate focused on the nature of the Third World, the manner in which Moscow should try to exploit new opportunities, the scope of those opportunities, and the utility of old instruments of policy.

Soviet analysts had long recognized the major trends complicating Moscow's Third World environment. Their discussion of declining opportunities to aid liberation struggles and the implications of Soviet economic problems on its foreign economic aid capabilities had also opened to question the merits of orthodox assumptions about Third World development and the utility of certain policies.

Two broad schools of thought were involved in the debate, which became intense during the late 1970s and early 1980s.[23] The traditional Soviet view held that the Third World states would develop according to Marxist patterns along the path to socialism. A more skeptical view was held by those who doubted both the prospects for socialism in backward countries and the longevity of radical regimes; these writers drew attention to the reverse trend—the increasing integration of Third World states into the Western-dominated world market. The latter school typically found the Soviet Union at a disadvantage in economic competition with the West in the developing world and tended to argue that elements of capitalism could benefit Third World development.

The pessimism of the latter view had an impact on the Soviet leadership even before the advent of the Gorbachev regime. At the 25th Party Congress in 1976, Brezhnev was optimistic as he argued that the trend toward socialism was prevalent in the Third World. At the 26th Party Congress in 1981, however, he conceded that the situation was "variegated" and indicated that Third World states would have to be more self-sufficient.

Brezhnev's death in 1982 permitted an even more thorough airing of various policy issues, including the rising economic cost of Moscow's Third World empire, the impact on US-Soviet relations of Moscow's activism in the Third World, and the poor economic and political performance of Moscow's recently acquired Third World allies. Soviet General Secretary Andropov wrote in 1983 that "it is one thing to proclaim socialism as one's aim and quite another to build it."[24]

SHIFTING PRIORITIES AND EMPHASIS

The history of Soviet–Third World relations is one of constantly shifting priorities and approaches. Lenin had recognized the importance of the Third World in the struggle between East and West and, at the Second Congress of the Communist International in July 1920, urged that all Communist parties support national movements of liberation. The Soviet Union lacked the resources to pursue such a policy actively, however, and was, in any case, preoccupied with internal problems and external pressures. In the early post-war period, Stalin rejected any alliance with the national bourgeoisie and argued that liberation of oppressed peoples was impossible without a proletarian revolution and the overthrow of imperialism. He thus failed to seek advantage from emerging Third World nationalism and focused instead on world revolution, encouraging communist insurrections in both colonial areas and those under national rule. This approach proved counterproductive, alienating natural allies among nationalist forces—both those in power and those pursuing power.

Khrushchev transformed Soviet policy toward the Third World, rejecting Stalin's strictly bipolar view and portraying a more complex world in which the Communist world and the emerging anti-Western Third World nations would cooperate to shift the "correlation of forces" in favor of socialism. This approach required some ideological adjustments. The "national bourgeoisie" now became acceptable allies—if they were pursuing the proper development policies (such as nationalization, expansion of the state sector, an anti-imperialist foreign policy, and the granting of democratic rights to "progressive domestic elements, including the Communist Party". This approach opened the way for the flexible and opportunistic Third World policy that marked the Khrushchev years.

During the decade from 1955 to 1964, the Soviets focused their attention primarily on South and Southeast Asia and the Middle East, with Afghanistan, India, Indonesia, Iran, and Egypt receiving the bulk of their attention. Their main instrument of policy was economic and military aid. They extended more than $5 billion in economic credits and grants to non-Communist Third World countries during this period, often for the construction of dramatic projects (e.g., the Aswan Dam in Egypt and the Bhilai steel mill in India); they also extended about $4 billion in military assistance.[25]

Following the removal of Khrushchev in 1964 for "hare-brained schemes," the Soviets re-evaluated their policies in the Third World, focusing on the obstacles created by anticommunism, excessive expectations, corruption, and the unpredictability of the regimes with which they were dealing. The result was the adoption of a less optimistic, even more pragmatic and realistic strategy. Where Khrushchev had been willing to incur economic cost for anticipated political or economic gain, Brezhnev was more businesslike, expecting a demonstrated—not just a potential—return on investment.

The Brezhnev approach was also less doctrinaire with respect to the development path required of Third World countries. Assumptions about the need for industrialization, nationalization, and expanded state controls gave way to more realistic views about the utility of private investment and the development of successful agricultural programs to build viable economies. The grading of Third World nations according to their level of socialism and their pro-Soviet policies was discontinued, and, although Brezhnev did not renounce the Soviet commitment to world revolution, expectations were lowered considerably. Khrushchev had been denounced for "adventurism;" the Brezhnev approach was marked by patience.

Despite the downgrading of Soviet ideological expectations and priorities under Brezhnev, Soviet strategic interest in the Third World did not diminish. Moscow remained committed to advancing its influence and presence at US expense, particularly in regions of geopolitical importance. While the primary focus of attention continued to be the Middle East and South Asia, the Soviets demonstrated a willingness to exploit opportunities that developed elsewhere (e.g., Angola, Ethiopia, Nicaragua).

The use of Soviet policy instruments shifted during the Brezhnev era, reflecting the general move toward rationality. Greater emphasis was put on economically feasible, as opposed to dramatic, projects. Economic assistance went primarily to close allies (Cuba and Vietnam). Economic aid declined and military assistance assumed greater importance as the Soviets recognized the broad range of benefits to be gained thereby. The focus shifted from the extension of assistance to the negotiation of hard-currency contracts. The use of surrogate forces was initiated in the 1970s, when Cuban troops were sent to both Angola and Ethiopia. Finally, the direct use of Soviet troops in a Third World nation occurred for the first (and thus far only) time, when the Soviets invaded Afghanistan in December 1979.

There was little change in policy during the transition period between Brezhnev and Gorbachev. While, as noted above, the academic literature became more openly critical of existing problems and trends, the Andropov interregnum was too brief to have a significant impact on policy, and Chernenko was not inclined to change. Thus, most of the trends of the Brezhnev era continued.

While encouraging their clients to develop the institutions that would enable them to provide continuity of policy from leader to leader, the Soviets did not encourage them to move rapidly toward socialism. The primary example of this was Ethiopia, where the Soviets pushed Mengistu to establish a Vanguard Party, but were reluctant to recognize Ethiopia as a socialist state because this would have committed them to the regime's survival. In this way, Moscow moved still further away from its ideological commitment to expand the world socialist community while maintaining its national, great-power goals and status.

THE US FACTOR AND DÉTENTE

East-West relations, and particularly the US-Soviet strategic relationship, have been of primary importance in Moscow's perception of its foreign policy interests. Thus, it was logical to anticipate that the Soviets would be willing to subordinate their ambitions in the Third World to the advancement of their interests in the West. Yet, as we have seen, the era of détente in Soviet-US relations (roughly 1969–1974) failed to moderate Soviet expansionism in the Third World. Despite the signing in 1972 of the SALT treaty limiting strategic arms and the Basic Principles Agreement (BPA), pointing to codes of conduct for crisis prevention in Third World areas, Moscow continued to view the United States as its adversary and to pursue opportunities for projecting its power in the Third World when they arose.

Soviet actions and US perceptions of those actions stemmed in part from the differing concepts of détente held by Moscow and Washington. For the Soviets, détente meant that they had achieved recognized nuclear parity and political equality with the United States, that the United States would play a more modest role in world politics, and, consequently, that Moscow would find it easier to advance its influence in the Third World. The Soviets anticipated, for example, that US efforts to dominate them in important arenas, such as the Middle East, would end and that their role as coequal would be recognized. At the same time, Moscow maintained its view that competition between the forces of socialism and imperialism would continue unabated, notwithstanding the new era of bilateral détente, making it highly unlikely that Moscow would abandon its aspirations in the Third World or change its perceptions of the role of power in international politics.

The United States, on the other hand, did not attach *de facto* political equality to its recognition of Soviet strategic parity and consequently failed to give the same political significance to détente as Moscow. Washington envisaged détente as a way of managing the emergence of Soviet power and assumed that détente would act as a restraint on Soviet behavior in the Third World. Thus, precisely as Moscow was preparing to enhance its position in the Third World, Washington was preparing to reduce Soviet influence in key Third World areas—particularly the Middle East.

During the period of détente, Moscow and Washington both pursued policies in the Third World which undermined the other's expectations. For its part, the United States:

- Continued to escalate its involvement in Southeast Asia, mining Haiphong Harbor in May 1972, on the eve of President Nixon's scheduled visit to Moscow.
- Pursued a rapprochement with the USSR's other adversary, China, with Kissinger's visit occurring in July 1971 and Nixon's in February 1972.
- Helped to undermine the Marxist government of Salvador Allende in Chile.
- Excluded the Soviet Union from the negotiating process following the Middle East war of October 1973 and moved to establish close ties to Egypt, formerly Moscow's most important Third World client.

During the same period, the Soviets took actions in the Third World that created strong doubt in the United States about Moscow's intentions. They

- Proceeded with plans to build a nuclear submarine base in Cienfuegos, Cuba, pulling back only after a diplomatic confrontation with the United States in 1970.
- Committed fighter pilots and thousands of air-defense troops to support Egypt in the War of Attrition with Israel in 1970.
- Continued large-scale arms assistance to Vietnam.
- Failed to warn the United States of Egypt's intentions to attack Israel in October 1973, despite the BPA signed in 1972, and threatened to intervene unilaterally during the war.

There were a number of other issues which undermined détente, such as the questions of Jewish emigration from the USSR and the extension of US credits to the Soviet Union. From the Soviet point of view, the most devastating blow was Congressional approval, in December 1974, of the Stevenson Amendment to the Export-Import Bank Bill, which restricted credit allocation to the Soviets to a four-year total of $300 million—a pittance compared to Soviet expectations. Immediately thereafter, Moscow repudiated commitments it had given to increase Jewish emigration as well as the 1972 US-Soviet Trade Agreement. At this point, despite the signing of the SALT II accord at Vladivostok in November 1974, the Soviets had probably dismissed the utility of détente.

For the United States, real disillusionment came with Soviet actions in the Third World—Angola in 1975, Ethiopia in 1977, and, most importantly, Afghanistan in 1979. These events fed the growing perception that Soviet actions in the Third World would not be constrained by closer US-Soviet relations.

NOTES

1. See Alvin Z. Rubinstein, *Soviet Foreign Policy Since World War II: Imperial and Global* (Boston: Little, Brown and Company, 1985), pp. 165–169.

2. See Joseph G. Whelan, and Michael J. Dixon, *The Soviet Union in the Third World: Threat to World Peace?* (Washington, DC: Pergamon-Brassey's International Defense Publications, Inc., 1986), pp. 5–8; Seweryn Bialer, *The Soviet Paradox* (New York: Alfred A. Knopf, 1986), pp. 259–272.

3. See Peter Zwick, *National Communism* (Boulder, CO: Westview Press, 1983).

4. On communism's remarkable adaptability, see Tony Smith, *Thinking Like a Communist: State and Legitimacy in the Soviet Union, China, and Cuba* (New York: W. W. Norton, and Co., 1987).

5. See Karl Dietrich Bracher, *The Age of Ideologies: A History of Political Thought in the Twentieth Century,* Translated from the German by Ewald Osers (New York: St. Martin's Press, 1984).

6. Smith, *Thinking Like a Communist.*

7. *Ibid.*; and Bracher, *The Age of Ideologies.*

8. The key exceptions were Israel, South Africa, Chile, and Saudi Arabia as well as several smaller Gulf states.

9. While these treaties are largely symbolic in nature, serving to legitimize the USSR's ties to a given state and enhance its global image, they also help block what Moscow perceives to be US efforts to create anti-Soviet regional alliances and to bolster its treaty partners. The terms of these treaties typically provide for mutual consultation in the event of hostilities but guarantee no specific support. Treaties were signed with Egypt, India, Iraq, and Somalia by 1974, later repudiated by Egypt and Somalia. Later treaties were signed with Angola, Mozambique, The Congo, South Yemen, North Yemen, Ethiopia, Syria, Afghanistan, and Vietnam.

10. See Melvin A. Goodman, "The Soviet Union and the Third World: The Military Dimension," in *The Soviet Union and the Third World: The Last Three Decades*, ed. Andrzej Korbonski and Francis Fukuyama (Ithaca and London: Cornell University Press, 1987).

11. See Abraham S. Becker, "The Soviet Union and the Third World: The Economic Dimension," in *The Soviet Union and the Third World: The Last Three Decades*, ed. Andrzej Korbonski and Francis Fukuyama (Ithaca and London: Cornell University Press, 1987), Ch. 40.

12. *Ibid.*

13. Table 2.3 is especially noteworthy in view of the sharp increase in Soviet economic aid extended during 1987–1988, a period in which it increased from just over $2 billion to over $7 billion. This dramatic jump is explained by $3.9 billion extended to India, to be drawn over a 20-year period, for a nuclear plant; $1.0 billion to Afghanistan; and about $1.2 billion to Nicaragua, to be drawn over a three year period. As these figures suggest, Gorbachev intends to continue to support, rather than abandon, key clients. In the case of India, however, he probably hopes increased aid will yield trade and commodities supporting a Soviet economic recovery.

14. Harry Gelman, *The Brezhnev Politburo and the Decline of Detente* (Ithaca: Cornell University Press, 1984), pp. 26–27.

15. Key examples were Ben Bella in Algeria (1965), Sukarno in Indonesia (1965), Nkrumah in Ghana (1966), Keita in Mali (1968), and Nasser in Egypt (1970).

16. The Soviets had access to facilities in Egypt as well as a sizable physical presence. The loss of access to Alexandria was a significant setback. The total number of Soviet naval aircraft deployed in the Third World did not return to the 1970 level until 1984, when increased use of Cam Ranh Bay made up the difference. Perhaps most importantly, the Soviets had considered Egypt the key regional state in an area of great importance—and thus lost what they perceived to be a major geopolitical advantage.

17. In this case, Moscow clearly had decided that Ethiopia had more potential as a client than Somalia and made a calculated choice—although it may have hoped to retain assets in both states.

18. *Handbook of Economic Statistics: A Reference Aid* (Washington, DC: Central Intelligence Agency, 1989).

19. Charles Wolf, *The Costs of Soviet Empire* (Santa Monica, CA: The RAND Corporation, September 1983), p. 19.

20. Bracher, *The Age of Ideologies.*

21. Douglas Pike, *Vietnam and the Soviet Union* (Boulder, CO: Westview Press, 1987), p. 133.

22. Charles McGregor, "The Sino-Vietnamese Relationship and the Soviet Union," *Adelphi Papers* 232 (Autumn 1988), p. 73.

23. See Elizabeth K. Valkenier, *The Soviet Union and the Third World: An Economic Bind* (New York: Praeger, 1983); Jerry F. Hough, *The Struggle for the Third World: Soviet Debates and American Options* (Washington, DC: Brookings, 1986).

24. *Pravda*, June 16, 1983.

25. Leo Tansky, *Report to U.S. Congress, Joint Economic Committee* (Washington, DC: US Government Printing Office, 1966).

3

GORBACHEV'S "NEW THINKING": ECONOMIC AND STRATEGIC PRIORITIES

Soviet policy toward Third World states must be viewed in the context of Moscow's fundamental security concerns—defending the homeland, sustaining economic growth, and protecting the Soviet political system. These vital interests have driven Soviet foreign policy since Lenin. Mikhail Gorbachev's dramatic initiatives in domestic and foreign policy, his focus on new economic and strategic priorities are but the latest stage of Soviet policy-making in pursuit of traditional national interests. In understanding how Gorbachev's "New Thinking" has affected Soviet–Third World relations, we first need to examine how "New Thinking" has itself been shaped by broader national security and domestic economic concerns.

"NEW THINKING" AXIOMS

Revitalizing and Restructuring the Soviet Economy

Gorbachev's "New Thinking" is driven by a number of axioms.[1] First is the urgent drive to revitalize and restructure the sagging Soviet economy (*perestroika*). Saving an economy in crisis has superseded any external military threat as the primary Soviet concern. In a departure from his predecessors' emphasis on military capability and competition, Gorbachev has argued that it is the civilian, scientific, technological, and agricultural sectors of the economy that provide the essential base on which security and global influence ultimately depend.

The priority of economic development was made clear by Gorbachev in his *Political Report of the CPSU Central Committee to the 27th CPSU Congress* in February 1986. "Today," he said, "it is a primary task for the party and for the whole people to produce a decisive change from the unfavorable tendencies in economic development. . . . There is no other path."[2] Echoing this theme are statements by other top Soviet officials. Prime Minister Nikolai Ryzhkov:

> In implementing the very important restructuring in our society, the party singles out the main directions and the key areas on which maximum efforts must be concentrated. The economy is one of the most important of these. . . . It is the basis of the might of our homeland. The most strenuous and uncommonly difficult work is now unfolding here. . . . What is restructuring in the economy? It is primarily the radical reshaping of the entire system of economic relations. . . .[3]

Although there are differences within the Soviet leadership about many aspects of new thinking, Gorbachev's drive to transform economic strength into long-term national security and to modernize the Soviet economy has been endorsed by his colleagues. Resolutions approved by the special Communist Party Conference in July 1988 gave Gorbachev a strong mandate to press on with his proposed plans for economic revival.

Soviet National Security Through "Mutual Security" and "Reasonable Sufficiency"

A second axiom at work in "New Thinking," linked to the quest for economic revival, is the need for an international environment conducive to Soviet economic growth—that is, a nonthreatening environment that will not demand and drain Soviet resources. Gorbachev realizes that Soviet economic development and strategic priorities are closely linked and that both must be pursued in a complex and interdependent world. A successful foreign policy, designed to maximize economic development and national security, must therefore take into account the views of other actors. Gorbachev and his colleagues have stated that Soviet security is not a zero-sum game—that it cannot be assured by depriving others of their security.

Gorbachev has stressed the theme of *mutual security*. He has repeatedly stated that, in the modern age, no state can defend itself solely by military-technical means; that security cannot be built on the fear of retribution or the doctrine of deterrence; that security cannot be limited to the superpowers but must be attainable on a universal basis; and that for anyone to feel secure, all must feel secure. In his 27th Party Congress speech, he called for a "world security system" to provide guidelines for dialogue among leaders of the world community. In this context, he urged the renunciation of war, a series of confidence-building measures, establishment of a new world economic order, and cooperation in the humanitarian sphere to eliminate such atrocities as genocide and apartheid. While none of these themes was completely new, Gorbachev's packaging of them was; and, because they have gained currency among Soviet officials, they have taken on a new vitality.

Vadim Zagladin, then First Deputy Chairman of the CPSU International Department, writing about the Soviet Party Conference of June 1988, stated that one aspect of Soviet international policy that was becoming clear was the fact that it is necessary to take into account not only the interests of the USSR but also the interests of all members of the world community.[4] And in a series of articles in 1987–1988, three members of the USSR's USA Institute argued that any state that relies exclusively on its military power for security "sets its own security against international security" and that the search for security requires negotiations with adversaries and both concessions and compromises that accommodate the interests of those adversaries. They argued that security is indivisible and that all must have it—or none.[5]

The Gorbachev regime also has stressed the related concept of *reasonable sufficiency* in military policy—meaning the possession of sufficient military means to defend against attack but not enough to gain victory through aggressive actions.[6] As one top spokesman, Yevgeniy Primakov, has said, "Searches for military superiority will inevitably backfire against those who make them—after all, the other side will inevitably search for and find countermeasures."[7]

Domestic and Foreign Policy Interconnections

Gorbachev's emphasis on national security through international security is closely linked to the quest for economic revival. His aim is to reduce East-West tensions, lessen the costs of competing in a "no-win" precarious arms race, and create a more favorable international economic environment, thereby enhancing prospects of increased credits and trade with the West. Economic and strategic priorities go hand in hand.

Thus, the third axiom of new thinking is that domestic economic strength and the international system are fundamentally interconnected. Unlike previous Soviet leaders who tended to view Moscow's internal domestic capabilities separately from the external international system, Gorbachev has placed new emphasis on the need for the USSR to work within the international economic system. Gorbachev and his followers perceive Soviet foreign policy as a means to tap international opportunities and to advance Soviet economic priorities. This perception has been expressed by a number of top Politburo members, including Eduard Shevardnadze in a 1987 speech to top decision-makers of the Ministry of Foreign Affairs:

> If the idea that foreign policy is an extension of domestic policy is true—and it undoubtedly is true—and if the thesis that the goal of diplomacy is to form an external environment that is favorable for internal development is correct—and it undoubtedly is correct, then we are compelled to recognize that the backwardness of our power and its steady loss of status is partially our fault too. . . .[8]

Linking this line of thought with the importance of foreign policy in advancing Soviet economic strength, Shevardnadze stated:

> the time has come today to introduce economics into Soviet foreign policy for, until it merges completely with economics, it will not be able to assist in restructuring the Soviet internal economy and society in general and as a whole, which otherwise will not be able to participate on equal terms in the competitive political struggle for making its social and political model of development attractive. . . .[9]

Thus "New Thinking" emphasizes the interaction of domestic and foreign policy to advance the economic dimensions of Soviet security—reducing international tensions in the hope of reducing military spending, increasing investment in the civilian sector, and opening up opportunities for increased trade in the international economic system. The anticipated result is the ability to focus on "butter" rather than "guns," to convert much of the more efficient military industry to support for the civilian sector, and to bolster the Soviet economic infrastructure.

Politics and Diplomacy over Military Competition

A fourth axiom of New Thinking is that diplomacy, political skill, and shrewd leadership—not military competition—are the appropriate base of a successful foreign policy. Soviet analysts have correctly perceived that the Soviet military build-up and expansionism of the 1970s fostered a Western view of the USSR as a dangerous power bent on the spread of communism and on pursuit of conventional and nuclear superiority. The results were chronic East-West tensions, Western military expansion and modernization, and a US commitment to its Strategic Defense Initiative (SDI). All presented Moscow with the need to sustain a costly arms program—which its struggling economy could ill afford. Having reached the conclusion that Moscow's previous military competition and foreign adventures had been counterproductive, Gorbachev revised the content of foreign policy to emphasize political activism and problem-solving diplomacy as the means of ensuring security.[10] Bringing political measures to the fore meant using diplomacy to reduce East-West tensions, pressing arms control to curtail the arms race, maximizing opportunities for cooperation with the international community, de-emphasizing ideology and, in other political/diplomatic ways, harmonizing Soviet and Western interests.

The Quest for "Stable Coexistence"

Fifth, "New Thinking" entails the search for what Gorbachev and the Politburo elite have termed "stable coexistence." By "stable coexistence" is meant an end to the East-West arms race and demilitarized and de-ideologized competition—replaced by political equilibrium between East and West and stability in military relations.[11] Stability includes demilitarizing and defusing adversarial relations between the Warsaw Pact and North

Atlantic Treaty Organization (NATO); one Soviet official has termed a confrontational structure in Central Europe superfluous, excessively expensive, and irrational.[12] Recognizing the mutual vulnerabilities and interdependence of the USSR and the United States, stable coexistence means an end to the Cold War and steps to improve dialogue and understanding between the Soviet Union and the United States.[13] As explained by Soviet Foreign Minister Shevardnadze in his report to a Foreign Ministry conference on July 25, 1988:

> . . . the new political thinking views peaceful coexistence in the context of the realities of the nuclear age. We are fully justified in refusing to see in it a special form of class struggle. . . . The struggle between two opposing systems is no longer a determining tendency of the present-day era.[14]

BACKDROP TO "NEW THINKING"

Gorbachev's new thinking on economic and strategic priorities is hardly surprising. His arrival on the scene found the Soviet economy in deep trouble. As one observer stated, Gorbachev inherited an "exhausted empire"—making necessary his coming to grips with its failures.[15] Moscow and its buffer states in Eastern Europe faced economic decline with backward technologies—with the exception of weapons and outer space—while the world around them was exploding with advanced information processing and communications systems, genetic engineering and biotechnologies, global trade and international financial systems. While actively involved in world communist affairs, Moscow had remained insular in many other international respects—reflecting its deep suspicions of foreigners and foreign countries. In what had become a highly interdependent world experiencing revolutions in science and technology, the USSR was paying a high price for its insularity.

A look at the rest of the world dramatized Moscow's dilemma. The People's Republic of China, with its dramatic reforms, was outpacing the USSR in productivity and moving toward economic superpower status. Newly industrializing countries (NICs) in the Far East were adopting new generations of microcomputers, integrated circuitry, and robotics—making the Soviet Union appear weak and feeble.

Nor was Soviet military technology keeping pace. In response to the USSR's deployment of SS-20 missiles during the 1970s, West Europe had accepted short range cruise and Pershing II nuclear missiles on its territory and was planning force modernization. The United States was increasing its own military spending and was pressing forward with plans for a new 600-ship maritime force, a Strategic Defense Initiative (SDI) for weapons in outer space, and new generations of precision-guided munitions (PGMs) with pinpoint—computer guided—accuracy and high explosive power. If the Soviets did not step up both their economy and computer-based information processing and communications systems, even their vaunted

TABLE 3.1 Average Annual Growth Rates of Real GNP (percent)

	1961–1965	1966–1970	1971–1975	1976–1980	1981–1985
USSR	4.8	4.9	3.1	2.1	1.9
United States	4.7	3.0	2.5	3.4	2.4
Japan	10.0	11.0	4.3	4.0	3.9
France	5.8	5.4	4.0	3.3	1.2[a]
West Germany	4.8	4.2	2.1	3.3	1.2
Italy	5.2	6.2	2.4	3.8	0.8[a]
UK	3.2	2.5	2.1	1.6	1.7[a]

[a] Data are for gross domestic product (GDP). The difference between GNP and GDP, net factor income from abroad, is small.

Growth rates are measured in national currencies.

Growth rates for the USSR in subsequent years were: 1986 (4.0), 1987 (1.3), and 1988 (1.5).

Sources: USSR: Central Intelligence Agency estimates. Western countries: 1961–1980, Organization of Economic Cooperation and Development, *National Accounts;* 1981–1985, International Monetary Fund, *International Financial Statistics.*

military strength would be overtaken by scientific and technological revolutions abroad.

Inheriting the Past

When Mikhail Gorbachev assumed power in March 1985, Soviet relations with its main adversary were at an impasse. In many respects the Soviets had come a long way during the post–World War II period, attaining strategic parity with the United States, achieving great power status, and acquiring a Third World empire. But these gains had produced ominous reactions from the United States—forward deployment of short-range nuclear missiles in Central Europe; new air, land, and naval weapons systems; SDI technological advancements; and a renewed Cold War with revised US nuclear strategies suggesting a willingness to engage in limited nuclear war against the "evil empire."

Economic Failure and the International Economy

Moscow's sinking economy was also a matter of concern long before Gorbachev's assumption of power. By the late 1970s—as Gorbachev writes in his book, *Perestroika*—signs of lost momentum were clearly indicated by declining productivity, huge grain imports, aging capital stock, hard currency shortfalls, lagging oil production, and an inability to keep up with the scientific and technological development of the West and Far East.[16] Table 3.1 indicates the steady decline in Soviet average annual growth rates in real gross national product since the late 1960s. As US government estimates show, by the time Gorbachev assumed power, the Soviet economy was experiencing a decade long slump, averaging just over two percent GNP growth per year in 1976–1985.[17] Economic erosion had generated growing domestic disillusionment—underscored by rising corruption, alcoholism, job absenteeism, and abortions—hardly an endorsement of the Soviet model or an inspiration for other revolutions.[18] Yuri Andropov, who followed Leonid Brezhnev as Party Secretary in November 1982, represented those individuals in the USSR who saw the Party's primary task as one of getting the country moving again. Before his death in early 1984, Andropov had launched a series of initiatives to raise productivity, reduce corruption, tighten discipline in the workplace, stimulate greater frankness between leaders and the led, and generally shake the Party from its lethargy. These moves were the precursors of Gorbachev's subsequent reforms.

In debating how to energize the economy, a number of foreign policy analysts urged fresh international policy directions based upon new perceptions of the realities of economic life. Many observers in the USSR had come to realize during the 1970s that the international economy operated more as a single interdependent system than as two opposed socialist and capitalist systems.[19] By using an obsolete model of two opposing networks, the Soviets had been left behind. They were outside the major international lending institutions, despite their efforts to gain membership, not participating in the General Agreement on Tariffs and Trade (GATT) or the International Monetary Fund (IMF), and relatively isolated from the trade and commerce generated by the rapid scientific and technological progress of the capitalist system. By the 1970s, Soviet writers were conversant with the internationalization of the world economy, the mutual dependence of countries of different political and social systems, and the interconnections arising from global food, pollution, energy, and oceanic issues.[20] Gorbachev inherited these ideas and began to respond to them as soon as he became General Secretary.

Military-Strategic Relations

During the 1970s the idea had caught on in Soviet analytic circles that, although political struggle with the United States would continue indefinitely, the value of military force in the nuclear age was declining.[21] Among the leading proponents of this view was Georgiy Arbatov, Director of the Institute of the USA and Canada, who ruled out nuclear war as a feasible instrument of foreign policy.[22] For Arbatov and others who took this position, the important question was how to move competition from the military arena to the political—because any use of military force in the nuclear age carried with it the possibility of a nuclear war.[23] The threat of nuclear war, coupled with Soviet economic difficulties and the challenge of keeping up with US increases in military spending, bolstered the view that Soviet security was closely tied to international and global security.[24]

Foreign Political Relations

The impact of revised thinking about the international economic system and strategic-military competition was far-reaching. Soviet writers began to focus on the need to think more about the *political*, than the *military* balance of power, about substituting political for military competition, and about the need to mobilize political power through collaborative efforts with non-socialist states.[25] Now Moscow would use politics to enhance its economic strength and strategic leverage, politics to amplify its overall security and power position in the international arena, and politics to gain a relaxation of East-West tensions and widened access to non-socialist resources and markets.

"NEW THINKING" IN PRACTICE

The first thing to understand about Gorbachev's domestic and international priorities is their continuity with lines of thought that were being debated within Soviet foreign policy circles well before Gorbachev assumed power in March 1985. Indeed, many of Gorbachev's policy initiatives—especially those regarding the links between the revitalizing of Moscow's stagnating economy and the need for a more stable international system, including détente with the United States—reflect views held by early Soviet decision-makers. The reform era of the 1920s produced the first experimentation with détente as the Soviets sought improved trade relations with the Western capitalist countries. Khrushchev's internal reforms led to an upscaled version of detente with the West, Brezhnev pursued detente in the 1970s, and Gorbachev's reforms were anticipated during Yuri Andropov's brief tenure (1982–1984). From this perspective, Gorbachev's policies are not a total break with the past. They are new, however, in their scope, substance, and style.

De-Stalinizing the Soviet Economy and Polity

Gorbachev's "New Thinking" involves the radical de-Stalinizing of the Soviet economic and political system. Operating under the assumption that rigid centralization of political rule and economic decision-making lie at the roots of Soviet economic stagnation, Gorbachev pressed an array of measures to eradicate the remnants of Stalinism that still marked many aspects of the Soviet system when he came to power. These included:[26]

- Extreme centralization and concentration of economic decision-making.
- Total control of the political over the economic order.
- The dead hand of centralized and entrenched Communist Party control over all major economic and political decisions.
- An economy whose allocation of resources favored the enhancement of military power over the objectives of economic growth.
- A decadent and corrupt system of stratified status determined essentially by political power.

- Cultural rigidity presenting an artificial sense of optimism, defined as "socialist realism."
- Autarchy in economic planning, isolation of the Soviet public from foreign influences, and extreme conservatism regarding attitudes toward change and innovation in existing institutions.

These and other aspects of the Stalinist command economy have demonstrated a remarkable resiliency against change over the years despite on-again, off-again anti-Stalinist campaigns, including those of Khrushchev and Andropov.

In terms of their scope and substance, Gorbachev's reforms range across a broad spectrum and cut deeply into Stalinist institutions, cultures, and structures. In addressing the central problem, "acceleration of the socioeconomic development of the country," as he told the 27th Party Congress in February 1987, Gorbachev has attacked laziness and inefficiency, poor work discipline and low productivity, absenteeism and alcoholism.[27] At the Central Committee's plenary meeting in June 1987, he laid out far-reaching proposals to make:

- Central planning agencies less responsible for day-to-day management of individual enterprises.
- Profitability, not plan fulfillment, the key criterion of economic performance.
- Profit the basis for bonuses.
- Productivity the criterion for determining a worker's value.
- Autonomy the golden rule for individual enterprises.
- Managers responsible for determining how they will spend their profits.
- Local managers elected, not appointed.
- Outside inspections to oversee the quality of production.
- Prices more accurately reflecting costs.
- State subsidies to factories subject to cut-backs.[28]

In the field of agriculture, the new Soviet chief launched a new program to put food on Soviet tables. After years of relying on Stalin's concept of big state farms (*sovkhozes*) and collective farms (*kolkhozes,*) Gorbachev assailed collective farms as a resounding failure and called instead for smaller units farmed by individual families.[29] Taking a note from Chinese reforms, Gorbachev urged individual families to rent plots from the state and pursue their own farming interests.

In an effort to prevent, or at least limit, the stultifying hand of Party bureaucracy from blocking implementation of economic reforms—the new Party Secretary also set about de-Stalinizing the political system. In June 1988 the 57-year-old Kremlin chief presented a plan for strengthening the post of state president (which he then assumed), establishing a new national legislature with broad authority, limiting terms of office for government officials to ten years, requiring competitive elections, and making judges more independent and stronger. These changes, approved by the Soviet legislature in December 1988, represent the most sweeping realignment of power since Stalin formulated the current system nearly 60 years ago.

The scope and substance of other political reforms is also impressive. Gorbachev introduced multiple competing candidates in local party elections, called for *glasnost*—"openness" which has inspired criticism of factory, government, and party life, and, perhaps most impressive of all, unveiled many of Joseph Stalin's sins in an effort to get at the "truth" of the Soviet past.[30] Although not as progressive as other aspects of *glasnost* and *perestroika* Gorbachev's increased permissiveness for religious institutions—whether Russian Orthodox, Muslim, or Jewish underscores how far he is prepared to go with his reform movement.[31] So, too, does his more progressive attitude toward human rights, perhaps the most difficult single issue in the liberalization process.

Enhancing External Trade Opportunities

In the external trade arena, Gorbachev has launched a number of broad-gauged programs. They include removing many administrative bottlenecks and allowing Soviet firms to deal with outside companies rather than going through state organizations. Joint ventures with foreign firms, once totally unacceptable, have been legalized, with foreigners able to own up to 49 percent of Soviet enterprises—potentially opening the door to needed technology and know-how from the West, Japan, and the NICs.[32] How well and how quickly the huge Soviet bureaucratic organizations can absorb new technology, knowledge, communications and information systems remains to be seen.

Mutual Security Through Arms Control and Disarmament

Arms control—an effort to gain a breathing space and reduce investment in military expansion—has figured prominently in Gorbachev's strategic priorities. By pressing arms control Gorbachev has tried to undercut the logic for SDI and an expensive arms race in outer space, slow down new weapons procurement in the United States, and prevent force modernization in Europe. Eliminating intermediate-range nuclear forces (INF) in Central Europe was the first priority. The INF Treaty was initialed by Gorbachev and Reagan in December 1987, subsequently approved by the US Senate, and signed in Moscow in May 1988.[33] The treaty called for destruction within three years of all US Pershing IA, Pershing II, and ground-launched cruise missiles; in return, the Soviets pledged to destroy all SS-4, SS-5, SS-12, SS-20, and SS-23 missiles. Moscow also promised to destroy its experimental new cruise missile, as did the United States its experimental new Pershing missile—the IB.[34]

Gorbachev is the first Soviet General Secretary to take a comprehensive approach to arms control. Beyond agreeing in the INF Treaty to scrap many more missiles and warheads than the United States (1500 warheads to 350), he allowed a US congressional delegation to tour the Soviet radar installation at Krasnoyarsk in Siberia and agreed to permit on-site inspections of military installations to verify compliance with the INF agreement—an impressively sharp departure from previous Soviet practice.[35] Moscow also cooperated in establishing "nuclear risk" reduction centers—as a way to smooth communications between the two countries.[36] Gorbachev opened the Soviet chemical warfare center in Shikhaniy to foreign disarmament negotiators, striving to convince the West of Soviet desire to destroy chemical weapons along with others, and in his speech to the United Nations in September 1989, Foreign Minister Shevardnadze called for the abolition of chemical weapons.[37]

These steps reflected the significant shift in Soviet military doctrine which had begun in the late 1970s. Where Moscow used to stress parity in nuclear balances with the US and the West, the Soviets now officially advocate "reasonable sufficiency."[38] Toward that end, they accepted asymmetric nuclear weapons reductions in the 1987 INF accord. Moreover, they revised their thinking on the inevitability of escalation in a nuclear war, stressing the immense costs of a nuclear "victory"—a revision already accepted by Brezhnev, who discarded Moscow's long-held principle of "first strike."[39] In attempting to avoid nuclear devastation, Soviet leaders adopted the position that there can be no victors in a nuclear war, that disarmament is the key to preventing its outbreak, and that escalation must be avoided if war should occur.[40] The leitmotiv of Gorbachev's nuclear doctrine was to downplay any hint of first use that might precipitate a NATO or US decision to attack Russia.[41]

Political Flexibility and Diplomacy in Foreign Policy

Gorbachev stated at the 27th Party Congress in 1986 that, "security is increasingly a political function that can be accomplished only by political means."[42] How this more flexible and comprehensive approach to national security plays out in terms of Soviet-US competition in the Third World poses one of the more interesting questions of international affairs during the last years of the twentieth century.

Certainly Moscow's revised national security priorities began to produce increased flexibility and sophistication not only in relations with the Third World, but in policy toward most regions of the world. In Eastern Europe, Gorbachev has repudiated the Brezhnev doctrine—which purported to legitimize the invasion of Czechoslovakia of 1968[43]—and instead has encouraged East European versions of *perestroika*.[44]

In Western Europe, the smiling and hand-shaking Mr. Gorbachev has pursued an active personal diplomacy, portraying the USSR not as a threat to West European security, but as a purely defense-oriented, non-aggressive power interested only in peaceful relations with its neighbors.[45]

His more sophisticated approach to West Europe has included promises never to begin armed action in Central Europe, support for increased contacts between East and West Germany, and an emphasis on the importance of arms control.[46]

Gorbachev's foreign policy flexibility in dealing with Western Europe has paid dividends in trade and credits. His stepped-up diplomacy—including numerous trips to West European capitals—has received a favorable response from West European leaders. The visit to the USSR by West German Chancellor Helmut Kohl in October 1988 highlighted Gorbachev's success. The visit ended a five-year chill in West German–USSR relations and resulted in 16 contracts including agreement to build a high-technology nuclear reactor in the USSR by a West German–Swiss consortium. Another agreement called for West Germany's extension of a $1.7 billion credit line to the Soviets.[47] Gorbachev's visit to Bonn in June 1989, produced "Gorby Fever;" the Soviet leader was greeted by cheering masses, and a West German poll indicated that 90 percent of West Germans trusted Gorbachev, compared to 58 percent who had confidence in US President Bush and 50 percent in West German Chancellor Helmut Kohl.[48] Still, Gorbachev's visit to France in July 1989 did not produce the same level of "Gorby fever." Gorbachev's charisma did not wow the French as it had the West Germans, suggesting limits to his personalist brand of diplomacy.

Political Settlement of Regional Disputes. The Soviet withdrawal from Afghanistan—remarkable given Kabul's geostrategic location on the Soviet border—is the most dramatic demonstration to date of Gorbachev's commitment to the peaceful resolution of regional conflicts. This commitment has been played out in Southeast Asia (Vietnam's May 1988 announcement of its plans to withdraw troops from Cambodia) in Africa (Moscow's leaning on the MPLA and Cuba to reach agreements with South African–backed UNITA) and in support for political settlements in the Middle East and Central America.[49] This emphasis on political settlement of regional disputes—examined in more detail later—complements the Soviet effort to foster negotiations on arms control with the West and to reduce military weapons competition between the superpowers.

As one Soviet historian has observed,

> Though we were politically, militarily (via weapons supplies and advisers) and diplomatically involved in regional conflicts, we disregarded their influence on the relaxation of tensions between the USSR and the West and on their entire system of relationships. . . . To abate the arms race and make it pointless, you have to *remove political contradictions* and balance the sides' interests. . . . The *primacy of political issues is self-evident. . . . The main problem is whether a political modus vivendi is attainable between the USSR and the Western powers,* whether they can secure a high level of mutual trust.[50]

Gorbachev's Political Style. Gorbachev's charming and open political style is a major ingredient in the implementation of "New Thinking." His vitality and dynamism are a dramatic change from the ponderous, reclusive image of Moscow's previous aging leaders. Observers in Washington, D.C., watching Comrade Gorbachev bound out of his car in the downtown capital city during his visit in December 1987, were impressed with his dazzling public relations skills. Fiercely determined to overhaul the Soviet economic system, breathe fresh air into Soviet society and government, and pursue a flexible and sophisticated diplomacy abroad, Gorbachev represents a new generation of young, highly-motivated, creative, and energetic leaders. In the language of modern political psychology, Gorbachev is a classic "active positive" leader, deriving joy from his high profile and hard work, luxuriating in his capacity to bring change at a turning point in Soviet history.[51]

A New Brand of Pragmatic Realism. What is new about Gorbachev is the extent to which he has grafted an energized type of pragmatic realism onto Soviet policy. He has set about, among other things, "depriving the United States of an enemy" (to use a phrase coined by Georgiy Arbatov) and breaking the log jam in Soviet-US relations. He is pursuing primary state interests—economic revitalization and national security—through reduced tensions with the United States and Western Europe, arms control, more favorable commercial relations externally, and a reformed, market-oriented, economic system. He has relegated to a secondary role those less vital interests such as promoting communism abroad and bolstering economically weak and beleaguered pro-Soviet clients.

Foreign Policy for a Globally Interdependent System

Gorbachev's New Thinking reflects a globalist perspective of world affairs—emphasizing the risk of nuclear weapons and the need to avoid nuclear war; the dependence of most states on each other for resources, trade and commerce; and the importance of managing the interdependence of states with different political and social systems. Moscow admittedly retains a Marxist-Leninist perception of competition between communists and capitalists; Marxism-Leninism is by no means dead in the USSR. Nor have the Soviets given up military power as an instrument of foreign policy. But Gorbachev departs from older, more narrow and combative Marxist-Leninist strictures in his endorsement of flexible collaboration by communists and capitalists to insure mutual survival. A more sophisticated interpretation of international relations than traditionally found in an ideologically doctrinaire system, his is less belligerent in the game of power politics—an attitude that has far-reaching implications for Soviet relations with the Third World.

POLICY TECHNIQUES

Any discussion of Gorbachev's policy techniques in achieving strategic priorities and economic interests must address first his skilled orchestration of personal power. Power—defined as the capacity to influence favorable outcomes—comes in various forms and draws upon multiple resources. As Hedrick Smith, author of *The Power Game*, so ably states, power comes not simply from the office or title held, nor from constitutional legitimacy alone nor from elected or appointed authority.[52] Power derives from how the power game is played, in terms of:

- Access to information.
- Visibility.
- Sense of timing.
- Personal energy.
- Likability.
- Charm.
- Illusion of power.
- Ability to command public attention.
- Creating a winning image.

A quick scanning of this list indicates high marks for Gorbachev. Time and again, in one press conference after the other, Gorbachev has demonstrated his ability to argue his case, attract and work an audience, command public attention, and above all, charm his guests. Gorbachev's skill in the power game is demonstrated by his abilities in bargaining and persuasion, his adroit working of the mass media, and his personal charisma. Top US scholars come away from meetings with Gorbachev impressed by his command of the issues and his depth of knowledge, and much of the US public finds his "integrity" and charm compelling. Even President Reagan—who early in his presidency described the USSR as the "evil empire"—left his fourth summit meeting with Gorbachev convinced of the latter's "sincerity." In his emotional farewell speech in the Kremlin, President Reagan described Mr. Gorbachev as "a friend," saying he and Gorbachev had struggled together against "threats to peace and to liberty."[53]

Gorbachev has channeled his personal power skills into several policies designed to attain strategic and economic priorities. He launched a diplomatic blitz into the most important geographical areas—meeting himself or sending his diplomats to meet with top leaders in Eastern and Western Europe, the United States, China and Japan, South and Southeast Asia, the Middle East and Latin America. An able staff—featuring many old hands with extensive knowledge of America and the West—bolstered these efforts, as did new Foreign Minister Eduard Shevardnadze, a quick study in Gorbachev's brand of flexible sophistication in diplomacy. Shevardnadze makes an appropriate counterpart to Gorbachev in terms of visibility, energy, and charm.

Beyond diplomacy, Gorbachev initiated a media campaign stressing his agenda—arms control, detente, flexible and sophisticated diplomacy, management of global interdependence, and socioeconomic reform at home—in the press, radio, television, public forums in and outside the USSR, and, naturally, at official party conferences and government meetings. He has proved especially skillful at handling domestic and foreign press conferences.

In pressing for broader public approval of the new Soviet image, Gorbachev has taken surprising new steps. He hired a US public relations firm to help "market" Moscow's image during the fourth summit meeting with President Reagan. The media campaign included careful casting of news programming to fit western tastes, redesigning the coats of the omnipresent Soviet security forces, and selling "summit" T-shirts as souvenirs for visiting press reporters. And when Gorbachev wanted to expand business with the West, he ran nine pages of advertising in *The Wall Street Journal*.[54]

Gorbachev moved quickly to enhance his personal power, using available levers of power. He established his dominance over Politburo, Party, government, and military leadership, packing all with his supporters. He used his legitimate authority to lead reform of the economic and political system and his ideological leadership to justify these reforms. He pulled the country toward increased political participation, weakening the party and strengthening the government by enfranchising his popular base.

What he has told his high ranking military officers—to gain support for arms control and reduced military spending—is not known, but can be inferred from a number of events, including the spectacular appearance of Marshal Sergei F. Akhromeyev, Gorbachev's top military adviser, before the US House Armed Services Committee in July 1989. Akhromeyev stressed the importance of Soviet-US arms control cooperation, especially to reduce naval forces. In dealing with his military, Gorbachev surely has stressed the economic foundations of military power and warned that a cancerous economy can not support military strength over the long-run. Secondly, he probably has stressed another factor not always recognized among Western observers: US military power, seen from the USSR, is much stronger—and more threatening—than perceived in the United States. Gorbachev's reasons for slowing down arms competition with the West, reducing the threat and risk of war, and revitalizing the economy as the basis for future military building included US SDI progress, US naval plans, precision-guided munitions capabilities, cruise missiles, anti-submarine warfare (ASW) capabilities, thousands more nuclear warheads capable of delivery to Soviet targets, superiority in military aircraft capable of delivering nuclear warheads to Soviet territory, access to 967 bases (730 of which lay outside NATO, compared to Soviet access to 80 facilities beyond its national borders, 13 of which are outside the Warsaw Pact).[55]

These elements suggest a less enviable Soviet position in terms of the balance of nuclear and conventional forces with the United States than a superficial look at statistics would indicate. London's prestigious International Institute for Strategic Studies (IISS) added another dimension to a less secure portrait of Soviet power in 1987 by refining its measurement of conventional arms in Central Europe to include qualitative as well as quantitative factors in assessing the balances of forces.[56] While acknowledging the Warsaw Pact's numerical superiority to NATO in manpower and other categories of land-based weapons in Central Europe, it argued that these figures could be misconstrued. Other factors—less easy to measure—included morale, quality of equipment, mobilization capabilities, and resupply time.[57]

Moscow's military, notoriously weak in several respects, operates with many deficiencies. These include Russian officers commanding non-Russian enlisted men, with consequent ethnic tensions, linguistic problems, and class-based morale problems.[58] The highly touted Soviet defense system is apparently riddled with vulnerabilities, as demonstrated when young German pilot Mathias Rust flew his small plane straight into Soviet territory and landed in Red Square on 28 May 1987—the anniversary of border guards day! This event gave Gorbachev an opportunity, however, to shake up his military establishment.

SUCCESSES AND LIMITS TO "NEW THINKING"

"New Thinking" Successes

As Moscow's revisionist leader headed into the last decade of the twentieth century, his achievements were mixed. In relations with the United States and West, clearly he had broken Cold War perceptions and established a new political climate for détente, future arms control negotiations, and widened commercial and trade relations. His effort to reduce anti-Stalinism abroad had gone far in presenting a new image of a flexible, deideologized USSR ready to cooperate in the productive, mutually beneficial management of the international system. President Reagan, on completing his fourth summit with Gorbachev, fell short of announcing the end of the Cold War, but came close to proclaiming precisely that conclusion. Western public opinion polls gave new Soviet leader Gorbachev high marks for his integrity and peace initiatives. Gorbachev, utilizing his considerable personal powers in the world of rhetoric and high visibility in superpower relations, had crafted what many saw as a winning image. Gorbachev's charm and flexibility on arms control issues as well as the dramatic withdrawal from Afghanistan, earned Moscow new credit and trade agreements with West Germany and Great Britain.

One of Gorbachev's more spectacular bids to reduce East-West tensions and seize the initiative in superpower peace-making came at his address to the United Nations General Assembly on December 7, 1988, the anniversary of Pearl Harbor. Gorbachev announced that over the next two years the USSR would unilaterally reduce its military forces by 500,000 men and 10,000 tanks, disbanding approximately one half its tanks in Eastern Europe and returning home "a major portion" of forces stationed on the Chinese border.[59] These cuts represent approximately 10 percent of total Soviet military manpower and about 25 percent of the Kremlin's tank forces in Central Europe.[60] They are designed to lend credibility to major aspects of Gorbachev's "New Thinking," including its:

- Rejection of war as an instrument of foreign policy.
- Belief that fighting a nuclear war is suicidal.
- Acceptance of the fact that the United States does not intend to attack the USSR.
- Faith in "reasonable sufficiency" as a sound military doctrine.
- Assumption that militarized foreign policy and previous Soviet foreign adventures were counterproductive.
- Disclaimer of intent to export revolution and socialism.

Constraints on "New Thinking"

Despite the dynamism of Gorbachev's personality and the momentum his policies have created, many constraints to "New Thinking" remain. Bureaucratic interest groups and worker resistance continue to plague Gorbachev's reforms at home. The conservative legacy of the past—secrecy and order, stability versus freedom, entrenched party control, fear of change and loss of security, suspicion of foreign ways—still permeate the system Gorbachev is trying to change. The most daring and innovative Soviet leader since Lenin, Gorbachev nevertheless faces pervasive inertia within the economy, worker and manager resistance, and rising expectations unmatched by significant increases in productivity, food supplies, housing, and consumer goods.[61]

Of the many risks facing Gorbachev in his reform efforts, one stands out dramatically—the release of counterproductive and uncontrollable forces as a consequence of *glasnost* and *perestroika*. Openness and reform essential to rebuilding, combined with a deteriorating economy, may unleash what could prove to be unmanageable social pressures. Worker discontent with food shortages and poor living conditions—sparking a wildcat coal miners strike in Siberia affecting 100,000 workers that shut down the Siberian coal fields in July 1989 and spread to the country's richest coal fields in the Ukraine—point toward future difficulties. Rising public discontent with continued housing and consumer goods shortfalls and public criticism and counter-cultures may prove unacceptable to party officials. An even more threatening challenge lies in ethnic nationalism, already erupting violently among Azerbaijanis and Armenians and simmering among Estonians, Latvians, Lithuanians, Tatars, Uzbeks, Tajiks, and Kazakhs. Nor should we forget the Soviet military which undoubtedly view with concern Gorbachev's downgrading of its interests. Gorbachev's announced unilateral cut of 500,000 military personnel in December 1988 produced sharp criticism by high ranking military officers of how previous troop reductions were managed.[62] Letters of complaint were published in the armed forces newspaper, *Red Star,* although none of them directly criticized Gorbachev's plan.

Unforeseen economic problems must be added to economic constraints hindering Mr. Gorbachev's economic revival efforts. A classic example is the December 1988 earthquake that caused considerable destruction in Armenia. The earthquake, leaving tens of thousands dead and approximately 400,000 homeless, is certain to require several billions of rubles in costs.[63]

Izvestia, the government newspaper, reported that early estimates for reconstruction started at five billion rubles, or around $8.4 billion, but that actual costs probably would be higher.[64] By comparison, the 1986 Chernobyl nuclear accident, another severe blow to Gorbachev's economic revival program, cost around $8 billion rubles, or approximately $12.8 billion.[65] These problems are made worse by the predicted deficit of 36 billion rubles for 1989, spawned in part by the collapse of international oil prices. Moscow lost over 40 billion rubles in revenue from petroleum exports during 1985–1988, according to economists.[66] And the Soviet economy has suffered an additional 36 billion ruble shortfall from its crackdown on drinking by raising the price of vodka, which led to a fall in sales.

PROSPECTS

How successfully Gorbachev's policy innovations will achieve stated objectives is an open question. Certainly his policies will be conditioned by numerous factors not completely under his control. Can the "dead hand" of the Stalinist-inherited Communist Party bureaucracy be overcome on the march toward more market incentives and "democratic" politics? Will a conservative and disaffected citizenry catch the fire in Gorbachev's belly? Will Western trade credits stimulate trading policies translated into Soviet economic development? Under the best of conditions, will Soviet technology be able to catch up with Western and East Asian scientific and technological development? Will the West respond to Gorbachev's arms reduction proposals that provide him with foreign policy "successes" and more flexible use of resources to be used to strengthen his domestic power base at home? Or will the reverse occur—lack of foreign policy "successes," and a weakened internal power base on which to orchestrate his *perestroika* and *glasnost*-driven reforms at home?

While Gorbachev clearly has launched a new era in Soviet economic and strategic priorities, his policy successes will be shaped not only by his leadership skill, but by domestic and foreign responses to his initiatives, how Soviet attitudes and institutions adapt to change, and the policies pursued toward the USSR by Western and Far Eastern countries. One factor not under his control, for example, is how the United States will interpret continuing high transfers of Soviet military weapons to preferred clients. While the total value of Soviet arms agreements fell in 1988—from $19.4 billion in 1987 to $9.9 billion—they continued to attract US attention. In 1988, the Soviets still accounted for about 34 percent of world arms transfer agreements compared to 31 percent for the United States.[67]

"New Thinking" in Soviet foreign policy has been crafted to manage East-West relations more effectively in quest of economic and strategic priorities. East-West relations during the post–World War II period had been a mix of cooperation and conflict—passing through distinct cycles of tension and relaxation—shifting from intense adversarial positions to the more stable relations associated with detente and back again. In 1985

Gorbachev set about revising the relationship, putting it on a more stable, long-term basis.

One thing is certain: Gorbachev's East-West priorities in foreign policy affect his approach to the Third World, just as Khrushchev's and Brezhnev's Third World postures were preconditioned by East-West relations. But Gorbachev's Third World activities differ from his predecessors. In earlier eras, the Soviet view of East-West détente was decoupled from Moscow's Third World activities (with detente in fact acting as a backdrop for expanded activities in Third World arenas) Gorbachev has coupled the settlement of East-West strategic issues and East-West competition in the Third World. Neither Khrushchev's free-wheeling Third World gambits—based on East-West "peaceful coexistence" announced at the 20th Party Congress in 1956—nor Brezhnev's loosely articulated "codes of conduct" in the Third World, essentially a green light for Soviet freedom of action, especially in the Middle East—linked to East-West détente in SALT I (1972)—made the connection between East-West détente and settlement of Third World regional disputes. The Soviet withdrawal from Afghanistan is instructive. As Gorbachev told members of the 11th annual meeting of members of the US–Soviet Trade and Economic Council (ASTEC) in Moscow in April 1988, "We hope that the signature of the Geneva accords on Afghanistan will lend an impulse to the process of settling regional conflicts."[68]

With this assessment of Soviet economic and strategic priorities in focus, we can now turn our attention to how, and in what ways, Gorbachev links pursuit of primary strategic priorities and economic interests in East-West relations with pursuit of less vital interests in the Third World.

NOTES

1. See *Highlights of the Atlantic Council–Soviet Union Third Dialogue: Mid September 1988*, October 12, 1988, unpublished comments, Atlantic Council, Washington, DC, p. 2.

2. See Gorbachev's Political Report of the CPSU Central Committee to the 27th CPSU Congress, Moscow, *Pravda* in Russian, Foreign Broadcast Information Service (FBIS), Daily Report, Soviet Union, March 28, 1986, Supplement. Hereafter cited as FBIS.

3. Report by N. I. Ryzhkov at a ceremonial meeting at the Kremlin Palace of Congresses, April 22, 1967, Moscow *Pravda*, in FBIS, Soviet Union, April 24, 1987, pp. R 2 ff.

4. Vadim Zagladin, *Sovetskaya Rossiya*, June 23, 1988, p. 1.

5. Deputy Director Vitaliy Zhurkin, Section Head Sergey Karaganov, and Senior Research Andry Kortunov, *Kommunist*, January 1988, pp. 42–50; *New Times*, October 12, 1987.

6. See Yevgeniy Primakov, "A New Philosophy in Soviet Foreign Policy," *Pravda*, July 10, 1987, p. 4; in *Current Digest of the Soviet Press*, Vol. 39, No. 28 (August 12, 1987), pp. 1–4.

7. *Ibid*.

8. Eduard Shevardnadze's speech at the Soviet Ministry of Foreign Affairs, June 27, 1987, FBIS, Soviet Union, October 27, 1987.

9. Eduard Shevardnadze, speech entitled "An Unconditional Requirement—Turn to Face the Economy," July 4, 1987, in FBIS, Soviet Union, October 30, 1987.

10. See Yevgeniy Primakov, "To Stem Arms Race's Drain on Economy, New Thinking Accents Political Means of Ensuring Security," *Pravda*, January 8, 1988, p. 4; *Current Digest of the Soviet Press*, Vol. 40, No. 1 (1988), pp. 1–4.

11. Joint United States–Soviet Recommendations for Stable Coexistence, *Congressional Record*, Proceedings and Debates of the 100th Congress, Second Session, Vol. 134, No. 63, Washington, DC, May 9, 1988. The American Committee on U.S.-Soviet Relations and the U.S.A.-Canada Institute began a series of discussions in 1985, a joint project combining US-Soviet efforts to examine requirements for mutual survival and make recommendations for joint action.

12. Atlantic Council, *Highlights of the Atlantic Council–Soviet Union Third Dialogue.*

13. *Congressional Record*, Joint United States–Soviet Union Recommendations for Stable Coexistence.

14. Ministry of Foreign Affairs Bulletin, August 1988.

15. Robert Kaiser, *The Washington Post*, September 23, 1984.

16. Mikhail Gorbachev, *Perestroika: New Thinking for Our Country and the World* (New York: Harper and Row, 1987).

17. *Allocation of Resources in the Soviet Union and China—1986*, Hearings before the Subcommittee on National Security Economics of the Joint Economic Committee, Congress of the United States, 100th Congress, first session, Part 12, March 19 and August 3, 1987, p. 11.

18. Gorbachev, *Perestroika.*

19. See Elizabeth Valkenier, *The Soviet Union and the Third World: An Economic Bind* (New York: Praeger, 1983), Chs. 2–3.

20. *Ibid.*

21. Jerry F. Hough, *The Struggle for the Third World: Soviet Debates and American Options* (Washington, DC: The Brookings Institution, 1986), pp. 205 ff.

22. *Ibid.*, p. 211.

23. *Ibid.*, pp. 211–212.

24. *Ibid.*, p. 216.

25. See Gorbachev's Political Report of the CPSU Central Committee, *op. cit.*

26. On these and other characteristics of the Soviet Stalinist system, see Seweryn Bialer's insightful work, *The Soviet Paradox: External Expansion, Internal Decline* (New York: Vintage Books, 1986), Ch. 1.

27. Gorbachev's Political Report of the CPSU Central Committee, *op. cit.*

28. See "On the tasks of the party for the radical restructuring of the management of the economy." Report of the General Secretary of the Central Committee of the CPSU M. S. Gorbachev to the Plenum of the Central Committee of the CPSU, June 25, 1987, *Pravda*, June 26, 1987. For a sophisticated analysis of Gorbachev's economic reforms, see Ed A. Hewett, *Reforming the Soviet Economy: Equality Versus Efficiency* (Washington, DC: The Brookings Institutions, 1988), Ch. 7. See also coverage of the June 1987 meetings in *The New York Times*, June 26, 1987; *The Washington Post*, June 26, 1987, and *The Christian Science Monitor*, June 26, 1987.

29. *The Washington Post*, October 14, 1988.

30. See *ibid.*, March 15, 1987.

31. See Daniel N. Nelson and Roger B. Anderson, eds., *Soviet-American Relations: Understanding Differences, Avoiding Conflicts* (Wilmington, DE: Scholarly Resources Books, 1988), pp. 70-71.

32. *Ibid.*, October 29, 1988.

33. See *The Washington Post,* December 9, 1987.

34. *Ibid.*

35. *The Christian Science Monitor,* December 2, 1987.

36. *The Washington Post,* September 10, 1987.

37. *The New York Times,* October 5, 1987.

38. On shifting Soviet military doctrine, see Michael MccGwire, *Military Objectives in Soviet Foreign Policy* (Washington, DC: The Brookings Institution, 1987).

39. *The Christian Science Monitor,* December 2, 1987.

40. See MccGwire, *Military Objectives.*

41. *Ibid.*

42. See Gorbachev's Political Report of the CPSU Central Committee, *op. cit.*

43. In a speech in Italy in September 1989, the Head of the Soviet Foreign Ministry's Information Department, Gennediy Gerasimov, said that the Soviet Union has "replaced the Brezhnev doctrine, which exists no longer and perhaps never existed, with the Frank Sinatra Doctrine from the title of one of his famous songs, 'I did it my way'" (Rome *Ansa,* September 8, 1989).

44. On the effects of Gorbachev's reforms in Eastern Europe, see Nicholas N. Kittrie and Ivan Volgyes, *The Uncertain Future: Gorbachev's Eastern Bloc* (New York: Paragon House, 1988).

45. For background reading on Soviet relations with the west, see Jerry Hough, *Russia and the West* (New York: Simon and Schuster, 1988).

46. *Ibid.*

47. *The Washington Post,* October 25, 1988.

48. During his June 1989 four-day tour in West Germany, Gorbachev stressed "common European values" and a "shared European home." Eleven agreements were signed on bilateral economic and cultural exchange as was a wide-ranging document on German-Soviet relations in which the two countries vow to eliminate obstacles separating Europe. See *The Christian Science Monitor,* June 12 and 15, 1989.

49. These issues are covered more in depth in subsequent chapters.

50. Professor Vyacheslav Dashishev, "East-West: Quest for New Relations. On the Priorities of the Soviet State's Foreign Policy," Moscow, *Literaturnaya Gazeta,* May 18, 1988, p. 14; in FBIS, Soviet Union, May 20, 1988, p. 4.

51. See James David Barber, *The Presidential Character* (Englewood Cliffs, NJ: Prentice-Hall, 1977, 2nd ed.).

52. Hedrick Smith, *The Power Game: How Washington Works* (New York: Random House, 1988).

53. *The Washington Post,* June 3, 1988.

54. See *The Wall Street Journal,* November 27–December 2, 1987.

55. See Tom Gervasi, *Soviet Military Power: The Pentagon's Propaganda Document, Annotated and Corrected* (New York: Vintage Books, 1988).

56. See The International Institute for Stratetgic Studies, *The Military Balance: 1987–88* London, 1988, Part I.

57. See Tom Gervasi, *The Myth of Soviet Military Supremacy* (New York: Harper and Row, 1987).

58. *Ibid.*
59. *The New York Times,* December 8, 1988.
60. *Ibid.*
61. *Allocation of Resources in the Soviet Union and China—1986.*
62. *The Washington Post,* December 16, 1988.
63. *Ibid.*, December 10, 1988.
64. *Ibid.*, December 14, 1988.
65. *Ibid.*, December 10, 1988.
66. *Ibid.*
67. Still the Soviets' percent of world arms transfer agreements dropped from 50.3 percent in 1987 to 33.4 percent in 1988. See Richard F. Grimmett, *Trends in Conventional Arms Transfers to the Third World by Major Supplier, 1981–1988* (Library of Congress: Congressional Research Service, July 31, 1989), pp. 2–3.
68. *News and Views from the USSR,* April 14, 1988, p. 5.

4

"NEW THINKING" IN SOVIET–THIRD WORLD POLICY

THE THIRD WORLD IN BROADER POLICY PERSPECTIVE

In his speech to the 27th Communist Party Congress in February 1986, Gorbachev made it clear that the Third World was low in the new regime's list of priorities. He subordinated the promotion of revolutionary change and the advancement of Soviet power in the Third World areas to the pursuit of domestic objectives and broader foreign policy goals. He indicated that the restructuring of the Soviet political and economic infrastructure was his primary goal and that, in support of his domestic agenda, he would seek improved relations with the West, particularly the United States. While critical of US policy in the Third World, he emphasized Moscow's interest in cooperating with the United States to resolve regional conflicts in order to create a more relaxed international environment. In his only reference to a specific Third World problem area, Gorbachev declared that Moscow wanted to withdraw its troops from Afghanistan as soon as possible.[1]

Creating a more relaxed international environment and easing superpower tensions has become the centerpiece of Moscow's foreign policy as it has sought to reduce pressures for military force modernization and gain access to Western credit and technology. The Third World, previously considered a major battle ground for superpower competition—where Soviet influence could be pursued without dire consequences for Moscow's broader economic and strategic priorities—must now be viewed, according to the regime's "new thinking," in the context of broader Soviet economic and strategic interests. Linkage between Soviet–Third World activities and more pressing national security interests has become a dominant feature of the Gorbachev era. As one observer states, ". . . the Third World, under the rubric of 'regional issues' has increasingly been placed in the context of US-Soviet relations as Moscow has come to accept—and use—the concept of linkage."[2]

East-West and Third World Linkage Before Gorbachev

This is not to argue that Moscow previously had pursued Third World policies without regard for either East-West relations or broader economic and strategic priorities. In fact, Soviet relations with the Third World always have been linked in some respects to East-West policies and working assumptions about the Soviet economy and strategic goals. These connections must be examined in order to understand how linkage under Gorbachev differs from linkage under his predecessors.

Third World Policies Conditioned by East-West Relations. Soviet policies in Third World arenas have always been conditioned by Moscow's relations with the West and by perceptions of the East-West balance of power. It is important to note that the West, not the Third World, was always the most important geographic region for Soviet policymakers. Moscow, more than once, demonstrated its willingness to sacrifice Third World positions—as in Cuba in the 1962 missile crisis—for more important interests in the West.

The pre-Gorbachev linkage focused on the opportunities that might be successfully pursued in the Third World (and the risks to be avoided) given prevailing conditions at home and in East-West affairs. It did not focus on the negative impact of its policies on both East-West relations and its own economy (as Gorbachev subsequently would do). Nikita Khrushchev's activist policies in the Middle East, Africa, and Latin America, for example, flowed from his growing confidence that the USSR had entered a new epoch of increased security as a result of economic reforms and advances in weaponry capable of protecting the world socialist system.

After Khrushchev brought the USSR and the United States to the brink of nuclear war in 1962, the Soviets under Leonid Brezhnev pursued a more conservative and cautious Third World course. Moscow emphasized the development of close state-to-state relations with a growing number of developing countries, de-emphasized support for radical nationalist leaders, scaled back outright economic aid, and concentrated on trying to collect some of the debts arising from Khrushchev's policies. Brezhnev's Third World posture from the mid-1960s to the mid-1970s reflected overall Soviet economic and strategic priorities. He sought to enhance security by pursuing a less aggressive East-West posture so that Moscow could catch up with the United States in conventional and strategic forces deployment.

Brezhnev's adoption of a more aggressive Third World policy in the mid-1970s again reflected prevailing Soviet assumptions about broad economic and strategic priorities. When Brezhnev embarked on a military intervention in Angola in 1975, he assumed that Soviet economic conditions were healthy enough to bear the costs and that East-West detente was sufficiently established to prevent direct confrontation with the United States. After all, this was a period when the Soviet economy was enjoying hard currency earnings as a result of the Organization of Petroleum Exporting Countries' (OPEC) oil price hikes of the early 1970s and lucrative weapons sales to oil rich Third World states. Detente with the United States—embodied in the Strategic Arms Limitations Agreements (SALT I and SALT II) of 1972 and 1974—seemed to provide a green light for increased Soviet activism and Moscow may have assumed that Washington was sufficiently chastened by its setback in Vietnam to prevent its active response to Soviet activism.[3]

Much of Soviet expansionism in the Third World after 1954–1955 proceeded on the basis of relative security in Central Europe, a strengthened defensive posture vis-à-vis the West, and a strong economy. Soviet relations with Western Europe were more or less stable, defined by the balance of power between North Atlantic Treaty Organization (NATO) and Warsaw Pact forces. Soviet nuclear weapons development, especially as Moscow moved toward parity with the United States, helped secure Soviet territory against the West and Far East, while conventional weapons strength provided a strong defensive position in Central Europe. The German question seemed to be under control, and Soviet economic growth was proceeding, if not spectacularly, at least at a satisfactory pace. This left Moscow relatively free to pursue more ambitious policies in Third World arenas.

Thus, in the pre-Gorbachev years, Soviet–Third World relations passed through numerous cycles, with shifts in Soviet national security priorities affecting Moscow's tactics and strategy in the Third World. When the Soviets experienced pressure from the arms race, economic problems on the home front requiring reform, overextended alliance commitments, and negative East-West fallout from Third World conflict—as occurred following the ill-fated Cuban missile crisis—they concentrated on addressing those issues and reduced their expectations of revolutionary change in the developing world.[4]

The Third World as an Arena for East-West Competition. A second kind of linkage was shaped by Soviet pursuit of East-West competition in Third World settings. This link dates back to 1954–1955, when Khrushchev first envisioned the Third World as an arena where competition with the West could be advanced under his new formula of peaceful coexistence, without danger of direct East-West confrontation.[5] Moscow traditionally sought openings where Western influence, especially that of the United States, could be undermined, if not replaced, by Soviet influence. By supporting national liberation movements, radical nationalist movements, and anti-Western/anti-colonialist sentiments, Moscow could use the Third World to advance its position and shift the correlation of forces in its favor. Even as Brezhnev signed a 1972 memorandum of understanding regarding "codes of conduct" for superpower cooperation in the Third World, he continued to aggressively pursue Soviet interests—supplying Cuba, Vietnam, Syria, and Libya with arms and exploiting a wide range of opportunities to expand the Soviet presence and influence in the Third World.[6] By the early 1980s, however, even Brezhnev had begun to see the negative consequences of Soviet Third World adventurism.

Policy Techniques Transferred to Third World. Another type of linkage between East-West relations and the Third World was Moscow's transferrence to the Third World of policy techniques crafted in the search for strategic security against the West. This pattern—illustrating how strategic issues have set Third World agendas—was evident in Soviet military and security policies, emphasis on the role of communist parties, and intelligence activities. The USSR extended huge amounts of military aid to developing countries in an effort to build its own political influence and undermine the West's strategic positions. It sought to expand its power projection capabilities and establish its credentials as a global superpower—the equal of the United States. Soviet military aid to Third World states in many respects reflected Moscow's view of its own military posture against the West and China—essentially defensive in nature, designed to protect clients and defend Third World regimes much as Soviet strategic weapons were designed to deter attacks against the Russian homeland.[7]

Soviet security-seeking—in terms of Moscow's history of establishing pro-Soviet communist governments in Eastern Europe and backing vanguard communist parties in Western Europe since World War II—also conditioned its security-seeking measures in Third World states. Moscow's pressing for vanguard Leninist parties as the best leadership for pro-Soviet clients—in Angola, Ethiopia, Mozambique, Cuba, Grenada (1970–1973), South Yemen, and Vietnam—stemmed from Communist ideological tenets applied politically over the years in countries closer to home.

Finally, Moscow transferred to the Third World the legacy of security seeking through intelligence activities. The Soviets trained client state leaders in intelligence, police, and other security matters—frequently using East Germany for these purposes—while infiltrating Third World military and intelligence forces with their own personnel. Cuba is a classic model of this situation; Cuba's Revolutionary Armed Forces (FAR) are commanded by Raul Castro, and the General Directorate of Intelligence (DGI) security apparatus is permeated with Soviet military and intelligence officers.[8]

Soviet–Third World relations, then, clearly have long been conditioned by key security concerns centering on the nature of East-West tensions, nuclear and conventional weapons balances, and economic considerations. The Third World was not hermetically sealed off from Moscow's primary strategic priorities and economic interests, and it would be a mistake to portray policies in these regions before Gorbachev as if they were detached from the operative assumptions driving Soviet foreign policy goals and techniques associated with East-West affairs.

Economic and Strategic Priorities Unaffected By Soviet Behavior in the Third World. What does emerge from this analysis of Moscow's pre-Gorbachev approach to the Third World, however, is that the Soviets did not consider their activities in these regions as having an adverse effect on Soviet economic and strategic priorities. Gorbachev's predecessors, while recognizing on occasion that there were counterproductive consequences resulting from activities in the Third World, basically rejected the notion of reverse linkage—that Soviet behavior in the Third World had important implications for its economic and strategic priorities. The Soviets seemed to believe they could act with impunity in Third World settings, that behavior in the developing countries had little impact on Soviet-US bilateral ties, Moscow's economic strength, and, ultimately, on their broad security interests.[9]

Recognition of Past Mistakes

Gorbachev has changed this outlook dramatically, concluding that adverse trends in Soviet-Third World relations have been undermining Moscow's economic and strategic priorities. The Soviets now recognize reverse linkage; in this context, Third World policies cannot be orchestrated as a spin-off of more dominant East-West relations, but must be viewed in terms of how they affect central economic and strategic interests.

Gorbachev's "new thinking" as it pertains to the Third World involves the incorporation of previous academic writings into official Soviet policy. The views of academics who argued in the 1960s and 1970s that Third World countries were complex and diverse and not necessarily ready for socialism, that gains and setbacks in such an environment were difficult to predict, that sustaining clients could prove difficult and costly, and that conflict situations might offer opportunities but could also interfere with broader interests have now been incorporated into Soviet policy.

The academic literature of the Gorbachev era, in turn, has gone on to break new ground as commentators argue that past Soviet foreign policy "mistakes" heightened Western perceptions of the Soviet threat and undermined detente. The benchmark article in this new approach was written by Vyacheslav Dashishev of the Institute of the Economics of the World Socialist System.[10] In his May 1988 article in *Literaturnaya Gazeta,* Dashishev argued that Moscow's aggressive policies during the post-war era had undermined its security interests and provoked the formation of rival coalitions seeking to counteract perceived Soviet expansionism. He charged that Moscow had created the impression that the USSR was a dangerous power—seeking to eliminate bourgeois democracies and establish communism throughout the world. He accused Brezhnev of squandering opportunities created by the attainment of strategic parity with the United States and the ensuing detente of the 1970s; he said Brezhnev had exploited detente to build up Soviet military forces, thus unleashing a massive arms race which undermined the weaker Soviet economy. Dashishev also condemned past Soviet policy in the Third World, arguing that the Soviet leadership had no clear ideas about the USSR's state interests when it embarked on its Third World policy in the 1970s and that it had squandered material resources in the pursuit of petty gains.[11]

Various commentators have criticized specific Soviet policies. In an article in *Izvestiya* in June 1988, for example, commentator Aleksandr Bovin argued that the Soviet decision to deploy the SS-20 missile had been a serious mistake as had the invasion of Afghanistan. He said both had achieved their objectives but at the expense of great damage to Soviet international prestige. In both cases, he stated, Moscow had driven itself into a corner and created situations from which there was no exit in the framework of old thinking. Only new thinking—the decision to support the "zero option" in INF negotiations and the decision to withdraw from Afghanistan—corrected the negative situations.[12]

Recognition of Third World Diversity

Under Gorbachev, Soviet officials have adopted a view long advanced by Soviet academics—that the Third World is diverse, with various states in different stages of development. Soviets now openly concede that international institutions dominated by the capitalist world have in the past and will continue to contribute constructively to the economies and stability of Third World states. They also admit that countries following the capitalist pattern often have done better than those of socialist orientation.

Soviet commentary now routinely states that the Third World has proved a major disappointment for the USSR. In an interview with the Italian paper *La Republica* in December 1987, academician Georgiy Mirskiy called Khrushchev the "last of the great optimists." He said that there remained little Soviet optimism regarding regional matters. He argued that it is not easy to build socialism in backward countries and that the theoretical misconception that the colonies would be dragged into revolution by revolution in the parent nation has disappeared. In fact, he stated, the situation is the opposite. The colonies liberated themselves politically, but have remained economically dependent on the former parent nations. Many of these states are themselves following the path of capitalist development. According to Mirskiy, the Soviet Union failed to build sufficient economic strength to keep the left-wing countries of the Third World in tow and to integrate them into the socialist world system. Soviet economic achievements are modest, he maintained, and the USSR cannot replace the West as the developing countries' principal partner. Because Moscow is not in a position to extricate the Third World from the deep abyss in which their economies find themselves, it should not advise them to sever all ties with capitalism.[13]

NEW THEMES IN SOVIET RHETORIC

The guidelines for Moscow's new approach to Third World issues were laid down by Gorbachev at the 27th Party Congress and were elaborated upon in his speech to the United Nations in December 1988. His themes of interdependence, globalism, deideologization of interstate relations, and the need for comprehensive security have replaced the previous "two-world" framework of Soviet analysis in which the world was divided into two world systems, capitalism and socialism, permanently locked in the struggle to gain new adherents and to alter the correlation of forces.

Interdependence

The concept of interdependence has become a key element in Gorbachev's "new thinking," replacing the Khrushchevian term "peaceful coexistence."[14] According to the latter, while military confrontation between the superpowers was no longer inevitable, all other modes of struggle between the capitalist and socialist systems were required, and the two remained locked in a prolonged struggle from which one would emerge victorious. In contrast, the theme of interdependence suggests that the two opposing world systems need no longer compete in political and economic (as well as military) affairs and that such competition as there is should be generally limited to the ideological arena. Carried to its logical extreme it negates the standard Marxist-Leninist view of the inevitable triumph of socialism.

At the 27th Party Congress, Gorbachev emphasized the growing tendency toward global interdependence which, he said, was leading toward a largely "integral world." While this formulation was not included in the party programs ratified at the party congress, it was repeated in the official resolution of the congress and in the authoritative *Pravda* editorial on the congress. Major media commentaries endorsed the approach,[15] and Gorbachev himself subsequently elaborated on it. In a speech on March 12, 1986, for example, he stated that the old order of things—under which national security was seen as primarily lying in the realm of military-technical solutions and power politics—must give way to an all-embracing security system covering all spheres of international relations.

Yevgeniy Primakov, then Director of the World Institute for Economics and International Relations (IMEMO), in discussing Gorbachev's formulation stated that it had "rectified the distortion whereby the examination of the confrontation between the two world systems—the socialist and the capitalist systems—had ignored their interdependence."[16] Primakov, who was subsequently elected Chairman of the Council of Union, one of the two main bodies of the New Supreme Soviet and, in September 1989, became a candidate member of the Communist Party Politburo, argued that this increasing interdependence was not limited to the problem of survival but was also evident in the development of the world economy, the protection of the natural environment, the elimination of backwardness in the Third World, the search for new sources of energy, the battle to conquer disease, and so on.

The Kremlin's chief ideologist, Vadim A. Medvedev, promoted to the Politburo in late September 1988 and named chairman of a commission to oversee the party line, also has advanced the theme of interdependence. Rejecting the idea of world struggle against the West, Medvedev instead began to stress a new concept of socialism, one borrowing ideas from other socialist countries—and, remarkably, from the West itself. "In working out the socialist perspective and formulating a modern concept of socialism, we cannot ignore the experience of mankind as a whole, including the nonsocialist world," he argued in October 1988.[17] These views were a clear repudiation of those held by the man he replaced, Yegor K. Ligachev, whose more orthodox views of Soviet ideology frequently clashed with positions taken by Gorbachev. In calling for a "new conception of socialism," Medvedev asserted, "the idea that socialism and capitalism are mutually exclusive is outdated."

Deideologization of Interstate Relations

In his speech to the United Nations in December 1988, Gorbachev stated that

> The deideologization of interstate relations has become a requirement of the new phase. We are not abandoning our convictions . . . and we are not urging anyone to abandon theirs . . . [but] this struggle must not be carried over to relations between states.[18]

He elaborated on this theme in his address to the USSR Congress of Peoples Deputies in May 1989, arguing that new thinking is based on the primacy of human values, freedom of political choice precluding interference in the affairs of any state, and the necessity of deideologization of interstate relations.[19]

Comprehensive International Security

Closely associated with the theme of interdependence is the concept of the need for mutual security. Gorbachev and his followers have made it clear—as discussed in Chapter 3—that in today's world, the security of some cannot be ensured at the expense of others, that security must be universalized and made comprehensive. In rejecting one-sided security—and the attempt to gain it, which will only backfire—Gorbachev's team has stressed that all must feel secure if anyone is to feel secure. The new Soviet conceptualization of security is global in scope, has moved away from zero-sum thinking (e.g., security gains by one superpower do not produce automatic gains for the other), and incorporates the notion that security should extend to all geographic regions and must include not only the military, but the economic, the political, and the humanitarian spheres.[20]

The new approach to mutual security applied in the Third World has generated numerous policy shifts, detailed in the regional analyses that follow. Soviet decision-makers recognize that the long record of direct and indirect military intervention in Third World conflicts by both the Soviet Union and the United States have contributed to the perpetuation of mistrust on both sides, brought the superpowers into near direct confrontation, and fueled Cold War tensions by clandestine political warfare and efforts to control—and, at times, overthrow legitimate governments.[21] Acknowledging that military intervention in regional conflicts is perilous in the nuclear age and that the costs of these interventions have exceeded benefits, Gorbachev and his colleagues have repeatedly stated their desire to forge a new international security system based upon demilitarized norms of behavior and problem-solving approaches.

The Superpower Equation: The Reagan Doctrine and Neo-Globalism

The Reagan Doctrine and the term neo-globalism have been used interchangeably by Soviet commentators to describe the alleged US interest in claiming the whole world as its sphere of interest.[22] Yevgeniy Primakov has defined neo-globalism as the doctrine which justifies the United States in its organizing, arming, and inspiring of external and internal forces against the governments of those countries which have taken a line independent of US "imperialism." He argues that US policies in Nicaragua, Afghanistan, and Cambodia fall into this category as did its attack on Libya in the spring of 1986.[23]

The emergence of the term "neo-globalism" reflected the shift in the Soviet perception of world trends—from the optimism of the 1970s to the pessimism of the 1980s. Viewed as having a declining impact on Third World affairs earlier, the United States is now considered by Soviet commentators to be exerting a high degree of initiative. The reverse side of this coin is that the Third World is a difficult arena for the Soviet Union and that caution and restraint are required. The use of the term neo-globalism is designed to depict the United States as the destabilizing superpower and to emphasize Moscow's comparatively benign intentions.

In an article in *Izvestiya* in December 1987, commentator Dmitriy Volskiy argued that the US approach to regional conflict lacked realism. He used as his examples continuing US support for the Nicaraguan contras even as regional states were trying to advance a peace plan for Central America.[24] Commentator Askold Biryukov charged in May 1988 that, in his speech to the US Congress earlier in the year, President Reagan had reaffirmed his commitment to neo-globalism, publicly stating his support for so-called "freedom-fighters" in Nicaragua, Angola, and Afghanistan.[25] In a March 1989 article, commentator Aleksandr Golts called on the new administration in Washington to review its military aid to Pakistan and Central America—to stop feeding the "fire of the undeclared wars."[26]

Cooperation to Resolve Disputes

While condemning US policy toward the Third World, the Gorbachev regime also has stressed that the United States is becoming more realistic in its approach to regional conflicts and that cooperation between the two superpowers is both desirable and possible. Following the US-Soviet summit in December 1987, for example, Gorbachev stated that the two superpowers need to consider a joint approach to the solution of regional conflicts and that, although there has not been much headway, he felt "the US administration has started approaching regional problems somewhat more realistically."[27] He also stated that, in his discussions with President Reagan, he had drawn attention to the need for a "joint approach" to regional problems based on the "unquestionable striving of the world community" to solve regional conflicts by "political means."[28] Foreign Minister Shevardnadze reinforced the argument that the prospects for cooperation with the United States were improving when he stated in early 1988 that talks with Secretary of State Shultz had taken on a "different quality" and that there was now a "different level of interest in finding a common basis for possible joint or parallel actions."[29]

In numerous speeches and articles, Gorbachev and other Soviet officials and commentators have made the call for an irrevocable break with past thinking that war is an admissible way to resolve conflicts and for recognition that conflicts must be resolved through negotiation.[30] Dmitriy Volskiy, in his December 1987 article in *Izvestiya,* called for cooperation in the approach to regional disputes. He argued that everything in the world is interlinked and that a local armed clash can cause a chain reaction threatening international security. He used as his example the dangerous situation in the Persian Gulf and the build-up of US forces there, and he urged the use of constructive diplomacy rather than gambling on force. He said that turning regional conflicts into an object of rivalry between the USSR and the United States is fraught with increasing risks and argued for the use of other instruments, such as the United Nations.[31] In an article written in the same month in *USA,* the organ of the USA and Canada Institute, A. V. Nikiforov advocated the acceptance of all foreign policy based on "compromises and mutual concessions for the common good."

Political Settlement of Regional Conflict

In pressing the concept of superpower cooperation to resolve disputes, Gorbachev's team has increasingly advocated political settlement of regional conflict. Gorbachev has cooperated with the United States and United Nations in the Afghanistan pull-out, worked with the United States in pressing for a political solution to the Angolan conflict, and urged Vietnam to withdraw from Cambodia. Gorbachev's stress on politically resolving Third World regional conflicts is consistent with other major themes in the new superpower equation—from "stable coexistence" to demilitarized USSR-US competition, deideologized relations, and ending zero-sum notions of security.

National Reconciliation

Arguing that conflicts in Afghanistan, Cambodia, Angola, and Nicaragua have caused a heavy loss of life and colossal material damage, the Soviets under Gorbachev have argued that these conflicts have caused a break in socio-economic development in those countries and have urged pursuit of a policy of national reconciliation (or power sharing) as an alternative to military confrontation. The pursuit of such a policy was pressed on Afghanistan, with the regime in Kabul calling for national reconciliation in January 1987. A policy of national reconciliation has also been pursued in Cambodia where such an approach was endorsed by Vietnam and Cambodia in mid-1987. In August and October 1987, the Cambodians called for talks with all opposition forces except Pol Pot—as well as for the withdrawal of Vietnamese forces simultaneously with ending outside interference and establishing a coalition government; this withdrawal was accomplished in September 1989. As for Nicaragua, the cooperation of the Sandinista government helped set up agreement on a regional settlement by the five Central American governments in August 1987. This facilitated direct talks between the government and the contras—which subsequently broke down. The concept of national reconciliation was used to move talks forward in Angola in 1989, setting up the conditions for the withdrawal of 52,000 Cuban troops from that country. The dramatic (if temporary) inclusion of UNITA leader Jonas Savimbi in talks with the Angolan government was brought about in June 1989 through the mediation efforts of African leaders.

Recognition of Third World Market Forces

Soviet leaders have increasingly acknowledged the viability of market forces as legitimate means of economic development, capable of coexisting with socialism. In his call for a "new conception of socialism," the Soviet Union's chief ideologist, Vadim Medvedev, has indicated that western capitalism holds valuable lessons for the Soviet Union. Indeed, he has gone so far as to call the law of supply and demand—typically associated with Western market economies—an "essential" of proper socialist economic management.[32] Rejecting the idea that capitalism and socialism are mutually exclusive, Medvedev argues that the two systems "will inevitably intersect."[33]

In arguing that socialism can draw lessons from capitalism, the Soviets in effect have recognized the limits of socialist models of development in the Third World. National communist countries from Nicaragua to Vietnam have been unable to convert socialist ideologies into viable paths of economic development, instead remaining dependent on Soviet aid. Moscow is well aware that as a result of beleaguered economies, most Third World national communist regimes have turned to market incentives and widened ties with Western capitalist states in an effort to stimulate economic growth. Vietnam has produced a number of liberalizing reforms paralleling Gorbachev's version of the Soviet evolving political economy. Angola has flirted with Western capitalist countries for new aid and investment opportunities—including efforts to join the International Monetary Fund—and is forging a new economic plan encouraging the private sector, private land owning, and foreign investment. Ethiopia has pursued a similar quest for closer relations with Western capitalist countries.

Given these trends, it is not surprising that Soviet observers have increasingly underscored the negative aspects of supporting non productive Third World countries. One regularly reads articles in *Pravda, Kommunist,* or *International Affairs* presenting scathing analyses of the foolishness and costs of a Soviet policy that supports non-capitalist modes of development in countries with dismal economic records.[34] In an *Izvestiya* article in June 1989, commentator B. Pilyatskin wrote that ". . . the principle we adopted many years ago of rendering technical assistance has not been justified in the majority of countries of Africa."[35] Thus the Soviets accept the bankruptcy of old thinking.

NEW DIRECTIONS IN POLICY

Personnel Changes

As in the area of domestic reform, changing the personnel charged with carrying out new policy approaches was Gorbachev's first priority. The process began in July 1985 with the removal of Andrei Gromyko from the Foreign Ministry and his "elevation" to the role of Chairman of the Presidium of the Supreme Soviet (the Soviet Presidency). Gromyko, as Soviet Foreign Minister over the years, had been so involved in the formulation of foreign policy and so identified with those policies that it would have been difficult for him to move energetically or credibly in Gorbachev's "new directions" even if he had wished to do so. When Gromyko died, in June 1989, he was given only perfunctory acknowledgement by Soviet leaders and was relegated to burial outside the Kremlin walls, symbolic of the discrediting of his policies.

Gromyko was replaced by Eduard Shevardnadze, a career party official whose lack of foreign policy experience presumably made him a credible purveyor of the new line. Under Shevardnadze's leadership, the entire upper echelon of the Soviet Foreign Ministry was changed.[36] New ambassadors were named to virtually all major countries, and the Foreign Ministry itself was reorganized.[37]

Gorbachev also replaced octogenarian Boris Ponomarev as Chief of the Communist Party Central Commttee's International Department. Ponomarev's roots were in the Cominterm and his orientation had been toward the promotion of communist and leftist elements in the Third World. He was replaced by Anatoliy Dobrynin, formerly Ambassador to the United States and a career foreign ministry official. Dobrynin, in contrast to Ponomarev, brought to the International Department a skill in traditional diplomacy and a stronger focus on the priority of the superpower relationship. Thus, whereas Ponomarev's Third World activities emphasized revolutionary change, Dobrynin concentrated on accommodating Moscow's Third World policies to its broader strategic objectives.

A second major reorganization of the party's foreign policy apparatus occurred in September 1988. Dobrynin was retired and replaced by Valentin Falin, a former Ambassador to West Germany and a vocal supporter of reform and detente. The International Department itself was made subordinate to the newly created International Policy Commission headed by Aleksandr Yakovlev, a Politburo member and probably the leading advocate of new thinking in the leadership. Dobrynin's removal was partly justified by his age and probably reflected the fact that younger figures like Shevardnadze and Yakovlev were ready to take responsibility for foreign policy.[38]

Gorbachev accompanied his 1986 shakeup of the foreign affairs establishment with the delivery of a clear message that Soviet foreign policy must be energized and made responsive to his "new thinking" policy agenda. In an address to an unusual Foreign Ministry conference in May 1986, Gorbachev delivered a critical appraisal of past policy and asserted the need for a new approach. He stressed that Soviet diplomacy must become more conciliatory, that the USSR must not be so obstinate in defending its positions, and that Soviet diplomats must look at issues in a broader context in order to understand the positions of others and meet their diplomatic partners halfway. Shevardnadze told an unprecedented conference of foreign ministry consular workers in December 1988 that the service must become "humanized," reflecting the processes of "renewal, democratization, and openness." And in an article in the weekly magazine *New Times* in July 1989, Shevardnadze emphasized that foreign policy would now be monitored "constitutionally" by the Supreme Soviet. He argued that this would exclude the risk of decisions taken behind closed doors, such as the invasion of Afghanistan.[39]

Diplomatic Activism

Gorbachev's new approach has involved a significant invigoration of Soviet diplomatic activity. Shevardnadze has visited the Far East, South America, and the Middle East. Gorbachev himself has taken numerous trips abroad, including two visits to India, a dramatic journey to China, and a visit to Cuba, in a clear effort to sell his new image. The general level of consultations and exchanges also has increased dramatically. The activity of Soviet ambassadors abroad has become more open as these spokesmen for "new thinking" now routinely grant interviews. One of the results of this approach is that different individuals are saying different things, emphasizing different aspects of policy, and therefore making Soviet policy appear more complex and differentiated than was previously the case.

Cooperation with the United States

Moscow has shown a greater willingness to engage in bilateral discussion of regional issues, to prepare new ideas for joint actions, and to seek to resolve disputes in cooperation with the United States. Gorbachev clearly wishes to prevent regional problems from undermining bilateral problems. During the early 1980s, US-Soviet dialogue was low-key; in 1985 the first set of regular bilateral talks on regional issues was held and they have since been held regularly.

Courting Third World States Previously Ignored

A distinct trend in Gorbachev's shifting Third World strategy has been the courtship of influential non-Marxist developing countries. In various articles, Karen Brutents, the First Deputy Chief of the Central Committee's International Department, has argued that the emphasis of Soviet policy should shift from weak Marxist-Leninist states to those relatively large and well-developed Third World states such as Mexico and Brazil.[40] Shevardnadze's visits to those countries during his Latin America tour demonstrated this policy in action. As the Soviets have become more sophisticated and subtle in their diplomacy they also have expanded contacts with such former "pariahs" as South Korea and South Africa and upgraded relations with Israel.

Efforts to Internationalize Policy

The party program adopted at the 27th Party Congress called for enhancement of the role of the United Nations, and Gorbachev emphasized the UN's importance in a letter to Secretary General Perez de Cuellar in 1986. In 1986, the Soviets gave credibility to their rhetoric, agreeing to pay their assessment for the UN's International Force in Lebanon (UNIFIL), which has been present in southern Lebanon since 1978 but which Moscow had refused to support. In 1987, Moscow further indicated that it would pay $225 million to the United Nations to cover its dues for the year as well as its assessment for past UN peacekeeping operations, including those in the Golan Heights.

In September 1987 Gorbachev made an 11-point proposal for strengthening the status and scope of the United Nations, including the creation of a multilateral center to manage conflicts. He also called for new UN functions such as verifying arms control agreements, investigating acts of international terrorism, and establishing international standards for human rights.[41]

In June 1988 the Soviet Union announced another shift in policy toward the United Nations, agreeing to allow its civil servants to join the organization on a long-term basis, thus becoming permanent international civil servants in accordance with the UN charter. This decision was responsive to a long-standing complaint that the USSR had filled UN posts with a succession of Soviet nationals who served for a brief term and carried out their duties on instructions from Moscow. The Soviet move had been long sought by the United States and other Western nations and represented an apparent Soviet effort to bolster the UN as a serious instrument for resolving regional conflicts around the world.[42]

The Soviets have indicated an increased willingness to involve the United Nations in conflict resolution—and to bolster their own political relevance simultaneously. Their endorsement in July 1987 of UN Resolution 598, designed to bring an end to the Iran-Iraq war; their efforts to use the UN framework for a conference on the Middle East; and their support for UN involvement in peacekeeping efforts—from Angola to Afghanistan—demonstrated this approach.

Globalism and Interdependence

Globalism and interdependence are, in fact, policy prescriptive and the Gorbachev regime has moved to give more support to various regional and international bodies and to support UN initiatives. Moscow also has used these slogans to reinforce previous calls for de-nuclearized and demilitarized zones. Much of this effect is propaganda, designed to put pressure on the United States to reduce its military presence in Third World regions; some is rhetorical, designed to enhance Moscow's image in the Third World; some may be genuinely aimed at reduction of tensions. The Soviets, under Gorbachev, have restated many old proposals and advanced some of their own. Some of these initiatives are:

- a call for the elimination of nuclear weapons in January 1986.
- the signing of the Delhi Declaration in India in late 1986.[43]
- the signing of the Raratonga Treaty, an attempt by the nations of Southeast Asia to turn the Pacific into a nuclear-free zone.
- a call for a Mediterranean conference, made in March 1986, to be attended by regional states as well as the United States and other interested countries.
- a proposal for an Asian security system arrangement, made in April 1986, and calling for cooperation of all Asian states to consider matters of security.
- numerous calls for denuclearization of the Indian Ocean.
- a call for Atlantic-to-the Urals conventional arms reduction, made in April 1986.
- a May 1986 proposal for an international conference and other steps for cooperation in the atomic energy field.
- a proposal that the United States and USSR freeze their naval forces in the Mediterranean—a repetition of Gorbachev's March 1986 proposal involving a consultative meeting for the Mediterranean.[44]

Withdrawal from Afghanistan

Moscow's decision to withdraw its military forces from Afghanistan is the most dramatic indication to date that it is prepared to implement its "new thinking" in the Third World. The Soviets have made clear that this decision also has implications for other regional conflicts. In his speech announcing the withdrawal in February 1988, Gorbachev stated that,

> when the Afghan knot is untied, it will have the most profound impact on other regional conflicts too. . . . Implementing a political settlement in

Afghanistan will be an important rupture in the chain of regional conflicts. . . .[45]

That Gorbachev meant what he said about the relevance of Soviet withdrawal from Afghanistan for other Third World conflicts was underscored by the long-awaited agreement for the phased withdrawal of Cuba's 50,000-man military force in Angola, which began in early January 1989, and the withdrawal of Vietnamese forces from Cambodia, which was completed in September 1989. Soviet pressure on its clients was instrumental in both cases.[46]

Reducing Provocative Actions by Soviet Radical Allies

Under Gorbachev, Moscow has taken a tougher stance with its radically-minded clients, whose provocative actions could undermine the broader Soviet agenda associated with "new thinking." It has warned Syria, long a "spoiler" of peace efforts in the Middle East, that it will not help it achieve strategic parity with Israel. It has told Libya not to create any "pretexts" for US military action and has heralded the Libyan-Chadian agreement of August 1989, presumably ending 16 years of hostility (caused by Libya's claims to Chadian territory).[47] As stated above, it has urged Cuba and Vietnam to withdraw their forces from Angola and Cambodia. And it has urged Nicaragua to seek a peaceful resolution of its conflict.

LIMITS OF CHANGE

Continuation of Gorbachev's new directions in the Third World is by no means guaranteed. There remain numerous obstacles to the translation of Gorbachev's initiatives into a redefined Soviet presence, a reduction of East-West tensions, and enhanced domestic economic development. While limits to change vary in terms of specific issues—and their strength and effect on Gorbachev's "new thinking" policies in the Third World—they merit attention as part of the overall assessment.

Among the obstacles to success must be included:

- Lack of control over the provocative behavior of Third World clients, as in Libya's dog fight with two US F-14s over the Mediterranean in January 1989 and Cuba's militant anti-Americanism.
- US action which may undermine Soviet efforts to resolve Third World conflicts, as in continuing US and Pakistani support for Afghanistan's mujahedin and US support for the contras aiming at the overthrow of Nicaragua's Sandinistas.
- Third party spoiling of Soviet initiatives, e.g., Syria and militant Palestinian factions opposing Moscow's efforts to move toward an international conference.

- The difficulty of reaching agreements with groups involved in national reconciliation negotiations, as in intra-mujahedin factionalism in the Afghanistan settlement.
- Nationalist, religious, and cultural antagonism toward Soviet ideology and suspicions of Soviet behavior.
- The legacy of Moscow's previous association with socialist regimes, which has left the latter economically impoverished with tens of thousands of their citizens dead or homeless as a result of war and poverty.
- The contradictions between Moscow's declared "peaceful intentions," and its continuing Third World clients actively engaged in supporting anti-Western national liberation movements, as in Cuba's backing of Central and South American leftists.
- The contradiction between Moscow's announced peaceful intentions and its continued shipment of sophisticated weapons to Third World clients.

CONCLUSION

There have been dramatic changes in Soviet policy toward the Third World under Gorbachev's leadership. Nonetheless, policy retains many old assumptions and threads. Soviet positions and actions in the Third World traditionally have been based on a long standing desire to compete with the United States, on Soviet perceptions of the world and how it operates, and on the domestic, foreign policy, and international environment in which Moscow has been operating. Given these obvious limits, however, the change has been extraordinary.

Gorbachev is a new leader, from an old system, looking at the existing world in a different way. His efforts to reshape Moscow's Third World presence will take time. Since he came to power Moscow has reassessed its Third World posture, balancing the arguments for scaling back—stagnating and costly Third World clients, domestic constraints inside the USSR, international priorities, and the lessons of the past *a la* Afghanistan—against the arguments for a sustained Third World role—Moscow's historical and ideological drive to push out and the felt need for strategic parity with the United States. The "new look" in Soviet–Third World relations reflects both these objectives. Gorbachev hopes to project an image of power but in a non-aggressive manner, while cutting the costs of foreign involvement. The new image is one of invigoration, featuring new personalities infused with renewed enthusiasm in pressing Gorbachev's initiatives. New themes are clear in Gorbachev's approach to the Third World—interdependence, peaceful solutions to regional conflicts, demilitarized and deideologized competition with the West, virtual abandonment of national liberation movements, and pursuit of a businesslike diplomacy designed to stimulate trade and commerce in a less tension-filled international setting. New foreign policy approaches have been adopted which embody these themes—withdrawal from Afghanistan, negotiation of peaceful settlements in Angola and Cambodia, and constraining the provocative actions of traditional clients.

At the same time, Gorbachev has not abandoned its Third World clients, for such a dramatic policy shift would signal lost power and prestige in superpower competition with the West. The USSR has maintained its commitments to close allies—illustrated by the approximately $5 billion in aid extended to Cuba, $1 billion to Afghanistan, $3.9 billion to India, and $1.2 billion to Nicaragua during 1988.[48] Thus, Moscow has signified that its effort to redefine its role in the world will not include complete retreat from established positions. The extent and the limits of Gorbachev's new thinking will be more rigorously examined in the regional chapters that follow.

NOTES

1. TASS, February 26, 1986. Earlier, in his January 15, 1986, disarmament proposals, Gorbachev implicitly criticized previous Soviet policy when he called for a "break with the past" in order to overcome the "negative, confrontational tendencies" that had developed in East-West relations. His report to the party congress built on this approach as he argued that changing the international environment was essential for the pursuit of Soviet domestic objectives.

2. See Wayne P. Limberg, "Moscow and Regional Conflicts: Linkage Revisited," a paper prepared for the APSA 1988 National Conference, Washington, DC, September 2, 1988, p. 1.

3. See Alexander L. George, *Managing U.S.-Soviet Rivalry: Problems of Crisis Prevention* (Boulder, CO: Westview Press, 1983).

4. George Breslauer, "Ideology and Learning in Soviet–Third World Policy," *World Politics* 34, No. 3 (April 1987), pp. 429, 444–445.

5. Moscow's Third World relations during the early post–World War Two period stemmed from a perceived—ideologically driven—improvement in the "correlation of forces" between world capitalism/imperialism and socialism/communism in favor of the latter. Proceeding from a more stable, less threatening, European climate after 1955, Soviet diplomacy began to cast a wider net beyond Europe's shores. See Stephen Sestanovich, "The Third World in Soviet Foreign Policy, 1955–1985," in Andrzej Korbonski and Francis Fukuyama, eds., *The Soviet Union and the Third World: The Last Three Decades* (Ithaca and London: Cornell University Press, 1987).

6. Limberg, *Moscow and Regional Politics: Linkage Revisited.*

7. Michael MccGwire, *Military Objectives in Soviet Foreign Policy* (Washington, DC: The Brookings Institution, 1987), pp. 222–223.

8. Leon Goure, "Soviet-Cuban Military Relations," in Irving Louis Horowitz, ed., *Cuban Communism* (New Brunswick: Transaction Books, 1988).

9. On pre-Gorbachev thinking about the Third World, see Elizabeth Kridl Valkenier, *The Soviet Union and the Third World: An Economic Bind* (New York: Praeger, 1983) and Jerry F. Hough, *The Struggle for the Third World: Soviet Debates and American Options* (Washington, DC: The Brookings Institution, 1986).

10. The head of the Institute, Oleg Bogomolov, published a letter in *Literaturnaya Gazeta* on March 16, 1986, in which he stated that his Institute had

argued against the Soviet intervention in Afghanistan on the grounds that it would undermine detente and damage the USSR's international stature.

11. Vyacheslav Dashishev, *Literaturnaya Gazeta*, May 18, 1988.

12. Aleksandr Bovin, *Izvestiya*, June 16, 1988, p. 5.

13. *La Republica*, December 5, 1987, p. 10; Foreign Broadcast Information Service (FBIS), Soviet Union, December 15, 1987.

14. The theme of interdependence had been discussed by Soviet theoreticians in the 1970s but was rejected as a concept justifying Western expansion into the Third World.

15. *Kommunist*, editorial, March 1986.

16. Yevgeniy Primakov, *Pravda*, July 9, 1987, p. 4.

17. *Pravda*, October 5, 1988.

18. TASS, December 7, 1988.

19. TASS, May 30, 1989.

20. Primakov, "New Flexibility in Soviet Foreign Policy," *Pravda*, July 10, 1987, p. 4.

21. American Committee on U.S.-Soviet Relations and the U.S.A.-Canada, Joint United States–Soviet Recommendations for Stable Coexistence, *Congressional Record*, Proceedings of the 100th Congress, Vol. 134, No. 63 (May 9, 1988), p. 5.

22. According to a Soviet academic writing in 1986, the Reagan Doctrine is an attempt to adapt the aggressive Truman Doctrine of the Cold War period to present-day conditions. A. Baychorov argued that the doctrine serves as a cover for efforts to mount a counterattack against the world's revolutionary process. He further stated that the US worldwide system of neoglobalism incorporates a wide variety of tactics designed to roll back the gains of revolution. A. Baychorov, *Aziya i Afrika Segodnya*, No. 9 (September 1986), pp. 5–8.

23. Primakov, *New Times*, No. 21. (June 2, 1986).

24. Dmitriy Volskiy, "In the Same Boat: About Regional Conflicts and Global Security," *Izvestiya*, December 24, 1987, p. 5.

25. TASS, May 17, 1988.

26. *Krasnaya Zvezda*, March 12, 1989, p. 3.

27. *Pravda*, December 12, 1987.

28. *Pravda*, December 10, 1987.

29. *Pravda*, February 24, 1988.

30. Gorbachev, TASS, February 25, 1986.

31. Volskiy, "In the Same Boat: About Regional Conflicts and Global Security," *Izvestiya*, December 24, 1987, p. 5.

32. See *The Washington Post*, October 6, 1988.

33. *The Washington Post*, October 6, 1988.

34. See for example, Alexsel Kiva, "Socialist Orientation: Reality and Illusion," *International Affairs* 7 (July 1988), pp. 78–86.

35. *Izvestiya*, June 20, 1989, p. 5.

36. Yuliy Vorontsov and Anatoliy Kovalev were named first deputy foreign ministers. Both had had extensive experience in East-West relations. Vorontsov had been ambassador to France and had served in Washington under Dobrynin in the 1970s. Kovalev had broad experience in European affairs. Four new deputy ministers also were named in 1986, including two (Aleksandr Bessmertnykh and Vladimir Petrovskiy) with broad East-West experience.

37. Various new functional units were added and existing departments were reorganized. There also were changes in the geographic bureaus, with new functional units created within them.

38. *The Washington Post,* October 1, 1988.
39. Cited in TASS, July 7, 1989.
40. *Pravda,* January 19, 1986; *Kommunist* 2 (February 1984).
41. *Pravda,* September 12, 1987.
42. *The New York Times,* June 4, 1988.
43. See Chapter 5.
44. *The Washington Post,* March 17, 1988.
45. *Moscow Radio,* February 8, 1988.
46. *The New York Times,* January 8, 1989.
47. TASS, September 1, 1989.
48. *Handbook of Economic Statistics: A Reference Aid* (Washington, DC: Central Intelligence Agency, 1989).

PART THREE

Regional Case Studies

5

AFGHANISTAN AND SOUTH ASIA

When Gorbachev came to power in March 1985, Afghanistan presented his most immediate foreign policy dilemma in the Third World. His approach to this problem provided the proof that "new thinking" did involve a substantive change in Soviet foreign policy and that Moscow would no longer allow secondary, regional issues to drive its foreign policy to the detriment of its primary objectives.

Gorbachev's policy toward Afghanistan provided a model for Moscow's subsequent approach to other regional conflicts. In Afghanistan, Gorbachev demonstrated that his commitment to the peaceful resolution of regional disputes was not rhetoric alone and that the drawdown of military force (with its reduction of risks and costs) was a primary objective. In Afghanistan, "national reconciliation" emerged as the favored Soviet political solution to those regional disputes in which Moscow sought a face-saving compromise. And, in Afghanistan, Moscow showed that, while it would seek to reduce the costs and risks associated with its Third World empire, it would continue to provide its clients with the necessary assistance to support themselves.

Moscow's decision to withdraw Soviet ground forces from Afghanistan was a tacit admission of its inability to suppress the insurgency. It was also an acknowledgment that the continued commitment of Soviet forces to an unwinnable conflict was a drain on scarce domestic resources and a costly embarrassment. Finally, the decision reflected Moscow's recognition that the presence of Soviet combat forces in Afghanistan was a major obstacle both to its long-term regional objectives and to the relaxation of the international environment which Gorbachev needed in order to pursue his domestic priorities.

A PYRRHIC VICTORY

Reasons to Invade

The decision to invade Afghanistan in December 1979 (which involved the first and thus far only use of Soviet ground troops in a Third World

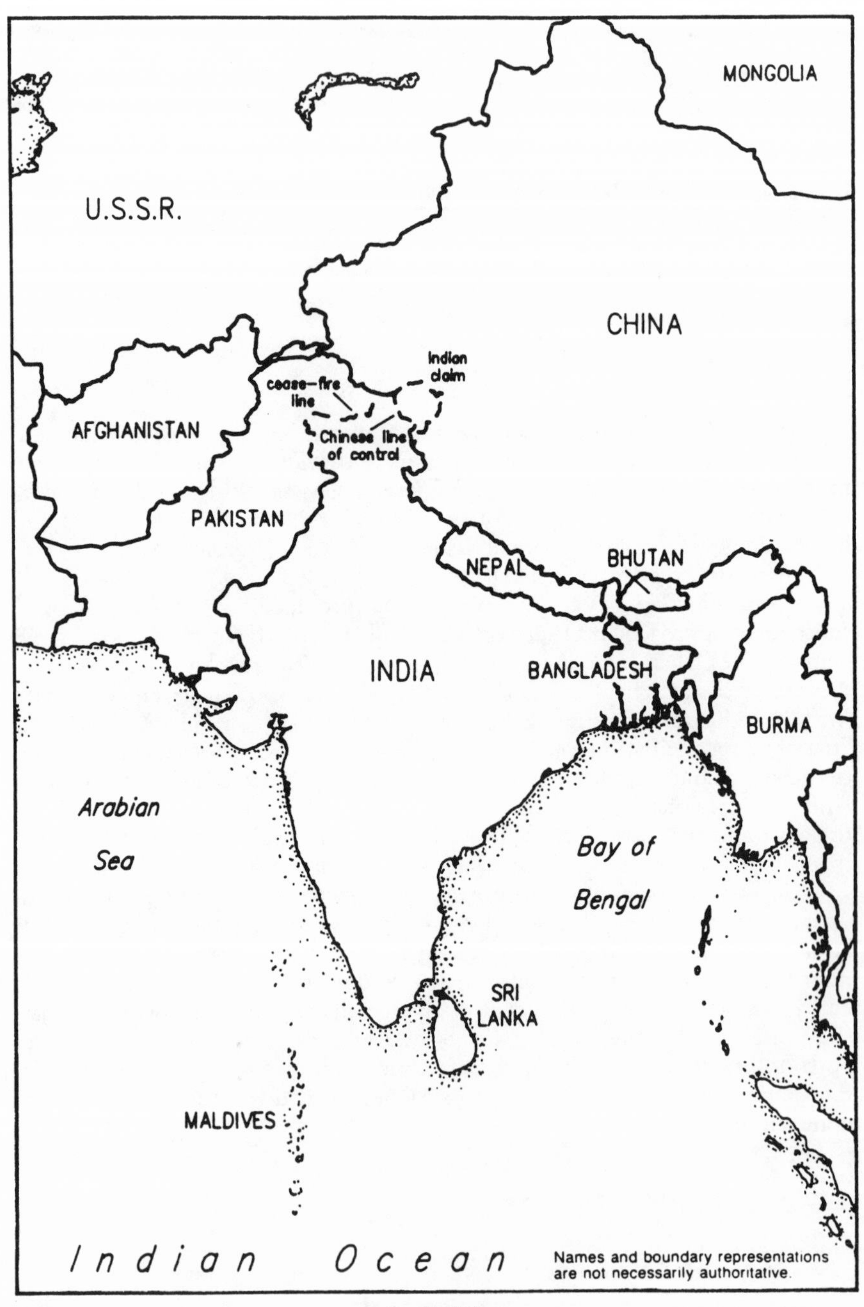
MONGOLIA
U.S.S.R.
CHINA
Indian claim
cease-fire line
Chinese line of control
AFGHANISTAN
PAKISTAN
NEPAL
BHUTAN
INDIA
BANGLADESH
BURMA
Arabian Sea
Bay of Bengal
SRI LANKA
MALDIVES
Indian Ocean
Names and boundary representations are not necessarily authoritative.

South Asia

country) resulted both from Moscow's perception that its own security was threatened and from its commitment to prevent the collapse of a communist government in a country on the Soviet border; in a sense, the so-called Brezhnev Doctrine with its implied assertion that the Soviet Union had a right to intervene to prevent the collapse of a communist regime in East Europe, had been extended beyond the Warsaw Pact.

The Soviets argue that they have legitimate security interests in South Asia[1]—a region geographically contiguous to the Soviet Union, with ethnic, religious, and cultural features similar to those of Soviet Central Asia. Moscow has opposed the expansion of US or Chinese influence and presence in this part of the world and has frequently expressed concern that hostile powers could use it as a base to threaten Soviet security. In the wake of the Iranian Revolution of early 1979, the Soviets had the additional concern that a fundamentalist Islamic regime might come to power in Kabul and either indirectly contribute to instability along the Soviet border or actively seek to export Islamic activism to Soviet Central Asia.

As elsewhere in the Third World, the Soviets have tried to foster leftist, pro-Soviet elements in South Asia. The communist takeover in Afghanistan in 1978 appeared to serve Moscow's objectives very well, and its decision to invade reflected both its extreme reluctance to have this gain "rolled back" and its concern that the successor to the communist regime might be pro-US, pro-Chinese, or fundamentalist.

Results of the Invasion

The Soviets undoubtedly anticipated that the invasion would insure the continuation of communist control in Kabul and probably hoped that this projection of force would enhance their political position in South Asia. They succeeded in the former, maintaining the People's Democratic Party of Afghanistan (PDPA) in a position of tenuous power in Kabul. But the costs of doing so were, in the end, too high and the second objective was frustrated. The regional and broader international ramifications of the invasion were overwhelmingly negative, creating ongoing problems for Moscow and preventing it from successfully pursuing more important goals.

Those Third World states that were both physically and psychologically far removed from Afghanistan deplored the brutality of the Soviet takeover, particularly the murder of Prime Minister Hafizullah Amin. The Islamic states of the Middle East, Persian Gulf, and Southwest Asia identified with the struggle of the Muslim mujahedin to eject the superpower (and atheist) invader. Some of them, most significantly Saudi Arabia and Egypt, contributed money and/or arms to the insurgents via Pakistan. Most Arab states either signed the initial request for an urgent Security Council meeting to condemn the Soviet presence or expressed official indignation in some other form. Each year for nearly ten years, the Islamic Conference Organization condemned the Soviet presence in Afghanistan and demanded the unconditional withdrawal of Soviet forces.[2] In 1981, the conservative states of the Persian Gulf formed the Gulf Cooperation Council (GCC) in an effort to coordinate their political, economic, and military responses to regional tensions. While the Iran-Iraq war was the proximate cause of the GCC's creation, the Soviet presence in Afghanistan was a contributing factor.[3]

Soviet relations with all of Afghanistan's immediate neighbors—Iran, Pakistan, and China—deteriorated as a result of the invasion. All of these countries condemned the Soviet action and provided support to the mujahedin; Pakistan became the sanctuary for over three million Afghan refugees and Iran for over one million; Pakistan became the staging area for the mujahedin, and Peshawar, Pakistan, became the "capital" for the opposition Afghan leaders in exile; both China and Pakistan improved their ties with the West, while Iran, despite the depth of its antipathy for the United States, maintained a hostile attitude toward Moscow. In short, by invading Afghanistan, the Soviet Union had provoked the formation of a loose, anti-Soviet alliance which included the United States, China, and most of the Islamic world and had undermined its ability to take advantage of the US setback in Iran.

The continuing Soviet military presence in Afghanistan served as a constant reminder of the potential military threat posed by Moscow and as a chronic impediment to improved political relations with numerous Third World nations. At the same time, the Soviet inability to defeat the insurgency and extend the control of the communist regime in Kabul beyond the major cities and into the Afghan countryside was an ongoing, embarrassing testimony to Soviet impotence. One unanticipated and ironic byproduct of the Soviet quagmire in Afghanistan was a shifting perception on the part of regional states of the threat posed by the Soviet Union; Moscow's inability to defeat the insurgency led to a reduction of concern about the credibility of the USSR's expansionist inclinations and to an increased willingness to deal with Moscow. Long before the Soviet withdrawal from Afghanistan, the conservative Persian Gulf states had begun to improve relations with the Soviet Union.

Reasons to Remain

When Gorbachev came to power, there remained a strong case against the withdrawal of Soviet forces from Afghanistan. After all, Moscow had managed modest improvements in bilateral relations with conservative Arab states (as well as with the United States and China) without implementing any significant troop withdrawals. The war clearly was not popular within the Soviet Union, but there seemed to be little effective domestic pressure for withdrawal.[4] The ineptitude of the Soviet-trained Afghan army and the probability that internal chaos and bloodshed would follow a Soviet withdrawal suggested the need for Soviet combat forces to remain in Afghanistan. Finally, the prestige and credibility of the Soviet Union were on the line, and Moscow undoubtedly wanted to avoid the humiliation of its own "Vietnam"—a forced retreat followed by the rapid collapse of its client.

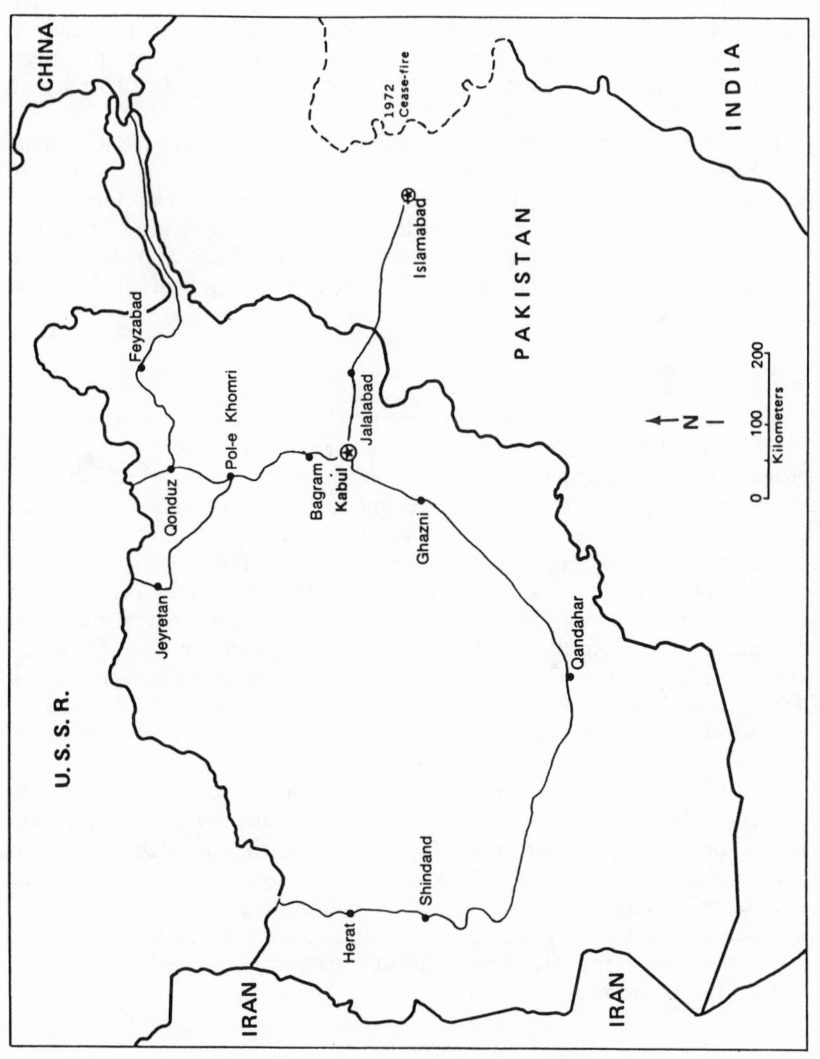

Afghanistan

"NEW THINKING" AND AFGHANISTAN

The "Bleeding Wound"

From the outset of his tenure in power, Gorbachev made it clear that he was aware of the problems created by the Soviet presence in Afghanistan and was anxious to reduce the Soviet commitment there. Gorbachev himself has reported that the shift in Soviet policy that led to the decision to withdraw began in April 1985 (only one month after he took power), when the Politburo "conducted a hard and impartial analysis of the Soviet position and started to see a way out of the situation."[5] In February 1986, in his report to the 27th CPSU Congress, Gorbachev publicly referred to the Afghan situation as a "bleeding wound" that had to be resolved. At the same time, he stated that the USSR and the Afghan government had worked out plans for a Soviet withdrawal of forces as soon as a political settlement had been achieved.[6]

Persuading Kabul

Following Gorbachev's pronouncement that Afghanistan was a problem in need of a political solution, the Soviets turned their energies to forging a settlement that would enable them to withdraw their ground troops. The first requirement was to persuade the regime in Kabul to accept the concepts of political compromise and Soviet withdrawal. In a demonstration of its determination to proceed, Moscow engineered a change in the leadership of the PDPA in May 1986. Babrak Karmal (who appeared less than enthusiastic about the new Soviet approach)[7] was removed as Afghan General Secretary and replaced by Najibullah, who proved more responsive to Moscow's directions. This did not end dissension within the traditionally factionalized PDPA, nor did it end PDPA opposition to policies advocated by Moscow.[8] But Moscow and Kabul were able to coordinate their approach sufficiently to proceed.

With Kabul on board, the Soviets began their pursuit of a negotiated settlement. Their optimum objective almost certainly was to attract key elements of the opposition into cooperation with the PDPA, thereby undermining the military threat to the Kabul regime and creating an environment conducive to the honorable withdrawal of Soviet forces. As it became clear that such a solution was unlikely, however, Moscow modified its requirements and proceeded toward its primary objective—the withdrawal of Soviet forces from Afghanistan.

MOSCOW'S CONCESSIONS

The Withdrawal Time Frame

Gorbachev's commitment to the withdrawal of Soviet combat forces from Afghanistan was clearly expressed in his major foreign policy speech in Vladivostok on July 29, 1986. In this speech, he gave the first public indication that Moscow might withdraw whether or not there was a political settlement. He announced that the USSR would withdraw a token six regiments (8,000 of an estimated 115,000 Soviet troops in Afghanistan).[9] The withdrawal was scheduled for the fall of 1986, and Gorbachev invited Western journalists to observe the movement of Soviet forces out of Afghanistan. There was considerable doubt that the Soviets had, in fact, reduced the total number of Soviet forces in Afghanistan as promised at this time (and charges that they had moved *in* as many troops as they moved out);[10] in hindsight, however, this episode was a harbinger of Gorbachev's intentions.[11]

During the next year and a half, while the issue of a political settlement remained stymied by the unwillingness of the resistance to compromise and the refusal of the Kabul regime to abdicate, the Soviets continued their efforts to extricate themselves militarily. The forum for negotiations was the UN-sponsored indirect (or proximity) talks between Afghanistan and Pakistan in Geneva. Crucial issues in these negotiations were the length of time to be involved in any Soviet withdrawal (Kabul naturally favored a prolonged timeframe; Pakistan and the Afghan mujahedin, represented by the leaders of the seven major resistance groups living in exile in Peshawar, demanded a rapid withdrawal) and the question of whether or not outside assistance to the insurgency had to be ended and a political solution found before a Soviet withdrawal could begin (Pakistan demanded that the Soviet withdrawal must occur first and without preconditions). From 1986 to 1988, the Soviets repeatedly modified their positions on both of these issues in order to move the process forward. With respect to the timetable for withdrawal, for example, Moscow had the Afghans offer a three-year timeframe in 1986; an 18-month timeframe in March 1987; and a 12-month timeframe in December 1987.[12] Finally, in February 1988, the Soviets themselves offered a 10-month timeframe.[13]

In a major policy statement on February 9, 1988, Gorbachev capitulated to Pakistan's demands, making several new and important concessions with respect to the above issues. In addition to reducing the timeframe for withdrawal by an additional two months, he gave the first specific date for the start of such a withdrawal (May 15, 1988), indicated that a "relatively larger portion" of the Soviet contingent could be withdrawn during the early stages of the withdrawal (as Pakistan and the United States demanded), and implicitly removed the condition that the Soviet withdrawal be preceded by the creation of an Afghan government acceptable to all parties to the conflict. In addition, Gorbachev noted, but did not demand, that the withdrawal should be linked to a ban on outside aid to the insurgents.[14] This statement was, in effect, the Soviet announcement that it would withdraw its military forces from Afghanistan in a relatively short period of time no matter what the situation on the ground might be.

Several months after this announcement, the Afghan government gave its official concurrence to the Soviet decision. In April 1988, Gorbachev and Najibullah met in Tashkent and issued a joint statement which endorsed the content of Gorbachev's February 8 announcement. The two further expressed approval of US and Soviet willingness to act as guarantors of the accord soon to be reached in Geneva. In addition, they glossed over the failure to reach a political settlement before the Soviet withdrawal, simply endorsing national reconciliation in Afghanistan and affirming that the final status of the country must be determined by the Afghan people themselves.[15]

The Geneva Accords

This Soviet (and PDPA) capitulation led to the signing of the Geneva Accords of April 14, 1988. Islamabad and Kabul formally agreed on a front-loaded Soviet troop withdrawal from Afghanistan (to begin on May 15, 1988, and to be completed by February 15, 1989). The agreement also provided for the return of the Afghan refugees to their homeland. In a separate agreement, the United States and the Soviet Union guaranteed their "noninterference and nonintervention" in the internal affairs of Afghanistan and Pakistan.[16]

By February 1989, in spite of the ongoing insurgent military challenge to the Kabul regime and Soviet threats to halt their withdrawal,[17] the Soviets had moved all of their troops out of Afghanistan. Thus, the decade that had begun in 1979 with the Soviet invasion of Afghanistan was ended by the General Secretary who had told the Soviet party congress in 1986 that the "bleeding" in Afghanistan must be stopped.

National Reconciliation

The bleeding did not stop, of course, as the PDPA and its mujahedin challengers remained implacably and violently opposed. Throughout the period of withdrawal, Moscow continued its efforts to find a political solution, hoping to gain some protection for its withdrawal, to save the PDPA from a humiliating collapse, and to insure reasonable Soviet relations with any successor government in Kabul. The rubric covering these Soviet initiatives was "national reconciliation." While Moscow's approach to military withdrawal had involved a series of retreats, its approach to national reconciliation involved a series of modifications, reflecting the fluctuations in its perception of the strength and viability of the PDPA.

In his February 1986 speech at Vladivostok, Gorbachev referred to the Afghan leadership's "line of national reconciliation" but gave it little emphasis, presenting it as a continuation of previous efforts to broaden the base of the regime by drawing non-PDPA (but non-militant elements within the country) into government participation.[18] Advocacy of a more profound national reconciliation was formalized by the Kabul regime in January 1987. At that time, Najibullah declared a six-month ceasefire (which was promptly rejected by the Peshawar Seven) and claimed that Kabul was ready to compromise with opposing Afghan elements located abroad (e.g., in Peshawar) to form a new government. Najibullah asserted, however, that the PDPA would remain the dominant force in any future government and insisted that, while the USSR and Afghanistan had agreed on a timetable for the withdrawal of Soviet forces, there would be no withdrawal until the mujahedin had ceased fighting.[19]

This basic formulation remained the position of both Moscow and Kabul throughout the period of negotiation leading up to the Geneva Accords of April 1988 and through the initial phase of the Soviet withdrawal. In late 1988, however, as Moscow moved toward total withdrawal and as the Kabul regime appeared particularly vulnerable to insurgent attacks on the cities still under its control, the Soviets tried to inject new life into the negotiating process.

The appointment of Soviet First Deputy Foreign Minister Yuliy Vorontsov as the new Ambassador to Kabul in October 1988 signalled a general intensification of Moscow's efforts to find a political solution in Afghanistan. During his extremely active, 11-month tenure in Afghanistan,[20] Vorontsov retained his title as First Deputy Foreign Minister, a fact which added to his credibility.

During this period (late 1988 through early 1989), Moscow reduced its rhetorical commitment to the PDPA and to its dominant role in a future Afghan coalition government. In his talks with Afghan Prime Minister Sharq in September 1988, according to *Pravda*, Gorbachev indicated that the role of the PDPA in any future government would depend on its "capacity for constructiveness" in the new situation.[21] Vorontsov's unexpected arrival in Kabul the following month was closely followed by the removal from power of Afghan critics of the policy of national reconciliation and by a reduction in the overtly communist character of the regime.[22] During his visit to Kabul in January 1989, Shevardnadze took another step away from the PDPA, giving only weak expressions of support for the Kabul regime. In an interview with the Afghan news agency BAKHTAR, Shevardnadze barely mentioned the PDPA at all, and his offers of support were directed to the Afghan people—not to its current government.[23]

By the summer of 1989, when the Kabul regime had managed to survive the Soviet withdrawal (to almost everyone's surprise), successfully countering the mujahedin drive to take Jalalabad, and as the mujahedin appeared to be increasingly riven by factionalism,[24] Moscow seemed to become more optimistic about PDPA prospects—although it remained flexible about the structure of an ultimate settlement. Its public insistence on PDPA inclusion in such a settlement rebounded somewhat. In a *Moscow World Service* broadcast on July 31, 1989, for example, Yuriy Soltan stated that US expectations that a political solution in Afghanistan means "the capitulation of the Kabul government are erroneous" and that "a settlement cannot be gained without the participation of the most powerful and well-organized political force, the Afghan Peoples Democratic Party, which has real authority and military power."[25] Soviet Foreign Ministry spokesman Gennadiy Gerasimov gave this position a more official endorsement in a press briefing in October 1989, stating that "it is impossible to attain peace . . . in Afghanistan while ignoring such a politically and militarily influential force as the legitimate government of the Afghan republic."[26]

Trying to take advantage of this improved position, Najibullah announced another diplomatic initiative in the late summer of 1989—and Moscow promptly endorsed it. The Afghan leader again proposed a six-month ceasefire and advanced a new formula for achieving reconciliation. The Soviets enthusiastically supported Najibullah's call for a dialogue between the PDPA and all other Afghan groups in the context of an all-Afghan peace conference.[27] The Peshawar Seven immediately rejected the proposal.

Negotiating with the Enemy

The Soviet Union's public dialogue with the Afghan resistance in late 1988 was another aspect of Moscow's effort to distance itself from the PDPA during its period of insecurity. The Soviets may have begun secret negotiations with the mujahedin even earlier; in April 1988, the Tehran news service IRNA cited Afghan resistance leader Rabbani to the effect that the Soviets had covertly approached the mujahedin seeking improved relations and a dialogue.[28] In the fall of 1988, however, the Soviets publicized their meetings with opposition elements in an effort to send a message of flexibility and openness to the international community as well as to Kabul.

Shortly after his arrival in Kabul, Vorontsov indicated that Moscow was pursuing direct contacts with guerrilla field commanders in an effort to draw them into a coalition government.[29] In early December, Vorontsov met openly in Saudi Arabia with the head of the insurgent alliance (Rabbani). In his subsequent public description of these meetings, Soviet Deputy Foreign Minister Petrovskiy said that they were designed to organize an inter-Afghan dialogue.[30] Following his meetings in Saudi Arabia, Vorontsov traveled to Rome to meet with former Afghan King Zahir Shah.[31] This marked yet another aspect of Moscow's effort to promote communication among the various Afghan factions and to broaden its own contacts with the potential successors to the PDPA. When the United States also sent an official to meet with Zahir Shah in Rome in September 1989, the Soviets welcomed the initiative.[32]

With the split in mujahedin ranks in the summer of 1989, precipitated by military clashes and the withdrawal of fundamentalist mujahedin leader Hekmatyar from the coalition, the Soviets began to express optimism that the split would lead to "the beginning of the collapse of the Peshawar Seven." A *Pravda* article of August 1989 argued that the resistance itself was beginning to realize the "futility of seeking a military solution to the Afghan problem."[33] And an *Izvestiya* article the same month speculated that the withdrawal of Hekmatyar, the most "intransigent of the mujahedin leaders," could "open up prospects for a compromise."[34]

GAINING INTERNATIONAL SUPPORT AND UN INVOLVEMENT

The Soviets accompanied their efforts to achieve a political solution with a campaign designed to gain international support both for the PDPA as the legitimate government of Afghanistan and for the concept of national reconciliation. They tried to promote Afghan ties to third countries and, perhaps most importantly, they tried to internationalize their own preferred approach to the situation. By involving the international community in the process of negotiating a settlement and thereby giving it a stake in the success of that settlement, they hoped to legitimize and strengthen their position.

The United Nations was involved from the beginning in the mediation talks in Geneva which ultimately led to the April 1988 agreement, and it also played a role in monitoring the Soviet withdrawal. Moscow consistently has tried to pull it into subsequent phases of the process. In November 1988, as part of its diplomatic effort to salvage what it then considered to be a deteriorating situation in Afghanistan, Moscow proposed a UN-sponsored international conference to seek a neutral and demilitarized Afghanistan. Gorbachev repeated this suggestion in his speech to the United Nations on December 7, 1988. He also called again for a ceasefire,[35] urged that UN peacekeeping forces be sent to Kabul and other strategic centers, and requested an end to arms deliveries to all belligerent parties.[36]

In its government statement supporting Najibullah's August 1989 initiative, Moscow again asserted that the convening of an international conference on Afghanistan was a major and integral part of the effort to guarantee the permanent neutrality of Afghanistan, the non-militarization of the country, and the protection of the political rights of all members of Afghan society; it suggested that future Afghan elections should proceed under UN observation.[37]

AN UNRESOLVED ISSUE

The War Continues

The US and Soviet guarantees of noninterference in Afghanistan, given in the Geneva Accords of April 1988, represented the presumed resolution of the issue of military deliveries to the antagonists absent a political solution. In fact, however, both the United States and the Soviet Union retained their own interpretations of what was permissible. The Soviet Union claimed that it had a right, if not an obligation, to continue providing support to its beleaguered client in Kabul, and the United States claimed that it had similar rights and obligations with respect to the opposition.

The Soviets have insisted that the Geneva Accords included a commitment to ending the "undeclared war against Afghanistan" and the adoption of "essential measures to plug the source of that war in Pakistani territory."[38] A joint Soviet-Afghan statement of May 15, 1988, the day the Geneva Accords went into effect, stated that "the pivotal question" in the settlement remains "the cessation of external interference in Afghanistan's internal affairs" and argued that the pledges relating to that issue were "unequivocal."[39]

By August 1988, with half of their military contingent out of Afghanistan, the Soviets were loudly attacking Pakistan for its "blatant violations" of the Geneva Accords. Moscow warned Pakistan in a government statement that its continued "obstruction" of the agreements "cannot continue to be tolerated" and that the Soviet Union reserved "the right to take the measures which the situation dictates."[40] By October, Soviet commentary was harshly attacking both the United States and Pakistan for "hiring killers, flooding Afghanistan with advanced armaments," and supporting widespread "terror and subversion."[41]

When, by the spring of 1989, the Kabul regime had not collapsed, the Soviets may have been as surprised as everyone else; they certainly were relieved and pleased. In an article reviewing the year which had followed the signing of the Geneva Accords, commentator Aleksandr Bovin noted that "hopes that the Kabul authorities would collapse soon after the withdrawal of Soviet forces were not realized. . . . The apple did not ripen and did not fall."[42]

Continued Assistance to Kabul Regime

A major reason that the apple did not ripen and fall was that Moscow continued to pour large quantities of military equipment into Afghanistan. While demanding an end to outside support for the resistance, the Soviets insisted on their own right to support the Kabul regime and continued to provide extensive military aid. Moscow airlifted military equipment to Kabul at increasing levels in the wake of its withdrawal. According to *The Washington Post*, senior US government officials reported that this assistance increased in 1989 and that, between March and July 1989 alone, the Soviets shipped Kabul 550 SCUD missiles, 160 T-55 and T-62 tanks, 615 armored personnel carriers, and 1600 five-ton trucks.[43] Thus, Moscow's support of a peaceful solution to the conflict had *not* meant the abandonment of its client.

REACTION TO SOVIET WITHDRAWAL

Reaction to the Soviet troop withdrawal was almost universally favorable.[44] The withdrawal certainly contributed to the relaxation of relations with both the United States and China. In the case of the latter, it facilitated the broad normalization of relations that produced the summit of May 1989.[45] The conservative Arab Gulf states, already expanding contacts with the USSR, moved to further upgrade relations. Soviet-Iranian relations, strained by the Soviet presence in Afghanistan (among other things),[46] began to improve. Somewhat ironically, however, Soviet relations with the two other large states of the subcontinent, India and Pakistan, changed very little. The reasons for this lie in the fact that these relationships are shaped primarily by other factors.

BROADER REGIONAL IMPACT OF "NEW THINKING"

India

Since the 1950s, India has been one of Moscow's most important Third World clients as well as the focal point of Soviet attention in South Asia.[47] There are sound strategic and regional reasons for this—Moscow's overriding interest in insuring its security; its desire to compete with and contain the United States and China; its pursuit of presence and influence in Asia; and its drive to advance its goals within the Third World generally and the nonaligned movement specifically. All of these objectives have been served by a close relationship with India, the largest and most prestigious state in the region and the longtime "moral" leader of the nonaligned movement.

India's interests are compatible with those of the Soviet Union. It seeks to maintain its status as the major regional power in South Asia; it wants to fortify its military position vis-à-vis Pakistan (with whom it has fought three wars over the past 40 years); it too wants to contain China with which it has border disputes and regional differences; and it shares the Soviet interest in preventing US military expansion in the area. The fact that the Soviet Union has been a reliable and generous source of arms as well as a faithful political ally in times of crisis have secured the USSR's position as a close friend of New Delhi.[48]

The Nature of the Relationship

Ideology has never played a significant role in Moscow's approach to India. Geopolitical considerations, power politics, and pragmatism have been the dominant considerations.[49] This is one important reason why Gorbachev's more pragmatic approach to foreign policy has not involved a significant change in approach to India. During his visit to India in 1986, Gorbachev told the Indian parliament that Indo-Soviet relations had provided the first example of new thinking in international relations because "differences in socio-political systems and ideologies . . . have not hampered dialogue."[50]

Arms transfers have been the key to Moscow's success in the Third World and India may be the best example of this phenomenon. New Delhi has received large quantities of arms from Moscow; in the first half of the 1980s, it signed three arms agreements worth more than $1.6 billion each.

It also has received very sophisticated weapons systems such as the MIG-23 and MIG-29 fighter and interceptor aircraft, T-72 and T-80 tanks, Kilo-class attack submarines, and BMP armored personnel carriers. In some cases India has received this equipment before non-Soviet members of the Warsaw Pact.[51] In 1983, Soviet Defense Minister Ustinov even agreed to sell the MIG-29 to India before it had been delivered to the Soviet air force.[52] Subsequently, the Soviets allowed India to co-produce the MIG-29 in a successful effort to undermine India's discussions with France about the purchase of Mirage aircraft. India began receiving T-72 tanks before some of the Warsaw Pact and also entered into a co-production scheme for this weapons system.[53]

SOVIET-INDIAN RELATIONS IN THE ERA OF "NEW THINKING"

The Impact of Afghanistan

The Indians responded favorably to Moscow's withdrawal from Afghanistan. They had never endorsed the Soviet invasion or continuing presence in that country. They considered the Soviet action potentially destabilizing, were opposed to any military encroachment by a superpower in the region, and were concerned by the increasingly close US-Pakistani relationship which this invasion had prompted; they particularly opposed the delivery to Pakistan of large quantities of US military equipment. In addition, India always had been apprehensive about the dangers inherent in the US-Soviet rivalry being played out in South Asia, and the withdrawal reduced the potential for superpower confrontation.

Indian Concerns

At the same time, the Indians undoubtedly were concerned about many aspects of Gorbachev's new approach. They were generally supportive of most of the broad international themes advocated by Moscow (e.g., recognition of interdependence, the need for global cooperation, the internationalizing and peaceful resolution of regional conflicts, and arms control). But New Delhi certainly worried that the Soviet withdrawal from Afghanistan and the potential for improved Soviet-Chinese relations and/or improved Soviet-Pakistani relations would have a negative impact on Moscow's willingness to continue providing the military support that India feels it needs. The political implications of Moscow's policies were also potentially negative. A successful resolution of Moscow's border problems with China, for example, would make India the only country having a major border dispute with China, and the Indians now had to wonder if Moscow might make concessions in relations with India in order to improve relations with China.

Gorbachev's Visits

Gorbachev quickly made it clear that India's position as one of Moscow's most important Third World clients was secure. His first visit to an Asian country or to any Third World nation was to India, and it occurred in November 1986.[54] Gorbachev almost certainly wanted to reassure New Delhi that the content of his major speech at Vladivostok in July 1986 (with its clear overtures to China) would not harm Indian security interests or undermine the Soviet-Indian relationship. He expressed Moscow's shared concern with India over continuing US supplies of large quantities of weapons to Pakistan and affirmed that the Soviet Union "naturally sees the need to strengthen India's defensive capabilities."[55] At the same time, he may actually have reinforced some of India's fears by refusing to give an uncategorical commitment to support India in case of any Indo-Pakistani conflict. He also showed unusual restraint in his criticisms of Pakistan for its support of the Afghan mujahedin.

During the visit, Gorbachev sought and received Indian support for many of the broad, rhetorical themes of "new thinking." He and Gandhi signed the "Delhi Declaration," setting forth 10 "principles of peaceful coexistence." Moscow has subsequently touted the Delhi Declaration as the guiding document for international efforts to promote peace. In the wake of Gorbachev's second visit to India in November 1988, for example, Soviet commentary again extolled the virtues of the document. A *Pravda* editorial stressed that the declaration, with its appeal to build a world free of nuclear weapons and violence, had had a major impact on the world and that the USSR and India had helped to establish the principles of peaceful coexistence.[56]

The *Pravda* editorial cited above explicitly addressed "speculative talk that the USSR is changing its priorities and almost losing interest in India," terming such charges "groundless and malevolent."[57] It went on to cite the ongoing and regular summit meetings between Gorbachev and Gandhi as giving an unprecedented dynamism to Soviet-Indian relations.[58] Following Gandhi's electoral defeat in late 1989, Moscow moved quickly to demonstrate its continuing commitment to the bilateral relationship. First Deputy Foreign Minister Yuliy Vorontsov visited New Delhi to deliver Gorbachev's greetings to the new government.[59]

The Soviets have continued to give priority to Indian needs and wants, offering New Delhi highly sophisticated weapons systems and special arrangements such as co-production rights and generous financing for assistance. They also have tried to keep India as a major trading partner, extending credits and seeking expanded commercial relations. Their commitment to India was demonstrated by the extension of $3.9 billion in credits in 1989 (to be drawn over a 20-year period) for construction of a nuclear power plant.[60] Trade for the 1986–1990 period is projected (by the Soviets) to grow by 50–100% over the 1981–1985 period. At the same time, according to *Pravda*, the Soviet Union is seeking a shift in emphasis in its commercial relationship with India—from the exchange of goods to production sharing and pursuit of joint enterprises.[61]

Indian Relations with Pakistan and China

As the Soviet Union has moved to improve its relations with former adversaries such as China, India has expanded its own dialogue with its traditional enemies—China and Pakistan; the Soviets have endorsed and encouraged these efforts. Gandhi has met twice with Pakistani Prime Minister Benazir Bhutto. In December 1988 he became the first Indian Prime Minister to visit Pakistan in 28 years. In praising the Gandhi visit, an *Izvestiya* commentary stated that "there exists no logical alternative to peaceful cooperation. . . . The horizon over South Asia is brightening."[62] This meeting produced agreements on nonaggression against nuclear installations and on development of cultural and economic exchanges.[63] A subsequent meeting in July 1989 produced no further agreements, and relations between the two countries remained strained by continuing differences over Kashmir as well as by mutual suspicions about weapons deliveries, nuclear programs, and the development of ballistic missiles.

The Soviets under Gorbachev also have encouraged India to seek its own rapprochement with China. During his visit to New Delhi in November 1988, the Soviet leader rejected the notion that the Soviet Union was changing its priorities and moving closer to China at India's expense; he did, however, assert that all states should improve relations and that good relations among the USSR, India, and China are "extremely important for the fate of Asia and for progress the world over."[64] On the eve of Gandhi's visit to China in December 1988, the first by an Indian Prime Minister in 34 years, the Soviets applauded the move, repeating their call for better relations between the USSR, India, and China.[65]

PAKISTAN

Moscow's relations with Pakistan have been largely defined by its commitment to close ties to India, Pakistan's historic adversary.[66] The invasion of Afghanistan simply served to exacerbate an already strained relationship. Pakistan provided refuge to more than three million Afghan refugees, served as the main staging area for insurgent operations, and moved to the forefront of those Islamic nations demanding the withdrawal of Soviet forces. The Soviet military presence in Afghanistan threatened Islamabad's security and increased its fear of the USSR. During the 10-year period from 1979 to 1989, Pakistan drew closer to both the United States and China.[67]

The Soviets took a two-track approach to Pakistan during this period. On the one hand, they urged Islamabad to reach an accommodation with the regime in Kabul and held out the carrot of economic assistance. On the other hand, they put pressure on Pakistan to stop its aid, issuing repeated and strong warnings to Pakistan to stop aiding the mujahedin, charging Pakistan with serving as a "bridgehead for aggression" for the United States,[68] and using military pressure to try to bully Islamabad into acquiescence. Soviet and Afghan overflights of Pakistani territory and bombing operations against mujahedin camps in western Pakistan never seriously threatened the regime in Islamabad or its policies, but they certainly created problems for Pakistani decisionmaking.

Gorbachev's Approach: Little Change

When Gorbachev came to power in 1985, relations with Pakistan were at an all-time low. In his meeting with Pakistan's leader, General Zia ul-Haq, after Chernenko's funeral in March 1985, Gorbachev reportedly threatened the general with dire consequences if Pakistan continued its policies in Afghanistan.[69] Moscow then proceeded with its policy of combining blandishments and pressure to persuade Pakistan to limit its assistance to the Afghan insurgents. Even after the signing of the Geneva Accords, Soviet threats continued. In a Foreign Ministry statement of May 1988, the Soviets attacked Pakistan's "flagrant violations" of the accords and indicated that the Soviet Union "reserves the right to react as the situation warrants."[70] While applying military and political pressure on Islamabad, however, Moscow actually increased its economic assistance to Pakistan.

The Soviets undoubtedly hoped to take advantage of the change in Pakistan's leadership which followed the death of Zia ul-Haq in August 1988, and they may well have assumed that Benazir Bhutto would be more responsive to their approaches than Zia had been. Bhutto shared Zia's opposition to the pro-Soviet regime in Kabul, however, as well as the commitment to repatriate the over 3 million Afghan refugees present in Pakistan. After taking power, she quickly made clear her intention to continue close ties to the United States and China[71] and to maintain support for the Afghan mujahedin.[72]

Pakistan's distrust of India and the Indo-Soviet military relationship also remained strong and led Islamabad in the summer of 1989 to request an additional 60 US F-16 fighter aircraft to supplement the 40 already in its inventory.[73] The Soviets made clear their opposition to Pakistan's acquisition of more F-16s. A *Moscow World Service* broadcast of July 12, 1989, even contained a threat; the commentary indicated that the deliveries could lead the USSR to take corresponding steps, such as the transfer to Afghanistan of MIG-29s and other weapons systems it had thus far refrained from supplying.

NUCLEAR PROLIFERATION IN SOUTH ASIA

The Soviets have supported the principles of non-proliferation in South Asia. They have consistently attacked Pakistan for pursuing a nuclear capability and have criticized the United States for its "hypocrisy" in refusing to cut off aid to Pakistan despite the latter's nuclear program. Under Gorbachev, the Soviets apparently have put some pressure on India as well. New Delhi has refused to sign the non-proliferation treaty and, in 1974, exploded its own nuclear device. In the spring of 1989, India announced that it had fired its first medium-range ballistic missile, thus joining the United States, the USSR, China, Britain, France, and Israel as states with the capacity to produce surface-to-surface ballistic missiles.[74] In the spring of 1989, an Indian newspaper reported that the Soviet Union was urging India to sign the non-proliferation treaty and to limit its pursuit of a nuclear capability.[75]

OUTLOOK FOR SOVIET POLICY IN SOUTH ASIA

The Indian Sub-Continent

Gorbachev's accession to power and the advent of "new thinking" have not affected the Soviet Union's basic orientation in the sub-continent. The priority of retaining close ties to India is unchanged, and India will continue to be the focal point of Soviet attention in the region. India's location, international prestige, regional stature, and longstanding political and military ties to Moscow guarantee its position as one of Moscow's most valued friends.

Soviet goals with respect to India also are unlikely to change. Moscow will try to insure the stability of the bilateral relationship through strengthened political and economic ties as well as through the continued supply of the military equipment India wants; it will seek India's cooperation against any strengthening of US or Chinese positions in South Asia (through the advocacy of zones of peace and other demilitarization proposals); and it will cultivate Indian support for Soviet positions in the international community (as exemplified by the Delhi Declaration).

Moscow's focus on India will continue to shape Soviet policy with respect to the other nations of South Asia, particularly Pakistan. Although the Soviet withdrawal from Afghanistan should lead to a reduction in Soviet-Pakistani tensions, actual improvement in Soviet-Pakistani relations will be constrained by Moscow's reluctance to antagonize India. Soviet arms deliveries to India will reinforce both Pakistan's suspicions of Soviet intentions and its ties to the United States and China.

But "new thinking" has had an impact on South Asia, and the ripples begun by Gorbachev's new approach are contributing to a reshaping of regional politics. Moscow's withdrawal from Afghanistan and the improvement in its relations with China and the United States have affected regional perceptions of Moscow's intentions. Most importantly, they have raised questions in New Delhi about Soviet priorities and the implications that Gorbachev's policies will have for Indian interests.

Although the Soviets will continue to reassure the Indians that the bilateral relationship will not be adversely affected by Moscow's new policies, the Indians almost certainly will remain concerned. Their own efforts to improve relations with China and to establish a better dialogue with Pakistan demonstrate their own adjustment to the new environment being created by "new thinking."

Afghanistan as a Model

The Soviets will continue to use Afghanistan as a model for other regional conflicts; they have repeatedly suggested that the resolution of the Afghan situation can pave the way for increased efforts to settle other regional conflicts, including those in the Middle East. In an article in *Izvestiya* in April 1988, commentator Konstantin Geyvandov argued that the Geneva agreements on Afghanistan "can be seen as the first model for peaceful resolution of regional conflicts on the basis of the principles of new political thinking" and that the Soviet Union and the United States "as mediators and official guarantors of the settlement of the Afghan problem, have set a precedent for the constructive collaboration which is extremely necessary for the improvement of international relations as a whole."[76]

Moscow's approaches to other regional conflicts in which it has been either directly or indirectly embroiled (Angola, Cambodia, Ethiopia) contain virtually the same elements present in its approach to Afghanistan. These include putting pressure on their clients to accept and pursue "new thinking"; proceeding with the withdrawal of military forces (or those of Cuba or Vietnam); pursuing a policy of national reconciliation (preferably with the help of a legitimizing international forum); and continuing to provide necessary support to beleaguered clients.

NOTES

1. South Asia, as defined in this chapter, includes Afghanistan and the countries of the Indian sub-continent.

2. Only Libya, South Yemen, and Syria refused to support these resolutions; only South Yemen and Syria recognized the government in Kabul before the Soviet withdrawal in 1989.

3. The members of the GCC are Saudi Arabia, Kuwait, Bahrain, Qatar, the United Arab Emirates (UAE), and Oman.

4. As Gorbachev's policy developed, and in keeping with *glasnost*, the Soviet press published letters and articles questioning Soviet policy in Afghanistan. After Gorbachev's announcement in February 1988 that Soviet troops would be withdrawn from Afghanistan, articles also appeared indicating that there had been strong opposition within the Soviet Union to the original decision to invade. In a letter to the official Soviet weekly *Literaturnaya Gazeta* on March 17, 1988, Oleg Bogomolov, the Director of the Institute of the World Socialist System (IMEMO), stated that his institute had opposed the invasion, warning that it would damage relations with China and other countries. A year later, in an interview with the Soviet weekly magazine *Ogonyok* in March 1989, General Valentin Varennikov, First Deputy Chief of the General Staff of the Soviet Armed Forces, claimed that the Soviet General

Staff also had opposed the invasion (*The Washington Post,* March 17, 1988; *The Washington Post,* March 20, 1989).

5. *Pravda,* February 19, 1988.

6. *Pravda,* February 26, 1986.

7. In *his* speech to the 27th CPSU Congress, Karmal failed to mention plans for a Soviet withdrawal—even though Gorbachev had emphasized that the USSR and Afghanistan were in agreement (*Pravda,* March 1, 1986).

8. In an interview in October 1987, for example, Najibullah indicated that there were problems within the PDPA with respect to the question of power-sharing, and PDPA spokesmen continued to emphasize that, in any national reconciliation program, the PDPA would have to play a leading role (TASS, October 12, 1987).

9. *Pravda,* July 29, 1986.

10. *The Washington Post,* October 16, 1986.

11. It has been argued that the increase in US-supplied aid to the Afghan insurgents in the mid-1980s led to the Soviet decision to withdraw. There is no doubt that US-supplied equipment, particularly the Stinger anti-aircraft missile, enabled the mujahedin to perform more effectively—and to shoot down increasing numbers of Soviet aircraft and helicopters. While this may have reinforced the Soviet decision, it seems clear that Gorbachev had decided early on that the Soviet Union had to cut its losses and pull out of Afghanistan.

12. TASS, December 17, 1987.

13. TASS, February 9, 1988.

14. TASS, February 9, 1988.

15. TASS, April 7, 1988.

16. Paul Lewis, "Four Nations Sign Accords for Afghan Pullout," *The New York Times,* April 15, 1988, p. 1.

17. In November 1988, Soviet First Deputy Minister Aleksandr Bessmertnykh stated that the withdrawal had been suspended. Within days, however, Moscow had moved to reassure both its domestic and foreign audiences that the withdrawal would be completed on schedule (TASS, November 4, 1988; *Pravda,* November 13, 1988).

18. *Pravda,* February 26, 1986.

19. *The New York Times,* January 19, 1987.

20. Vorontsov served as Soviet Ambassador to Afghanistan from October 1988 to September 1989 (*Izvestiya,* September 14, 1989). When he returned to Moscow, he resumed his role as First Deputy Foreign Minister with responsibility for the Middle East and South Asia.

21. *Pravda,* September 21, 1988.

22. *The New York Times,* November 18, 1988.

23. *Pravda,* January 16, 1989.

24. Shortly after the Soviet withdrawal from Afghanistan, the seven resistance parties represented in Peshawar formed an "interim government" in exile. The leaders of eight Shiite insurgent groups formed their own alliance in Tehran. By the summer of 1989 the Peshawar groups had turned on each other, and Gilbuddin Hekmatyar, leader of the largest fundamentalist grouping (Hezb-e Eslami) had withdrawn from the interim government.

25. *Moscow World Service,* July 31, 1989.

26. TASS, October 10, 1989.

27. TASS, August 21, 1989.

28. IRNA, April 30, 1988.

29. Henry Kamm, "Moscow Hints at Contacts with Afghan Guerrillas," *The New York Times*, November 18, 1988.

30. TASS, December 2, 1988.

31. *Izvestiya*, December 30, 1988, p. 4.

32. TASS, September 12, 1989.

33. *Pravda*, August 31, 1989, p. 5.

34. *Izvestiya*, August 31, 1989, p. 1.

35. On New Year's Eve, Najibullah repeated the Soviet call for a ceasefire (*Pravda*, January 9, 1989.).

36. TASS, December 7, 1988.

37. TASS, August 21, 1989.

38. TASS, April 26, 1988.

39. *Izvestiya*, May 15, 1988.

40. *Izvestiya*, August 16, 1988, p. 1.

41. TASS, October 27, 1988.

42. *Izvestiya*, April 15, 1989, p. 4.

43. *The Washington Post*, September 2, 1989, p. 20.

44. Exceptions included Vietnam which was concerned about the implications for its own military presence in Cambodia. (See Chapter 7).

45. See Chapter 7 for further discussion of this point.

46. See Chapter 6 for further discussion.

47. In 1955, the year of the Soviet-Egyptian arms deal which is often heralded as the marker of Moscow's entry into the Third World arena, the Soviets extended a loan of $100 million to India to build a steel mill in Bhilai. This was just the beginning of a massive infusion of Soviet economic and military assistance to India which would make the latter the largest non-communist recipient of Soviet aid. Moscow actively helped the Indians to develop their economic infrastructure and, during the late 1970s and early 1980s, was India's largest trading partner; the United States assumed this position in 1984.

48. See Robert Horn, "The Soviet Union and South Asia: Moscow and New Delhi Standing Together," in *The Soviet Union and the Third World*, ed. by Andrzej Korbonski and Francis Fukuyama (Ithaca and London: Cornell University Press, 1987), p. 208–211.

49. Soviet support for the two Indian Communist Parties, for example, has typically been subordinated to its more important ties to the New Delhi government. In his trip to India in November 1988, Gorbachev emphasized this priority when he did not even bother to meet with Indian communist leaders as he had done two years earlier.

50. Francis Fukuyama, "Gorbachev and the Third World," *Foreign Affairs*, Volume 64, #4, Spring 1986, p. 721.

51. Horn, "The Soviet Union and South Asia," p. 212.

52. *The New York Times*, September 25, 1984, p. 7.

53. Andrew Cockburn, *The Threat: Inside the Soviet Military Machine* (New York: Random House, 1983), p. 83.

54. Gorbachev may also have wanted to establish a personal relationship with Indian Prime Minister Rajiv Gandhi. The assassination of Indira Gandhi and the accession to power of her son Rajiv in 1984 undoubtedly had caused some concern in Moscow. Indira had been a longtime friend of the Soviets and her relatively brief absence from power in the 1970s had seen some drift in Soviet-Indian relations. Early in his tenure, Rajiv did, in fact, appear to be less willing than his mother

to emphasize close Soviet-Indian relations and more open to a dialogue with the United States and Pakistan.

55. Yevgeniy Primakov, *Pravda*, "A Big Step Forward: Thoughts Following M.S. Gorbachev's Visit to India," January 5, 1987, p. 6.

56. *Pravda*, November 23, 1988, p. 1.

57. *Ibid.*

58. Gandhi visited Moscow in July 1989 and invited Gorbachev to visit India again in 1990 (TASS, July 15, 1989).

59. *Pravda*, December 23, 1989.

60. *Handbook of Economic Statistics: A Reference Aid* (Washington, DC: Central Intelligence Agency, 1989).

61. *Pravda*, November 23, 1988. p. 1.

62. *Izvestiya*, January 3, 1989.

63. TASS, December 31, 1988.

64. *Pravda*, November 20, 1988.

65. *Pravda*, November 28, 1988.

66. The Soviets have consistently made clear the priority of their relationship with India. In 1985, the Pakistan paper *Muslim* quoted Mikhail Kapitsa, then Soviet Deputy Foreign Minister as having said that the USSR wants good relations with all nations of the region, but it "will take India's side in any dispute with its neighbors" (cited by Horn, "The Soviet Union and South Asia," p. 220.).

67. The invasion of Afghanistan led the United States to reverse the Carter Administration's decision to cut off US military aid to Pakistan in retaliation for the latter's nuclear weapons program. The United States thus decided to subordinate its nonproliferation objectives to its goal of defeating the USSR in Afghanistan. During the 1980s, the United States has sent over $3 billion worth of military and economic aid to Pakistan.

68. *Pravda*, October 22, 1985; *Pravda*, May 8, 1987.

69. *Pravda*, May 20, 1985; June 6, 1985 (from Asian Survey, p. 1175).

70. *Pravda*, May 29, 1988.

71. Bhutto's first foreign trip after coming to power was to Beijing.

72. By late 1989 there had been some gradual improvement in the Soviet Pakistani dialogue with respect to Afghanistan. In October 1989, the two countries agreed to language for a UN resolution calling for a peaceful resolution to the conflict—although they continued to differ on what such a resolution would look like (*Islamabad Domestic Service*, October 2–4, 1989).

73. Bernard Weintraub, "Bush and Bhutto Agree on Afghan Aid," *The New York Times*, June 7, 1989, p. 3.

74. Barbara Crossett, "India Reports Successful Test of Mid-Range Missile," *The New York Times*, May 23, 1989, p. 9.

75. *Calcutta Ananda Bazar Patrika*, April 9, 1989.

76. *Izvestiya*, April 22, 1988, p. 5.

6

THE MIDDLE EAST

The Middle East has been the Third World region of primary interest to the Soviets since they first embarked on an active Third World course in the 1950s. Individual clients (such as India, Cuba, and Vietnam) subsequently became more central to Moscow's geostrategic position as well as to its posture in the Third World—and received the bulk of its assistance. In the 1980s, Afghanistan became its major Third World policy dilemma. But, as a region, the Middle East has been of greatest importance and concern because of its geographic proximity to the USSR; its strategic location and resources; the opportunities it has provided Moscow as a consequence of chronic Arab-Israeli tensions; the risk it has posed of possible confrontation with the United States; and the gains made there by the Soviets in terms of political ties, hard-currency earnings, and access to air and naval facilities on the Mediterranean, the Red Sea, and the Indian Ocean.

A RECORD OF SUCCESS

The overall Soviet record in the Middle East since the 1950s has been one of considerable success. The USSR has become an important regional player and, as recent events in Lebanon, Syria, and the Persian Gulf have demonstrated, cannot be ignored. It has used its support for the Arab cause (and US support for Israel) to bolster its own position and undermine that of the United States. Over the past two decades, the Soviets have been the major suppliers of military equipment to many Arab states, earning hard currency and establishing a sizable physical presence in the region as a result.

The Soviets have concluded treaties of friendship and cooperation with Egypt (since abrogated), Iraq, Syria, North Yemen, and South Yemen. They believe these treaties have helped legitimize their role in the region. And, at one time or another, they have had naval and naval air access to most of these states as well as to Libya.[1]

Soviet arms deals with Arab states have been particularly beneficial. Algeria, Iraq, Libya, and Syria all rely on Soviet weapons systems and have acquired a degree of dependence on Moscow for resupply, maintenance,

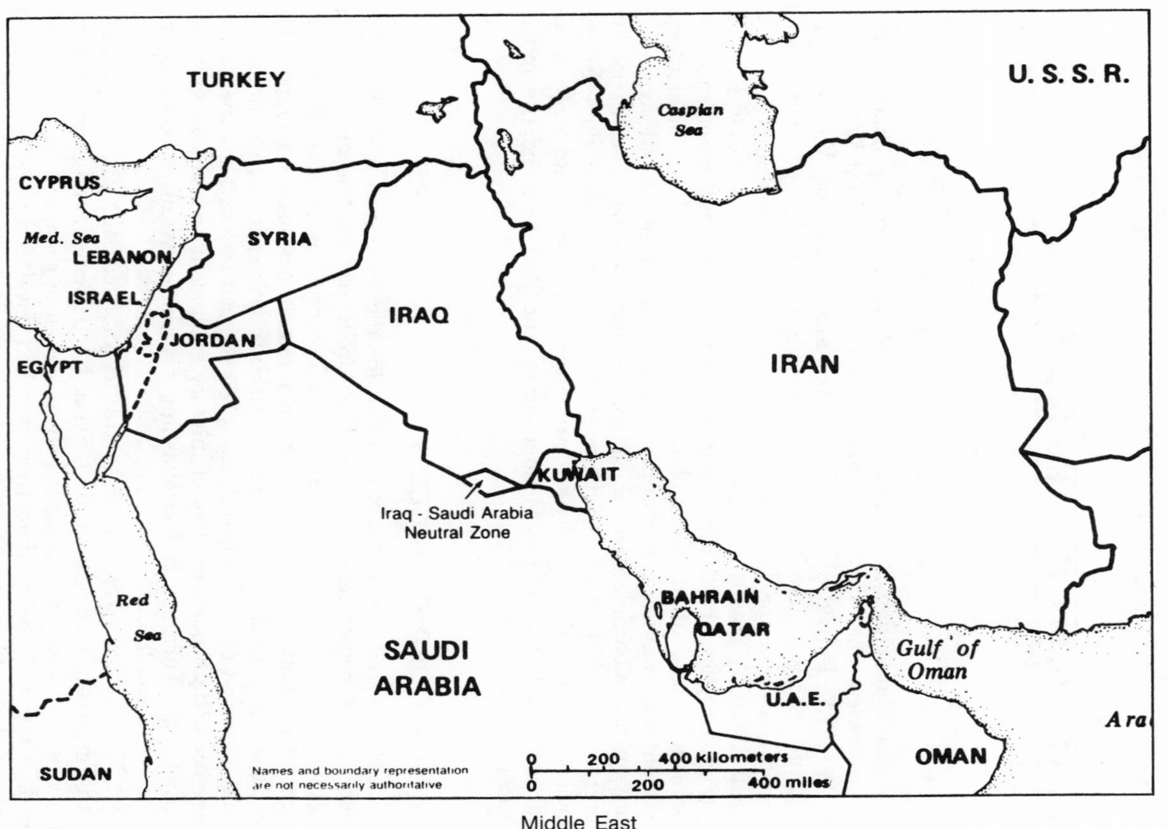
TURKEY
U. S. S. R.
Caspian Sea
CYPRUS
Med. Sea
LEBANON
SYRIA
ISRAEL
IRAQ
JORDAN
EGYPT
IRAN
KUWAIT
Iraq - Saudi Arabia Neutral Zone
Red Sea
BAHRAIN
QATAR
SAUDI ARABIA
Gulf of Oman
U.A.E.
OMAN
SUDAN
Names and boundary representation are not necessarily authoritative
0 200 400 kilometers
0 200 400 miles

Middle East

and training. This dependence, in turn, gives Moscow a certain political leverage. Despite serious strains in relations between Moscow and Baghdad in the early 1980s, for example, the arms relationship forced Iraq to moderate its hostility towards Moscow and sustain a degree of civility.

Soviet military equipment has allowed Moscow's clients to play enhanced regional roles, often complementing Soviet interests. Soviet arms have given Syria the confidence and credibility to pose a military threat to Israel as well as to Jordan and the Palestinians, enabling it to act as a spoiler of any Arab-Israeli negotiations which did not take its interests into account. Soviet arms gave Egypt a military capability sufficient to challenge Israeli superiority in 1973. Soviet arms enabled Iraq to wage a ground and air war against Iran for nearly eight years. Soviet arms bolstered Libyan leader Qadhafi's confidence and enabled him to pursue his regional ambitions.

AN ERA OF STAGNATION

Despite this impressive overall record, however, the Soviets have made no major political gains in the region since the early 1970s, and they may even have lost ground. The turning point occurred in 1972, when the new President of Egypt, Anwar Sadat, ordered the Soviets to remove their 15,000 military advisors from Egypt, transfer all Soviet military installations to Egyptian control, and either sell all Soviet-controlled military equipment to Egypt or remove it from the country. At the end of the Soviet withdrawal, only several hundred Soviet military personnel remained in Egypt and most Soviet-controlled military equipment had been withdrawn, including Soviet-piloted MIG-25 interceptors and TU-16 reconnaissance aircraft that had been used to monitor the US Sixth Fleet.[2] Sadat's rejection of the Soviets culminated in his 1976 unilateral abrogation of the Soviet-Egyptian Treaty of Friendship and Cooperation and his downgrading of bilateral diplomatic representation.

The deterioration of Soviet-Egyptian relations and Egypt's eventual turn toward the West had a number of consequences for Moscow's position in the Middle East—all of them negative. First of all, the Soviets had lost a significant military presence in the region, one which they have never regained.[3] Secondly, from this point on, the Soviets were to be excluded from the Arab-Israeli peace process, started by Secretary of State Henry Kissinger in the wake of the October 1973 war and culminating in the Camp David Agreements of 1978, orchestrated by President Jimmy Carter. Thirdly, the absence of a strong geopolitical position in Egypt—the key Arab actor in the region—was to seriously weaken Soviet efforts to counter Arab disunity in the region and to forge an organized, pro-Soviet, anti-US Arab position with respect to the Arab-Israeli conflict. Finally, the Soviets found themselves isolated with the radical states in the region—Syria, Libya, and South Yemen—and discovered that they had virtually no control over the unpredictable actions of these clients.

Numerous Syrian actions over the past 15 years have been opposed by the Soviets, including many of its policies in Lebanon (from its intervention in Lebanon in the mid-1970s against the Palestine Liberation Organization [PLO] to its current military operations); its hostility to PLO leader Arafat; and its diplomatic and military support for Iran's Ayatollah Khomeini during the Iran-Iraq war. Libya's policies also have created discomfort in Moscow. The Soviets gave little support to Libyan efforts to control Chad, and Qadhafi's support for international terrorism has been an embarrassment for the Soviets. Soviet efforts to influence South Yemen's political process served to exacerbate internal infighting in that country, and the tribal warfare which erupted in early 1986 caught Soviet policymakers by surprise.

In addition to the setbacks caused by the deterioration in Soviet-Egyptian relations, Moscow created its own problems in the Third World and the Islamic community with the invasion of Afghanistan in 1979. The eventual entry of more than 100,000 Soviet armed forces into Southwest Asia generated considerable Arab unity in international fora against the Soviet intervention and on behalf of the mujahedin resistance fighters.[4] The Soviet invasion of Afghanistan was one of the reasons the USSR was unable to capitalize on the US political setback in Iran in 1979. Support for the mujahedin included Iranian assistance as well as major amounts of Egyptian weaponry and Saudi Arabian financial assistance.

Over the years, the Soviets suffered from their unwillingness to provide direct military support to beleaguered Arab clients, particularly in confrontations with Israel. It was US pressure, for example, and not Soviet actions, that led to the end of the Israeli encirclement of the Egyptian Third Corps in October 1973, and both Syrians and Libyans were quick to remind the USSR of its unwillingness to come to their assistance in one-sided confrontations with Israel in 1982 and the United States in 1986 respectively. In addition, outside of the military and national security sectors, the Soviet model holds virtually no appeal for Islamic states opposed to atheistic Communist ideology and suspicious of Soviet intentions. Finally, the failure of the Soviets to extend more economic assistance in the Middle East, indeed in most of the Third World, has reinforced Arab perceptions that the Soviet Union has little of economic value to offer—save weapons.

GORBACHEV'S "NEW DIRECTIONS" IN THE MIDDLE EAST

In order to bolster Soviet policy interests, General Secretary Mikhail Gorbachev has made a series of interrelated moves designed to strengthen Moscow's political position in the Middle East, gain it a place at the Arab-Israeli bargaining table, and enhance the Soviet Union's image as a responsible superpower intent on pursuing constructive solutions to regional disputes.

Gorbachev's initiatives in the Middle East have not been as sweeping as his arms control proposals or as comprehensive as the approach toward Asia which he outlined in his speech at Vladivostok in 1986.[5] They appear to be based, however, on a similar perception that the USSR's strong military position has not been successfully transferred into political and diplomatic gains.

Over the past five years, the Soviets have pursued considerably more flexible policies with respect to a wide variety of Middle East issues, including relations with Israel and the moderate Arab states and a diplomatic solution to the longstanding Arab-Israeli conflict. These steps have been accompanied by the public airing of differences with such Arab clients as Libya and Syria over terrorism, military parity with Israel, and political relations with Israel.

An Opening to Israel

As Galia Golan of the Hebrew University of Jerusalem has noted, Moscow's moves toward an opening to Israel represented a "new direction" in Soviet policy toward Israel and a deliberate effort by Gorbachev to broaden Soviet options in the Middle East.[6] Moscow broke diplomatic relations with Israel in 1967 during the Six Day War in order to relieve the pressure being put on it by its Arab clients and to regain the credibility it had lost as a result of Israel's rapid and overwhelming success against its Soviet-supplied opponents. The move put the Soviet Union at a disadvantage vis-à-vis the United States in terms of mediating the Arab-Israeli conflict, however, and contributed to the stagnation of the Soviet political position in the Middle East. Gorbachev is the first General Secretary to actively pursue expanded ties with Tel Aviv and to offer concessions to Israel in order to enhance Moscow's regional flexibility and international credibility.

Gorbachev moved immediately to expand the diplomatic dialogue with Israel, sanctioning informal meetings in Paris and Washington between the Soviet and Israeli ambassadors in the summer of 1985 and allowing Poland and Hungary to arrange the establishment of interest sections in Israel. The Polish interest section opened in 1986, and the Hungarian interest section in 1988.[7] In September 1989, Hungary established diplomatic relations with Israel—a move the Soviets publicly endorsed.[8]

The first official meeting between Soviet and Israeli officials in nearly 20 years took place in Helsinki, Finland, in August 1986 and, the following month, Soviet Foreign Minister Shevardnadze and then Israeli Prime Minister Shimon Peres met at the United Nations, the highest-level meeting of Soviet and Israeli officials since 1967. Neither of these meetings accomplished much of a substantive nature, but they reflected the interest of both sides in pursuing a dialogue and they were followed by further contacts.

In a gesture to both Israeli and Western sensibilities, Gorbachev has allowed Soviet Jewish emigration to increase, first gradually and then dramatically. In 1987 over eight thousand Soviet Jews were allowed to leave compared with under a thousand the year before.[9] In 1988, almost 20,000 Soviet Jews left the Soviet Union, and in 1989, the number of Jewish emigres exceeded 70,000.[10] While this policy was probably aimed more at

Soviet relations with the United States than at relations with Israel, it had resonance in Israel; all Israeli leaders want to increase (and to take credit for increasing) the number of Soviet Jewish emigrants. Israel also wants Soviet assistance in getting more Soviet Jews to go to Israel rather than "dropping out" and going to the United States;[11] for this reason, all Israeli leaders have an interest in expanding relations with the Soviet Union.[12]

The most dramatic statement of Moscow's new determination to improve state-to-state ties with Israel came in Gorbachev's speech at a state dinner in the Kremlin in April 1987 for Syrian President Hafiz al-Assad, Moscow's most important ally in the Arab world and Israel's major foe. Gorbachev asserted that the absence of diplomatic relations between the Soviet Union and Israel "cannot be considered normal." He also emphasized that the concept of a military solution to the Arab-Israeli conflict had been discredited and that the conflict could only be resolved through political processes—an implicit rejection of Assad's efforts to achieve strategic parity with Israel.[13]

Three months after Gorbachev's remarks to Assad, in July 1987, a Soviet consular delegation arrived in Tel Aviv, becoming the first official Soviet delegation to visit Israel since the Six Day War of 1967. The arrival of the delegation was a victory of sorts for Soviet policy as Israel previously had linked such a visit to a reciprocal visit by an Israeli delegation or the resumption of full diplomatic relations. Israel's unconditional agreement to the visit (as well as its subsequent agreement to extend the delegation's stay for an additional three months) probably reflected Peres' optimism about improving relations with Moscow and his desire to use this relationship as well as increased Jewish emigration from the USSR to demonstrate the credibility of his claims to be the "peace" advocate in the Israeli cabinet.

In January 1988, when the Soviets requested another extension of visas for their delegation, the Israelis were less forthcoming. They provided a one-month extension and indicated that they expected the Soviets to approve a reciprocal Israeli visit. The implicit message was that the Soviet delegation would have to leave Israel unless Moscow responded favorably. In mid-January, the Soviets did respond favorably, indicating that an Israeli delegation could visit the USSR to inspect Tel Aviv's interests section at the Dutch embassy.[14] This delegation became first a *de facto* consular delegation and then a permanent presence.

Soviet-Israeli contacts expanded still further in 1988 and 1989. Tel Aviv's cooperation with Moscow in the apprehension and return of Soviet hijackers in December 1988 and its rehabilitation of a number of Armenian earthquake victims created a positive atmosphere for the further expansion of political, cultural, and economic relations. Commercial contacts began to develop[15] and tourist exchanges began. In the first five months of 1989, over 7000 Soviet tourists visited Israel,[16] and in May 1989, an Israeli tourist group visited the USSR for the first time.[17]

The political relationship also continued its gradual development. Shevardnadze met Israeli Foreign Minister Moshe Arens in Cairo in February

1989, and the two agreed to a meeting of experts to exchange information and evaluate the Middle East situation.[18] The two met again in September 1989 at the United Nations, where they discussed the question of direct flights for Soviet Jewish emigrants to Israel. In a statement that seemed to reaffirm the march toward the re-establishment of diplomatic relations, Soviet Foreign Ministry spokesman Gerasimov acknowledged in July 1989 that the Soviet and Israeli consular delegations were, in fact, engaged in substantive dialogue and were being "used as a channel of political communications."[19] In October 1989, for the first time in eight years, the Soviet Union refused to vote against Israel's membership in the United Nations.[20]

The January 1990 visit to Moscow by Israeli Minister of Science and Technology Ezer Weizman produced still another upgrade in bilateral relations. Shevardnadze told Weizman that the status of the Soviet and Israeli "consular groups" would be "regulated." This explicit recognition of consular status constituted an incremental step toward official diplomatic relations. The Soviets simultaneously upgraded the PLO mission in Moscow to embassy status as they continued efforts to maintain a balanced position.[21]

Thus the groundwork for the restoration of diplomatic relations with Israel had been well laid by 1990, and the question of whether and when to do so had become a matter of public debate. *Izvestiya* published an article by commentator Aleksandr Bovin in August 1989 which called for the restoration of relations. Bovin argued that the situation in the region was deadlocked—and was likely to remain so, but that the Arab-Israeli confrontation would continue and might well lead to escalation. Citing the dangers of this situation, Bovin argued that all possible steps should be taken to modify the situation—including the restoration of relations.[22]

Izvestiya subsequently carried several strong rebuttals to Bovin's article. The most interesting came from Soviet Ambassador to Syria Zotov, who had been one of the primary participants in the USSR's opening to Israel. Zotov argued that there was hope of a serious settlement to the conflict and that Soviet diplomacy must be constructively engaged in achieving it. He argued that the situation was deadlocked because "rightist Zionist circles" in Israel (e.g., the Likud bloc led by Prime Minister Shamir) dismiss a compromise based on land for peace and security. He maintained that political influence must be applied to these "rightists" and that the restoration of relations at this time would be premature. Such a restoration, he asserted, should be connected naturally to efforts to stimulate a just peace.[23]

Zotov's position remained that of the Soviet government into 1990. Moscow appeared committed to postpone diplomatic relations until Tel Aviv provided a *quid pro quo*—meaning, progress toward a legitimate negotiating process in which the USSR was involved. Shevardnadze took the occasion of his meeting with Arens in September 1989 to state that the restoration of diplomatic relations was not the important question; rather, he said, emphasis should be put on proceeding with negotiations—either through an international conference or the pursuit of positive elements in other proposals. Shevardnadze said that he had appealed to Arens to enter into direct contacts with the Palestine Liberation Organization (PLO) and had offered his services to organize such a meeting on Soviet territory.[24] Given the firm opposition of Israeli Prime Minister Shamir to an international conference or to any sort of direct or indirect negotiations with the PLO, progress in this respect seems highly unlikely as do the short-term prospects for a resumption of Soviet-Israeli diplomatic relations.

IMPROVED TIES WITH ARAB MODERATES

Egypt

As upgrading the dialogue with Israel serves Moscow's broader strategic and regional goals, so too does expanding contacts with moderate Arab regimes. Shortly after coming to power, the Gorbachev regime signaled that it was eager to move these relationships forward. The primary target of this approach was Egypt, whose gradual move back into the Arab fold during this period was consistent with Moscow's efforts to encourage a more united Arab approach to the conflict with Israel.

Under Egyptian President Mubarak, there had been only glacial improvement in Soviet-Egyptian relations. Mubarak had permitted the Soviet Ambassador to return to Cairo in mid-1985, but had allowed little other progress. A major obstacle to improved relations was disagreement over repayment terms for Egypt's large military debt to the USSR. Since 1977, Egypt had refused to make payments, while Moscow had made such payments a precondition to delivery of spare parts for Soviet-made military equipment and to improved commercial relations.[25]

The Soviets began making overtures to improve the climate of relations with Egypt in the fall of 1985 and, during the next year, there were numerous exchanges of visits and messages of good will. The appointment of a high-level foreign trade official (G. K. Zhuravlev, formerly a First Deputy Minister of Foreign Trade) as Ambassador to Cairo in September 1986 gave new impetus to the search for a solution to the debt problem.

In early 1987, Moscow basically agreed to Egypt's terms for repayment, including a six-year grace period and generous terms for the subsequent 19 years of repayment.[26] Soon after this agreement, the two sides signed new bilateral economic agreements and renewed discussions of military supply.[27] In October 1987, Egypt allowed the USSR to reopen its consulates in Alexandria and Port Said,[28] and, in March 1988, its Cultural Center in Cairo.[29]

The content of Soviet-Egyptian relations may have progressed very little,[30] but the atmospherics have improved considerably. In February 1989, Shevardnadze became the first Soviet foreign minister to visit Egypt in 15 years; the visit was highly publicized and Shevardnadze received a warm welcome in Cairo from President Mubarak. According to press reports, Mubarak will visit the Soviet Union in 1990.[31]

In response to the improvement in relations with the USSR, Egypt repeatedly has endorsed Moscow's calls for an international conference on the Middle East. In the wake of Shevardnadze's visit to Cairo, President Mubarak said that both superpowers must take part in resolving the Middle East problem.[32] Even after advancing his own negotiating initiative in September 1989,[33] Mubarak continued to insist that the USSR must play a leading role in any peace negotiations. Thus, even the modest improvement in bilateral relations with Egypt strengthened Moscow's claims to a mediating role in the Arab-Israeli conflict.

Jordan

The Soviets also have moved to improve state-to-state ties with Jordan. They gave red-carpet treatment to King Hussein in December 1987 (his first visit to Moscow since 1981), and press reports indicate that they offered to sell Amman the advanced MIG-29 fighter aircraft which only India, Syria, and Iraq currently possess.[34]

For a short period of time, Moscow even appeared to shift its support toward Jordan's position in the peace process. Its commitment to the PLO's role in the peace process became somewhat more ambiguous.[35] In the spring of 1987, Israeli Foreign Minister Peres reported that Shevardnadze had conveyed to him a flexible position with respect to Palestinian representation at an international conference, suggesting that Moscow was prepared, at that time, to drop its insistence that the PLO must directly represent the Palestinians at any Middle East peace conference.[36] This ambiguity presumably was designed to convey the impression that Moscow was open to any constructive approach to an international conference, including participation by a compromise Jordanian-Palestinian delegation.[37]

Shevardnadze visited Amman during his February 1989 tour of the Middle East—becoming the first Soviet Foreign Minister ever to visit Jordan. In the wake of the visit, King Hussein praised Soviet efforts in the Middle East, stating that Moscow was trying to work with the United States to achieve peace. He said Moscow's views were identical to those of Jordan and the majority of world leaders.[38]

Soviet-Jordanian relations continued to improve slowly during 1989. The new Joint Soviet-Jordanian Economic Commission met in the summer and agreed to expand trade to a level of $50 million annually.[39] Roving Ambassador Gennadiy Tarasov visited Amman twice for consultations on Middle East issues,[40] cultural exchanges were negotiated,[41] and, in August, the Soviets agreed to reschedule Jordan's debts.[42]

The Peace Process and the Palestinians

Under Gorbachev's leadership, the USSR has become more flexible toward virtually every question relating to the peace process and the Palestinian issue. It has modified its positions on the modalities of the negotiation process and an eventual settlement; given active support to moderate elements of the PLO (led by Yasir Arafat) in its power struggle with Syria and more radical Palestinian factions; and consistently urged the PLO to adopt a conciliatory posture. These policies have given credibility to Moscow's long-expressed willingness to use its good offices as well as its leverage to move the peace process forward. The new Soviet approach also has contributed to a shift in the regional political balance in favor of the Arab moderates.

Under Gorbachev, the Soviets have used persuasion and active diplomacy to encourage Palestinian moderation and conciliation. Their first initiative was to back the reunification of the PLO; their stated goal was to create a strong and viable Palestinian entity able to negotiate a peace settlement with Moscow. Moscow played an active role in the reunification of the PLO which occurred in Algiers in April 1987, encouraging their longtime clients, the Popular Front for the Liberation of Palestine (PFLP) and the Democratic Front for the Liberation of Palestine (DFLP), to cooperate in this process and urging Syria to acquiesce. Soviet lobbying may have contributed somewhat to the reunification; the PFLP, DFLP, and Syria may all have taken Soviet views, as well as those of other Arab actors, into account in deciding that it was better to go along in this case than to be isolated on the fringes of Arab politics.

Gorbachev's reception of Yasir Arafat in Moscow in November 1987 and April 1988 marked the formal restoration of Soviet support for the PLO under Arafat's leadership.[43] These were Arafat's first formal meetings with a Soviet general secretary in nearly five years. The creation in January 1989 of a joint Soviet-Palestinian Committee to coordinate policies raised the relationship to an even higher symbolic level.[44]

The Soviets also have put pressure on Syria to pursue a rapprochement with the PLO. Before Shevardnadze's visit to the Middle East in February 1989, the Soviets tried to arrange a meeting between the Soviet Foreign Minister, Syrian President Assad, and Arafat in Damascus. Arafat refused to go to Syria, however, without a direct invitation from Assad—and the latter was not prepared to issue one.[45] Shevardnadze did meet with Arafat in Cairo, however, and met separately with Shimon Peres. In the wake of these meetings, Arafat frequently referred to these talks as "indirect talks with Israel" arguing that Shevardnadze had played the role of go-between.[46]

By meeting with Arafat and putting pressure on Syria to accept a unified PLO under Arafat's leadership, the Gorbachev regime demonstrated its determination to have good relations with a key participant in the Middle East peace process and to avoid being isolated with those who take the most extreme positions toward the negotiating process.

These policies have been well received by the PLO because they reinforce its institutional role. But the Soviets also have put pressure on the PLO to moderate its policies and, by indicating flexibility in their own positions, have implied decreased support for some strongly-held Palestinian positions. The PLO certainly was not pleased by the warm reception the

Soviets gave Jordanian King Hussein in December 1987. Nor could it have been happy with the brief Soviet flirtation with the US- and Israeli-backed "Jordanian option" and Moscow's exploration of the possibility of a joint Palestinian-Jordanian delegation to an international conference—anathema to the PLO which consistently has insisted on its right to independent representation at a conference.[47]

With the *intifada,* beginning in early 1988, however, and King Hussein's July 1988 renunciation of responsibility for the Palestinians on the West Bank, the Jordanian option became obsolete. The Soviets themselves argued that Hussein's decision was intended both to dispel the illusion of a "Jordanian version" of a settlement and to demonstrate that the true participants in the peace negotiations must be Palestinians. At this point, Moscow returned to its original emphasis on the PLO as "the sole legitimate representative" of the Palestinian people.[48]

In the wake of the Hussein announcement, the Soviets urged the PLO to take a more "realistic" position based on recognition of Israel and a two-state solution and to make some conciliatory gestures in order to reactivate the peace conference and create a good environment for an international conference. They urged the PFLP and DFLP to maintain PLO unity and to acquiesce in the various decisions taken by the PLO to modify its position in late 1988; these included acceptance of UN Resolutions 242 and 338, renunciation of terrorism, and recognition of Israel's right to exist.[49]

Moscow also welcomed the opening of a dialogue between the United States and the PLO in Tunisia in early 1989. In an *Izvestiya* article in January, commentator Aleksandr Bovin argued that the moderate wing of the PLO had gained a major victory and criticized those who opposed this course. He said that many Arabs remain critical of Arafat's moderate policy (citing Syria and Libya as examples) and stated that even "solid Palestinian organizations such as the PFLP and DFLP" now warn the PLO against concessions even though "concessions to common sense harm only those who refuse to make them."[50]

Neither the USSR nor the PLO endorsed the election plan proposed by Israeli Prime Minister Shamir in early 1989. Both criticized the plan because it excluded them from the negotiating process, kept control of the process in Israel's hands, set unacceptable preconditions (such as the end of the *intifada,*) provided no assurance of movement beyond the elections themselves, and restricted the outcome of the process.[51] Neither rejected the plan outright, however, probably because of a desire to continue to project a conciliatory image and possibly because each believed the initiative was destined to fail without their outright opposition. The Soviets and the PLO also reacted cautiously to Mubarak's 10-point follow-up to the Israeli proposal in September 1989 and to the US 5-point proposal, advanced by Secretary of State Baker in October 1989—in both cases giving Israel the opportunity to reject the initiatives first.

New Support for United Nations

Moscow's courtship of Israel, Egypt, and Jordan broadened the base of Soviet political action in the Middle East and bolstered Gorbachev's emphasis on political regulation of disputes. The Soviets further enhanced the credibility of their claims to be a constructive political force in the region by giving new emphasis and support to the role of the United Nations. They laid the groundwork for this policy in 1986, when they unexpectedly agreed to pay their assessment for the United Nations International Force in Lebanon (UNIFIL), which has been present in southern Lebanon since 1978 but which Moscow had refused to support. In 1987, the Soviet Union announced that it would pay $225 million to the United Nations to cover the USSR's dues for the year as well as Moscow's assessment for past UN peacekeeping operations—including those in the Golan Heights.

In order to provide a UN framework for its policy in the Middle East, Moscow has favored an international conference since the failure of the Geneva Conference of 1973, at which Moscow and Washington were co-chairmen. In 1981, the late General Secretary Brezhnev strongly endorsed the idea at the 26th Party Congress of the Soviet Communist Party. Gorbachev returned to the proposal in July 1986, adding the suggestion of a preparatory meeting in order to circumvent the refusal of the United States and Israel to deal directly with the PLO. In January 1988, in a letter to the UN Secretary General, Soviet Foreign Minister Shevardnadze tried to put new life into the Soviet proposal (and to take advantage of Israel's handling of the West Bank and Gaza demonstrations) by urging immediate consultations in the UN and at the foreign minister level to convoke an international conference.[52]

PRESSURE ON RADICAL CLIENTS—SYRIA AND LIBYA

Syria

In reorienting Soviet policy toward the Middle East, Gorbachev has taken a firmer line toward Moscow's radical Arab clients, most importantly, Syria. He has made it clear that Soviet, not Arab, interests will dictate Moscow's foreign policy agenda—even in areas where Moscow had previously deferred to its clients. In the case of Syria, this had meant a tougher Soviet line with respect to military deliveries (Moscow now explicitly rejects Syria's efforts to achieve strategic parity with Israel), with respect to Syrian relations with other Arab entities (most importantly, the PLO and Iraq); and with respect to Lebanon (where the Soviets have sought to facilitate rather than exacerbate efforts to find a solution). In his speech during Assad's visit to the Soviet Union in April 1987, Gorbachev publicly introduced the new Soviet approach to some of these issues. In addition to emphasizing that the absence of relations with Israel was abnormal and rejecting "strategic parity," Gorbachev urged Syria to repair its relations with both the PLO and Iraq.[53]

The Problem of Lebanon

Moscow has had differences with Damascus over Lebanon ever since the Syrians first moved troops into Lebanon in the mid-1970s—ostensibly to help quell the civil war. The Soviets deferred to Syria both because they recognized that Lebanon was of more importance to Syria than to them and also because ongoing tensions in the region served Soviet as well as Syrian interests (by blocking US-backed efforts to pursue a settlement). The Soviets have reacted more constructively to the deterioration in Lebanon in the late 1980s, however, reflecting their new recognition that instability contains the danger of escalation and superpower confrontation and undermines Moscow's broader interests.

During 1989, the situation in Lebanon deteriorated following abortive elections and the establishment of two governments (one Christian and one Muslim). There was ongoing conflict between Lebanese groups seeking to strengthen their positions and there were recurring threats of escalation involving Syria and Iraq, Syria and the Lebanese Christians, and Syria and the French. In the past, Moscow might have tried to exploit these tensions to strengthen its own position vis-à-vis the United States; in this instance, it acted in a more straightforward and constructive manner, urging moderation on all parties, including Syria and Iraq.[54] At the same time, the Soviets did not become deeply involved in the situation, preferring to support the mediation efforts of others.

The Soviets sought international and bilateral statements of support for mediation. In May 1989, the Soviet Union and United States issued a joint statement on Lebanon—the first such statement issued by the two countries since Gorbachev took office. Washington and Moscow urged all parties to the conflict to adopt and observe a ceasefire, expressed support for the Arab League proposal to build a framework for national reconciliation, offered their good offices to help promote a political resolution and expressed support for the sovereignty, territorial integrity, and independence of Lebanon.[55] In July, the Soviets and the French issued an almost identical statement, but added a call for an end to arms deliveries to all Lebanese groupings—a reference to the new problems created by Iraqi arms deliveries to the Christian forces of General Aoun.[56]

In late September 1989, after their meeting in Wyoming, US Secretary of State Baker and Shevardnadze issued a second USSR-US joint statement on Lebanon. This statement reaffirmed the conviction of both sides that the problems of Lebanon did not have a military solution and called for a dialogue among the Lebanese. It welcomed the Arab League Tripartite Committee's renewed efforts to establish a ceasefire, lift the blockage, and begin the process of a settlement.[57] It is possible that this combination of US-Soviet pressure was sufficient to inhibit Syrian military action against General Aoun in late 1989.

Arms Deliveries

In a press conference in Moscow in September 1989, Soviet Ambassador to Syria Zotov indicated that Soviet military aid to Syria might be reduced. He said that the USSR was reviewing Syria's requests for military aid for the next five years and that these would be scrutinized critically; if there are changes, he said, they would be in favor of reductions. He argued that Syria's ability to pay is not unlimited.[58] An article in the military paper *Red Star* in the same month also stated that the USSR would "never" give Syria more advanced weapons.[59] These statements may not be born out, because of the pressure on Moscow to continue to deliver weapons to Syria and to demonstrate that Damascus remains its key ally in the Arab world. Zotov stated in a subsequent interview that Moscow would not abandon Syria but would provide it weapons based on a view of reasonable defense sufficiency—that is, enough to withstand an Israeli attack and mount a credible counterattack. This presumably was the rationale for Moscow's provision of SU-24 attack bombers to Syria in late 1989.[60]

Moscow has continued to deliver sophisticated weapons systems to Syria—and to Libya in spite of warnings to the latter about its policies.[61] In April 1989, a Soviet Foreign Ministry spokesman publicly admitted that the Soviet Union had delivered SU-24 Fencer fighter bombers to Libya. He said these deliveries were in accordance with contracts concluded previously and argued that these aircraft, in range, are inferior to aircraft already supplied to Libya and do not signify either a buildup of armaments or a possible change in the regional correlation of forces.[62] While the Soviets recognize that continuing arms deliveries to radical clients tend to undermine their claims of peaceful intentions, they clearly are not prepared to lose hard currency or to risk relations with their clients.

GORBACHEV'S "NEW DIRECTIONS" IN THE PERSIAN GULF

When Gorbachev came to power in 1985, the Soviet position in the Persian Gulf was very weak. Moscow had good relations with only two regional states (Iraq and Kuwait). Its relations with Iran were poor and it had no diplomatic relations at all with any of the conservative Arab Gulf states. Its position had been adversely affected by its invasion and occupation of Afghanistan and by the Iran-Iraq war. As elsewhere in the Third World, Gorbachev has tried to change regional perceptions of the Soviet Union and modify the environment in which Moscow is operating. By the end of 1989, the Soviet Union had made incremental gains in the region.

Relations with Iran and Iraq: A Balancing Act

The Iran-Iraq war complicated Moscow's efforts to pursue good relations with both Tehran and Baghdad. Iraq has had a prolonged relationship with the Soviet Union, based originally on a shared antipathy for the West and, in more recent years, on an extensive and mutually beneficial arms relationship. The two countries have a Friendship and Cooperation Treaty dating from 1972. Soviet relations with Iran during the years of the Shah were never close, although a workable economic relationship had been established and Moscow had supplied Iran with some military equipment.

The Iranian Revolution surprised Moscow as much as it did the West. Although the Soviets had reservations about the nature of a fundamentalist regime, they certainly were gratified by the setback suffered by the United States. Their efforts to take advantage of the apparent opening failed, however, as the Islamic Republic dismissed the Soviet Union as a "foreign devil" second only to the United States. The new Iranian leadership rejected godless communism and retained traditional Iranian suspicions of Soviet intentions. The Soviet invasion of Afghanistan (to support a communist regime against Islamic insurgents) provided another reason for antipathy—and the war with Iraq, a major recipient of arms from the Soviet Union, was the third major reason for Tehran's animosity towards Moscow.

The Iran-Iraq War

Throughout the Iran-Iraq war (which began in September 1980 and ended with a ceasefire in August 1988), the Soviets indicated that they wanted the war to end quickly—and without a clear victor. They did not want a stronger and more independent Iraq—with its apparent inclination to align itself with the West and the moderate Arabs. Nor did they want a strengthened Iran, antagonistic to the Soviet Union and capable of exporting Islamic fundamentalism in the region. During the period from 1980 until 1982, when Iraq seemed on the verge of a military victory, the Soviets implemented an arms embargo with respect to both parties to the conflict. This action was directed far more at Iraq, with which the USSR had an extensive arms supply relationship than at Iran. After 1982, when Iran expelled the Iraqis from its territory and moved its troops into Iraq, the Soviets supported the Iraqi position in the war.

Moscow's concern with new Iranian advances on the ground in Iraq in late 1986 and early 1987, particularly the threat to Basrah, led to increased Soviet support for Baghdad and increased pressure on Iran to end the war. The Soviets issued a government statement in January 1987, calling for an immediate end to the war, and they supported UN Resolution 598 which put pressure on both countries to end the war. They refused, however, to actively support sanctions against any party—in this case, Iran—which did not accept and implement 598. As UN efforts to negotiate a settlement stagnated during 1988 and 1989, the Soviets offered their good offices. In January 1990, both Baghdad and Tehran responded favorably to Moscow's proposal that it host a meeting of Iranian and Iraqi Foreign Ministers in the USSR.[63] Thus Moscow's balanced policy had paid political dividends as it was accepted as a mediator by the antagonists.

Relations with Iran

Moscow's support for Iraq, coupled with its agreement in early March 1987 to lease oil tankers to Kuwait (thereby providing some security support against possible Iranian attacks) fueled Iranian hostility to Moscow. This culminated in an Iranian attack on a Soviet ship in the Gulf in early May 1987.[64] By late May 1987, as the United States began to increase its naval presence in the Gulf and to stress its determination to defend US-flag vessels, Iran indicated its desire to limit the damage to its relations with the USSR in order to avoid confronting both superpowers simultaneously. The Soviets, also concerned by the increase in the US naval presence in the region, were responsive.[65]

During the summer and fall of 1987, Soviet-Iranian contacts increased considerably. Soviet First Deputy Foreign Minister Vorontsov visited Tehran three times, Iranian Deputy Foreign Minister Larijani visited Moscow twice, and numerous bilateral meetings were held at lower levels. The tone of rhetoric improved on both sides and, for the first time since 1982, there was some limited progress on substantive matters. Aeroflot resumed intermittent flights to Tehran in October,[66] and a trade protocol was signed to the effect that Iran would ship crude oil to the USSR in return for light oil products, machinery, and renewed help in industrial projects. (Tehran had long sought a return of Soviet experts to its power and steel plants; these experts had been withdrawn in the early years of the Iran-Iraq war).

The strong Iranian reaction to Iraq's use of Soviet-supplied SCUD ground-to-ground missiles to bomb Tehran in early 1988 again put a negative cast on bilateral relations.[67] At a press conference on March 24, 1988, Speaker of the Iranian Parliament (Majles) Rafsanjani accused the USSR of pursuing a policy of "hypocrisy and duplicity."[68] Agreements already reached were maintained, however, and the two countries continued to do business.[69]

With the Iran-Iraq ceasefire, both the Soviet Union and Iran expressed their interest in improving ties. Moscow reacted with "profound satisfaction" to Tehran's July 1988 acceptance of UN Resolution 598,[70] and, in a visit to Tehran shortly after the Iranian announcement, Soviet First Deputy Foreign Minister Vorontsov expressed Soviet willingness to expand relations with Iran.[71]

Motivated in part by a desire for Soviet support in negotiations with Iraq,[72] Tehran signalled its own interest in improved relations. In a letter delivered on January 4, 1989, Ayatollah Khomeini praised Gorbachev for "confronting realities" in the Soviet Union and for revising Soviet ideology. He also lectured Gorbachev on the need to seek truth and return God and religion to Soviet society.[73] This was the first letter Khomeini had sent to a foreign leader. The Iranian news service reported that Shevardnadze had told a group of Iranian reporters that the letter marked a "turning point" in Soviet-Iranian relations.[74]

The Soviets quickly responded to the Iranian gesture and, in February 1989, Shevardnadze became the first Soviet Foreign Minister to visit Iran in 70 years.[75] During the visit, the two countries agreed to regulate their political, cultural, and scientific contacts and to expand trade. They endorsed a conciliatory approach to Afghanistan, agreeing that it must be sovereign, independent, and nonaligned and that the bloodshed there must end.[76]

The death of Khomeini and the visit of Majles Speaker (soon to be President) Ali Akhbar Hashemi Rafsanjani to Moscow in June 1989 gave new impetus to the bilateral relationship as a number of economic and commercial agreements were reached. The most dramatic of the documents signed was a Declaration of Principles that included a Soviet agreement to "cooperate with the Iranian side with regard to strengthening its defense capability."[77]

The declaration did not indicate what military equipment the Soviets were prepared to deliver to Iran. Some press reports speculated that Moscow had agreed to provide sophisticated weapons in return for one or more favors (e.g., Tehran's promise not to interfere in Soviet Muslim areas, an irreversible end of the Iran-Iraq war, or an end to Iranian aid to Shia insurgents in Afghanistan).[78] Other press reports indicated, however, that Moscow had made it clear that any arms agreement with Iran would not disrupt the military balance or destabilize the region and that Moscow would not supply Iran with sophisticated offensive weapons, but only limited defensive weapons.[79]

Moscow may sell Iran ground forces equipment as it did in the 1970s and early 1980s. The Soviets may have decided that this is the best way to strengthen relations with Iran without severely straining relations with Iran's adversaries (Iraq and Saudi Arabia). It does seem clear that some weapons will be sold. Responding to a question from a Supreme Soviet Deputy about the morality of selling arms to Iran, Gorbachev defended it as part of the USSR's overall arms trade policy and said it did not conflict with efforts to secure a more peaceful international climate.[80]

Trade between the Soviet Union and Iran has increased gradually (reaching an estimated $350 million in 1988[81]—still well below the pre-revolution level of about $1 billion). The two countries have agreed on the renewal of Iranian natural gas sales to the Soviet Union in 1990—after an almost nine-year hiatus. The initial yearly sale will be 3 billion cubic meters (compared to 10 billion cubic meters before sales were stopped in 1980).[82] They have agreed to resume cooperation in expanding the Esfahan steel plant, originally built with Soviet help,[83] and to expand cooperation in ferrous metallurgy, heat and hydraulic power engineering, transportation, and industrial and housing construction.[84] The actual value of the agreements reached so far is not clear, but Iranian Economic Minister Iravani's claim that they are worth more than $6 billion seems greatly inflated.[85]

Afghanistan and Iraq (a Quid Pro Quo?)

Part of Moscow's rationale for pursuing closer ties to Iran was to try to draw Iran into cooperation in resolving the Afghan problem. Talking to visiting Deputy Foreign Minister Larijani in August 1988, for example, Shevardnadze "expressed hope that Iran would render assistance" to Soviet efforts in Afghanistan.[86] In January 1989, after meeting with the Afghan mujahedin leadership (representing the Peshawar Seven) in Taif, Saudi Arabia, Soviet First Deputy Foreign Minister and then Ambassador to Kabul Mikhail Vorontsov traveled to Iran, where he met with leaders of the Afghan Shia opposition groups based in Iran.[87] He also expressed the hope that Iran might contribute to the negotiating process.[88]

In late 1988, Moscow began to receive indications that Iran might be helpful. In a meeting with Soviet Ambassador Gudev in November, Iranian First Deputy Foreign Minister Besharati said that Iran was ready to cooperate for the immediate withdrawal of Soviet troops and would help Afghan Muslims determine their country's fate.[89]

In late January 1989, in a speech in Cuba, Larijani called Gorbachev's policy with respect to Afghanistan a great policy. He said Moscow should be able to withdraw its forces without losses and that the Soviet Union should not have to accept a hostile government in Kabul; he indicated that Iran would help to resolve these issues.[90] It is not at all clear, however, that Iran has ceased its support for the Shia mujahedin factions fighting in Afghanistan.

Moscow appears to have followed through with its part of the quid pro quo arrangement as its position with respect to the Iran-Iraq dispute again tilted toward Iran. On the eve of Rafsanjani's June 1989 visit to Moscow, Soviet foreign ministry spokesman Gerasimov told a press briefing that Iraqi troops should vacate occupied territory and return to the borders defined in the 1975 Algiers Accord.[91] While a Soviet official subsequently announced that Gerasimov had been expressing his personal view, the statement sent a clear message of support to Iran.

In spite of these signs of improving Soviet-Iranian contacts, there are inherent constraints to improving relations stemming primarily from Iran's fundamentalist ideology and its suspicions of Soviet intentions. Various issues continue to create strains—even during a period of rebuilding. For example, Iran has accused Moscow of supplying arms to Iranian terrorist groups, including Iranian leftist groups such as the Mujahedin-e Khalq and Baluchi groups.[92] Iran continues to repress the Iranian Tudeh Party, and the Soviets continually criticize this repression.[93] And the Soviets have criticized Tehran for its policy in Lebanon. In an October 1989 article in *Izvestiya*, commentator Konstantin Geyvandov accused Iran of trying to "rekindle" the Lebanese war. He said that Iran had appealed to Lebanese Muslims not to compromise with the Christians and charged that this was simply pouring oil on interreligious enmity in Lebanon.[94] Finally, Moscow's military intervention in Soviet Azerbaijan in January 1990 aroused Iranian anger over the USSR's treatment of its Muslim minority. While both countries currently have an interest in improved relations, over time their differences and mutual suspicions will act as a constraint to cooperation.

Relations with Iraq

Soviet-Iraqi relations tend to fluctuate in response to Soviet-Iranian relations. When Moscow's ties to Iran seem to be improving, its relationship with Baghdad suffers—and vice versa.

Soviet-Iraqi relations improved during the latter years of the Iran-Iraq war because of Soviet arms deliveries, credit extensions, and support for Iraqi efforts to end the war. The Iraqis, who had strongly criticized the Soviet invasion and occupation of Afghanistan, expressed their appreciation for Soviet help by signing an economic agreement with Afghanistan in 1987 (thus recognizing the Kabul regime and giving it the kind of legitimacy Moscow was seeking for it).[95]

As indicated above, in the wake of the Iran-Iraq ceasefire and as part of their effort to court Iran, the Soviets moved toward the Iranian position with respect to resolution of Iran-Iraq differences. In mid-1989, the Soviet press began to cite Iranian claims to have withdrawn from Iraqi territory, noting that Iraq had not followed Tehran's example.[96] This was followed by the Gerasimov statement appearing to endorse Iran's position with respect to its border with Iraq.

Iraq reacted negatively to this shift and even more angrily to the announcement that the Soviets were prepared to sell arms to Iran. The government-controlled newspaper *Al Iraq* carried several strong editorials critical of the USSR for its "opportunistic behavior" and for destabilizing the region. The paper charged that Moscow should not have made any move toward Iran without consulting Iraq because of the Soviet-Iraqi Friendship Treaty. And it reported that the Soviets had agreed to supply Iran with a number of weapons systems, including MIG-29 fighter aircraft. Such public criticism of the Soviet Union by Iraq is very unusual.[97]

By the end of 1989, Moscow and Baghdad had restored a semblance of civility to the relationship. Shevardnadze and Iraqi Deputy Foreign Minister Al-Faysal met amicably, and the two countries exchanged congratulatory messages on the occasion of the 45th anniversary of the establishment of diplomatic relations.[98] In a commentary that was both criticial and reassuring, *Moscow Radio* criticized Iraq's concern about improving Soviet-Iranian ties and confirmed that the USSR was prepared to help Iran strengthen its defense structure. The commentary stressed, however, that nothing in the agreement should cause concern in Baghdad—that this kind of cooperation had existed until 1982 and was simply being resumed. Moscow thus implied that the weapons sold to Iran would be ground force equipment (as in the pre-1982 period) and not sophisticated weapons (such as MIG-29s).[99]

Courtship of Conservative Gulf States

Moscow has benefited from a shifting perception among the conservative Gulf states about the nature of the Soviet threat. Even before the Soviet withdrawal from Afghanistan, Gulf state concern about Soviet intentions and capabilities had diminished because of Moscow's inability to prevail in Afghanistan. Since the Iranian Revolution, these states have considered Iran and fundamentalism (not the USSR and communism) the greatest threat to their stability. They also have become somewhat less certain about the durability of the US commitment to their interests and see some advantage in balancing their superpower relationships. The Soviets have tried to encourage this new perception through their rhetoric as well as by their withdrawal from Afghanistan. They also used their support for Iraq in the Gulf war to demonstrate their common interest with these states.

The Soviet agreement to lease three oil tankers to Kuwait in March 1987 was significant as it marked the USSR's first participation in the Gulf in a security role. It was followed by the US decision to reflag 11 Kuwaiti tankers and then its commitment to protect those vessels with US naval forces. The major US naval buildup in the Gulf during the summer of 1987 was an event the Soviets certainly would have preferred to prevent. Their preoccupation with the US presence and their efforts to have it reduced complicated their attempts to improve relations with the conservative Gulf states.[100] As noted above, as part of this effort, they shifted some of their support toward Iran in the Gulf war and resisted Gulf states pressures to impose sanctions on Tehran in compliance with Resolution 598.

As elsewhere in the Third World, the Soviets have tried to improve relations with the conservative states of the Gulf in a variety of ways. The rhetoric of new thinking combined with active diplomacy and a generally more responsible position with respect to Gulf issues helped to improve Moscow's image. The fact that the USSR did not take advantage of tensions during the Gulf war to strengthen its own naval forces in the region helped convince the conservative Gulf states that Moscow's intentions were, in fact, benign.

Since 1985, Soviet contacts with all the conservative Gulf states have intensified and relations with most have expanded. Kuwait has long had diplomatic relations with the USSR and often has served as a proponent of Soviet interests in the region. The two countries have had an arms supply relationship since the early 1970s, and, in July 1988, they signed a new $300 million arms contract for armored personnel carriers.[101] Kuwait has not as yet been particularly responsive to Soviet efforts to pursue joint projects and expand trade.

Oman and the United Arab Emirates (UAE) established diplomatic relations with the Soviet Union in the fall of 1985, and Qatar followed in August 1988.[102] While Soviet relations with Oman have not progressed appreciably,[103] the USSR and the UAE have had a number of contacts and reached several agreements; of most interest is an agreement allowing Soviet naval vessels to visit UAE ports.[104]

Saudi Arabia

The primary conservative Arab state in the Persian Gulf is Saudi Arabia. It has not yet established diplomatic relations with either China or the Soviet Union.[105] The Soviets certainly hope to expand their economic ties to Riyadh and ultimately expand their political and diplomatic relations. There is no question that the Saudis have become more responsive to Soviet overtures in recent years and that they are moving in the direction of restoring formal ties.[106]

As other Gulf states have done, Saudi Arabia moved first to improve ties with China. Riyadh's purchase of a missile system from Beijing, a decision which became public in March 1988 but must have been made a year earlier, revealed a new Saudi willingness to deal with communist states—even without diplomatic relations. In October 1988, Prince Bandar headed the first Saudi delegation to visit the PRC in a strictly bilateral context, and in April 1989 the Chinese reported that Saudi Arabia would open a trade office in Beijing in 1989.[107]

The Saudis also have expanded contacts with Moscow. In January 1988, Saudi Foreign Minister Sa'ud visited the USSR as the head of a Gulf Cooperation Council (GCC) delegation.[108] The following month Soviet envoy Vladmir Polyakov visited Riyadh, becoming the first Soviet to pay an official visit to Saudi Arabia in over 50 years.[109] Saudi Arabia hosted the meeting between Soviet First Deputy Minister Vorontsov and the Afghan mujahedin in Taif in December 1988, and Vorontsov subsequently met with King Fahd—becoming the first Soviet representative to meet with a Saudi King in 50 years.[110]

While it seems clear that diplomatic relations will ultimately be restored, numerous problems and differences continue to delay movement. Moscow was displeased by the rapid Saudi recognition of the Afghan interim government in March 1989. The Saudis were not happy with the Soviet sale of SU-24 Fencers to Libya, and they were annoyed by Soviet criticism of the Saudi purchase of Tornados from Great Britain. The Saudis continue to be critical of Soviet treatment of its Islamic population, and the conservative religious establishment in Saudi Arabia is opposed to improved Soviet-Saudi ties.

CONSTRAINTS TO SOVIET PROGRESS

While the Soviets can alter and modify their own policies, the environment in which they are operating remains complex, and many situations and leaders are intractable. Assad, Qadhafi, and Saddam Hussein may be dependent on the Soviet Union for military aid, but they continue to follow their own domestic and foreign policies with minimal regard for Soviet interests. The Soviets have tried very hard to improve relations with Iran and have had some success, but Moscow enjoyed a far more stable and beneficial relationship with Iran under the Shah than it has enjoyed at any time with the Islamic Republic. Gorbachev has increased Soviet Jewish emigration dramatically and upgraded the Soviet-Israeli dialogue since 1986, but the Israeli government remains adamantly opposed to a Soviet-backed international conference—or to any process involving the PLO.

Another variable working against Soviet interests in the Middle East is Arab disunity. Over the years, Moscow has had to choose between rival Baathist parties in Syria and Iraq, hostility between Syria and the PLO, tribal and territorial disputes between North and South Yemen, political differences between Algeria and Morocco, and provocations involving Egypt and Libya. Moscow has long argued that this disunity weakens Arab negotiating leverage with Israel.

Under Gorbachev, the Soviets have tried, with some success, to encourage and become the recognized ally of a moderate Arab coalition seeking a peaceful resolution of the Arab-Israeli conflict. Their role in any negotiating process has been endorsed by the moderate Arabs as has their specific call for an international conference. They have put pressure on Syria to pursue rapprochement with both Iraq and the PLO. Gorbachev used his meeting with Assad in April 1987, for example, to press Damascus to play a "special role" in promoting Arab unity, saying that this would constitute a "major historical achievement."[111] The joint Soviet-Syrian communique winding up the visit emphasized that the Arabs face the "urgent task" of "surmounting continued internecine conflict."[112] In spite of this apparent Syrian agreement to work for Arab unity (and Assad did subsequently meet with Iraqi President Saddam Hussein and did permit Arafat to visit Damascus), he reverted to his old positions as soon as it was prudent—and he continued to pursue an independent course in Lebanon in spite of the criticism of most of the Arab world.

CONCLUSIONS AND OUTLOOK

Although Soviet policy options and prospects will remain limited by the complex environment of the Middle East and Persian Gulf, Gorbachev has succeeded in injecting Soviet policy with new vitality and flexibility. Soviet diplomats are paying frequent visits to Arab capitals to explain Soviet views and proposals. The new Soviet policy toward Israel has increased Moscow's relevance to the Middle East peace process and enhanced its image in the United States and West Europe.

Moscow recognizes that its ability to influence the parties to the Arab-Israeli conflict is limited, and it will not waste the leverage that it does have on initiatives it considers unviable. Moscow will not, for example, try to force its clients to accept proposals (such as the Egyptian 10-point plan or the US 5-point plan) that clearly run counter to the clients' interests as well as its own. It will listen carefully to its clients before adopting a strong position with respect to any proposal and will continue to be careful not to get so far out in front of their clients that they lose their credibility with all parties to the negotiations.

At the same time, Moscow will continue to encourage clients such as the PLO to take conciliatory positions, hoping that at least the impression of momentum in the negotiating process can be maintained in order to prevent the increasing frustration and tension that produce instability and threaten peace.

Moscow's new policies have helped to shift the regional political balance in favor of the moderates. The Soviet role in mediating the reunification of the PLO in Algiers in 1987 and its encouragement of PLO moderation played an important part in these moves. The more moderate Soviet posture also may have contributed to the acceptance of Egypt back into the Arab fold at the Arab League summit in Casablanca in May 1989—with the acquiescence of Damascus if not its blessing—and to Syria's renewal of relations with Egypt in late 1989. In a general way, Moscow's support for moderate Arab positions has deprived the more radical Arab elements of a superpower champion and thus weakened their ability to undermine the political strategy of the moderates.

Moscow's use of the United Nations as an extension of its own policy interests has worked particularly well in the Middle East and Persian Gulf. Its proposal that the permanent members of the Security Council prepare for an international conference put it back in a prominent role in the Middle East and set the stage for ongoing diplomatic activity and follow-up proposals; it also helped in its courtship of moderate Arab states, particularly Egypt and Jordan. Its support for UN Resolution 598 gave its increased credibility with Iraq and the conservative Gulf states (although it squandered some of this good will by refusing to follow through with sanctions). Its decision to pay its UN debts also conveyed the impression of a new Soviet Union willing to play a responsible role in the world and to pursue constructive solutions to regional tensions.

These efforts, as well as the Soviet withdrawal from Afghanistan, are consistent with Soviet diplomatic efforts to stress the nonmilitary aspects of international security and to defuse regional conflicts that carry the risk of compromising US-Soviet relations. A series of articles by three members of the Soviet Union's USA Institute (Deputy Director Vitaliy Zhurkin, section head Sergey Karaganov, and senior researcher Andrey Kortunov) provided the rationale for this new Soviet approach. Although the threat of premeditated nuclear aggression is decreasing, they said, "the threat of war may be increasing in part due to the struggle in regional sectors." They argued that the search for peace requires concessions and compromises to interests of the adversaries.[113]

NOTES

1. The sole exception is North Yemen.

2. Jon Glassman, *Arms for the Arabs* (Baltimore, MD.: Johns Hopkins University Press, 1975), p. 96.

3. The Soviets had aircraft operating from seven Egyptian airfields as well as repair and supply facilities at the Egyptian ports of Alexandria, Port Said, Mersa Matruh, and Sollum. (Karen Dawisha, "The Soviet Union in the Middle East: Great Power in Search of a Leading Role," in *The Soviet Union in the Third World*

ed. E. J. Feuchtwanger and Peter Naila [New York: St. Martin's Press, 1981], p. 122).

4. See Chapter 4.

5. TASS, May 27, 1986.

6. *Foreign Affairs,* Fall 1987, p. 41.

7. Tel Aviv *Davar,* February 14, 1987.

8. *Komsomolskaya Pravda,* September 20, 1989.

9. *The New York Times,* March 6, 1988, p. 3.

10. *Wiener Zeitung,* February 4, 1990.

11. The drop out rate of Soviet Jewish emigres is very high; only about 10% actually go to Israel. Tel Aviv would like to solve this problem by having Soviet Jews flown directly to Israel (via Bucharest). Once Soviet Jews arrive in Israel, they lose their refugee status and, under US immigration laws, are ineligible to go to the United States. The United States has been a leading advocate of the right of Soviet Jewish emigres to choose their destination. Washington's limit of 50,000 refugees per year as of October 1989 appeared to open the way for a Soviet-Israeli agreement on direct flights. In a news conference in September 1989, Shevardnadze indicated that, in principle, the Soviet Union and Israel had agreed to resume talks on direct flights (TASS, September 29, 1989). In October Aeroflot and El Al agreed to begin flights in 1990 (*The Jerusalem Post,* October 19, 1989).

12. The Soviets have taken a number of other steps designed to improve relations with Israel—and, more importantly, with the United States. They have permitted prominent refuseniks to leave, allowed Soviet emigrants to return on visits, clarified emigration procedures somewhat, and permitted the improvement of religious conditions for Jews who remain in the USSR.

13. *Pravda,* April 25, 1987.

14. Soviet willingness to approve the Israeli request was particularly striking given the timing. Moscow had been extremely critical of Israel's handling of Palestinian demonstrations in the occupied territories and almost certainly would have preferred not to make any positive gestures toward Israel at this time. The fact that it did so reflects its clear commitment to sustaining a presence in Israel.

15. In August 1989, agreement was reached for the establishment of a joint company to set up agricultural projects in the Soviet Union (Tel Aviv *Davar,* August 13, 1989). In September the USSR and Israel agreed to establish a factory in the USSR—for the production of wheelchairs (Tel Aviv *Yedi'ot Aharonot,* September 7, 1989). Later that month, the Soviet Union and Israel held trade talks in Paris and agreed to the opening of trade missions (*Jerusalem Domestic Service,* September 26, 1989). In January 1990, the Soviet and Israeli chambers of commerce agreed to the development of trade and economic relations, 23 years after direct contacts were ended (TASS, January 23, 1990).

16. *The Jerusalem Post,* July 19, 1989.

17. Tel Aviv *Ma'ariv,* May 12, 1989.

18. TASS, February 22, 1989.

19. TASS, July 26, 1989.

20. *The Washington Post,* October 18, 1989.

21. TASS, January 10, 1990.

22. *Izvestiya,* August 26, 1989.

23. *Izvestiya,* September 22, 1989.

24. TASS, September 29, 1989.

25. Dawisha, "The Soviet Union in the Middle East," p. 126.

26. Cairo MENA, March 23, 1987.

27. Cairo MENA, April 7, 1987.

28. TASS, October 26, 1987.

29. *Izvestiya*, March 19, 1988.

30. On the economic front, the first exhibition of Soviet export goods was held in Cairo in April 1989, and the following month, (*Izvestiya*, April 11, 1989) the Joint Soviet-Eygptian Intergovernmental Commission for Economic, Commercial, Scientific, and Technology Cooperation held its first meeting in Cairo. Trade between the two countries has improved little, however.

31. Abu Dhabi *Al-Ittihad*, September 20, 1989.

32. Cairo MENA, February 25, 1989.

33. See the section "The Peace Process and the Palestinians."

34. Kuwait *Al-Qabas*, December 27, 1987.

35. In an article in *New Times* on November 27, 1987, Aleksandr Zotov, a member of the Central Committee's International Department, approached the Palestinian problem in a flexible way. He suggested that, having been given the right to create their own sovereign government, the Palestinians might in fact opt for a federation or confederation with Jordan. While he indicated that PLO participation in an international conference was necessary to insure that conference decisions be accepted by the Palestinians, he did not insist that the PLO be represented directly.

36. *The New York Times*, April 8, 1987.

37. For further discussion, see the section "The Peace Process and the Palestinians."

38. Amman Television Service, February 24, 1989.

39. Amman *Sawt Al-Sha'b*, August 21, 1989.

40. Amman Domestic Service, August 27, 1989.

41. Amman *Sawt Al-Sha'b*, May 30, 1989.

42. Amman *Jordan Times*, September 24, 1989.

43. In 1983, there was a split in the PLO, and Syria supported a dissident, anti-Arafat grouping. By keeping Arafat at arms length, the Soviets demonstrated their commitment to Damascus and also demonstrated their opposition to the Amman Accord of 1985 in which Arafat and King Hussein agreed on a joint Palestinian-Jordanian approach to talks with Israel. Arafat formally renounced the Accord before the meeting in Algiers in April 1987.

44. Kuwait *Al-Anba*, February 23, 1989.

45. *Radio Monte Carlo*, March 9, 1989.

46. Kuwait *Al-Watan*, February 26, 1989.

47. During Arafat's November 1987 visit to Moscow, Gorbachev stated publicly that the PLO should endorse UN Resolutions 242 and 338. He strongly backed the idea of an international conference under the aegis of the United Nations, and he indicated that a single Arab delegation to such a conference might be feasible. By avoiding phrases identifying the PLO as the "sole legitimate representative" of the Palestinian people and by not insisting that the PLO be directly represented at a conference, he gave an authoritative indication of a new flexible approach (TASS, April 9, 1988).

48. *Izvestiya*, September 18, 1988.

49. The Palestine National Council (PNC) met in Algiers in November 1988 and gave qualified endorsement to UN Resolutions 242 and 338, thereby implicitly accepting the existence of Israel; declared an independent state in the West Bank and Gaza with its capital in Jerusalem (citing UN Resolution 181 of 1947 which had called for a two-state solution to the Palestine dilemma); and called for a

confederation of Jordan and Palestine. In his address to the United Nations, meeting in Geneva in December 1988, Arafat also endorsed Israel's right to exist and renounced the use of terrorism. These actions opened the door to the beginning of the dialogue between the United States and the PLO in Tunis.

50. *Izvestiya*, January 7, 1989. Another conciliatory gesture made by the Soviets to the broader international community (and not appreciated by the PLO) was the decision not to support the PLO's application for membership in the World Health Organization in May 1989. In the wake of the Soviet decision, the PLO called for an urgent meeting of the Palestinian-Soviet Coordinating Committee to discuss relations (*Radio Monte Carlo*, May 12, 1989; Kuwait *Al-Anba*, May 16, 1989).

51. TASS, February 1, 1989.

52. TASS, January 22, 1988.

53. *Pravda*, April 25, 1987.

54. Abu Dhabi *Al-Ittihad*, June 4, 1989; Kuwait *Al-Qabas*, August 23, 1989.

55. TASS, May 11, 1989.

56. *Pravda*, July 6, 1989.

57. TASS, September 24, 1989.

58. Reuters, September 18, 1989.

59. *Red Star*, September 16, 1989.

60. *The Financial Times*, November 20, 1989.

61. In one of his first lectures to a Third World leader, Gorbachev lectured visiting Libyan leader Jallud in May 1986 about the need for "restraint and avoidance of any pretext for imperialist attacks," above all "terrorism in all its forms" (TASS, May 27, 1986).

62. TASS, April 7, 1989.

63. Baghdad INA, January 11, 1990, and Tehran IRNA, January 14, 1990.

64. TASS, May 14, 1987.

65. Iran had made a previous attempt to improve relations with the USSR. In February 1986, Soviet First Deputy Foreign Minister Korniyenko visited Tehran, and the following year Iranian Foreign Minister Velayatti visited the Soviet Union. These were the highest level visits since the revolution. After a six-year hiatus, the Permanent Committee for Economic Cooperation finally met in Moscow in December 1986. Thus there was improvement in rhetoric and an upgrading of contacts—but little substantive change in a basically very limited relationship.

66. *Moscow Domestic Service*, October 13, 1987.

67. IRNA reported on March 4, 1988, that Tehran residents chanting "Death to Russia" had marched toward the Soviet Embassy to "protest against Moscow's supply of long-range missiles" to Iraq. On March 6, the news service reported that the use of tear gas had been necessary to disperse a demonstration near the Soviet Consulate in Esfahan and that thousands of students had demonstrated at the Soviet embassy compound in Tehran.

68. *Tehran Television*, March 24, 1988.

69. The annual Soviet-Iranian Joint Commission on Economic Affairs held its meeting in Tehran in June 1988 and issued a protocol. The session discussed setting up joint shipping operations in the Caspian Sea (*Tehran Domestic Service*, June 9, 1988).

70. TASS, July 18, 1988.

71. IRNA, July 20, 1988.

72. Iran was particularly anxious to gain Soviet assistance in persuading Iraq to withdraw to the international borders (i.e., those established by the Iran-Iraq Algiers Accord of 1985).

73. *Tehran Radio,* January 8, 1989.

74. IRNA, January 9, 1989.

75. This was not the highest level visit in 70 years, however, as Prime Minister Kosygin had visited Iran in 1973.

76. IRNA, February 26, 1989; TASS, February 27, 1989.

77. TASS, June 22, 1989.

78. *Al-Qabas,* June 26, 1989; Abu Dhabi *Al-Ittihad,* June 25, 1989; London, *The Independent,* September 23, 1989.

79. *Al-Qabas,* July 26, 1989.

80. *Moscow Domestic Radio,* August 1, 1989.

81. IRNA, December 3, 1988.

82. IRNA, November 20, 1988.

83. IRNA, November 24, 1988.

84. TASS, December 8, 1988.

85. IRNA, June 24, 1989.

86. TASS, August 3, 1988.

87. *Moscow Domestic Service,* January 3, 1989.

88. IRNA, January 2, 1989.

89. IRNA, November 19, 1988.

90. *Pravda,* January 19, 1989.

91. Tehran *Ettela'at,* June 28, 1989.

92. IRNA, November 16, 1988.

93. *Pravda,* December 7, 1988; *Moscow Radio,* September 14, October 6, 1989.

94. *Izvestiya,* October 13, 1989.

95. *Pravda,* June 8, 1987.

96. *Moscow Radio,* April 2, 1989.

97. *Al Iraq,* July 2 and 3, 1989.

98. TASS, September 8 and 13, 1989.

99. *Moscow Radio Peace and Progress,* September 29, 1989.

100. In July 1987 the Soviets called for withdrawal of all foreign fleets from the Gulf and, in October, they proposed the creation of a United Nations naval force to replace the US, British, and French fleets in the region. While the Soviets were never clear about the objectives, composition, and duties of the force, it was clear that their objective was to gain a reduction of the US naval presence in the Gulf (*Pravda,* July 4, 1987 and October 18, 1987).

101. Kuwait, *Arab Times,* July 11, 1988.

102. The Soviet embassy in Doha opened in June 1989 (TASS, August 6, 1988; TASS, June 11, 1989).

103. The first visit by an Omani official to Moscow did not occur until January 1989 (*Al Ittihad,* January 16, 1989).

104. *Krasnaya Zvezda,* October 25, 1988.

105. The Soviet Union became one of the first nations to recognize Saudi Arabia as a sovereign nation in 1932, and the two countries established diplomatic relations and exchanged ambassadors. As relations became strained, the envoys were withdrawn and have never returned.

106. The Saudis do not seem to have criticized moves by the smaller Gulf states to expand relations with the USSR. Bahrain remains the only Gulf state, other than Saudi Arabia, that still does not have diplomatic relations with Moscow, and there are indications that it too is moving closer to formal ties. In June 1988, the Soviet Ambassador to Kuwait visited Bahrain. And, in the best indicator, Bahrain

established diplomatic relations with China in April 1989 (Manama WAKH, April 18, 1989).

107. *Xinhua*, April 1989.

108. Sa'ud also had visited Moscow in 1982 as a member of an Arab League delegation. During the 1988 visit, however, he was accompanied only by Saudi officials, and the visit was treated in the Soviet press as a bilateral exchange.

109. TASS, February 22, 1988.

110. Riyadh SPA, December 5, 1988.

111. *Pravda*, April 25, 1987.

112. *Pravda*, April 27, 1987.

113. *New Times*, October 12, 1987; *Kommunist*, January 1988.

7

ASIA

Although the Middle East historically has been the Third World region of greatest opportunity and danger for the Soviet Union, the Far East may now pose the greatest challenge and offer the most significant prospects. The Soviet Union, after all, is a major Asian power; one-third of its territory lies east of Irkutsk in east Asian Siberia, and some 20 percent of the Soviet population is Asian. It is contiguous to the states of East Asia and has a need to protect its eastern flanks. Its position in the region is of clear significance to its global competition with the United States, but, in spite of the USSR's military buildup in the region over the past 20 years, the United States remains the strongest military power in the Pacific. Finally, Moscow has a strong economic interest in the Far East. It seeks to develop Siberia (which contains a large proportion of Soviet natural resources), and it would like to capitalize on the enormous economic capability of the region to gain investment capital and expertise.[1]

THE RECORD

As General Secretary Mikhail Gorbachev looked at the Soviet position in Asia in 1985, he must have concluded that Moscow's policy had been a failure. Nowhere was the gap between the USSR's military strength and its political position more apparent. During the two decades which preceded Gorbachev's ascension to power, Moscow had steadily strengthened its military position in the region—massively augmenting its troop strength on the border with China,[2] fortifying its position in the Northern Territories facing Japan,[3] and establishing a military presence at Cam Ranh Bay in Vietnam.[4]

Moscow undoubtedly had anticipated that this military expansion would produce a corresponding improvement in its political position. It probably saw potential openings in the mounting political and economic friction between the United States and Japan, in long-term political instability in both South Korea and the Philippines, and in the rapidly evolving political situation in China. The Soviets may have assumed that the US setback in Vietnam would alter regional perceptions of the utility of close

Lake Baikal
U.S.S.R.
Ulaanbaatar
MONGOLIA
Beijing
NORTH KOREA
P'yongyang
Demarcation line
Seoul
SOUTH KOREA
JAPAN
Tokyo
Indian claim
CHINA
Chinese line of control
NEPAL
BHUTAN
Kathmandu
Thimphu
BANGLADESH
INDIA
Dhaka
Taiwan
Hanoi
BURMA
LAOS
Macau (Port.)
Hong Kong (U.K.)
Vientiane
Philippine Sea
Rangoon
THAILAND
VIETNAM
Bay of Bengal
Bangkok
Manila
CAMBODIA
Phnom Penh
PHILIPPINES
SRI LANKA
Colombo
BRUNEI
Kuala Lumpur
MALAYSIA
Bandar Seri Begawan
Singapore
SINGAPORE
Jakarta
INDONESIA
Names and boundary representation are not necessarily authoritative

East Asia

ties to the United States and that their own military buildup would lead both China and Japan to adjust their positions in Moscow's favor.

The results were the opposite, however. The Soviet military buildup pushed both China and Japan toward increased cooperation with the United States on Asian security issues. Each leg of the US, Chinese, Japanese triangle became stronger, and an informal anti-Soviet coalition emerged between these nations and both South Korea and the ASEAN states of Southeast Asia.[5] The invasion of Cambodia by Soviet-backed Vietnam in 1978, the Soviet invasion of Afghanistan in 1979, and Moscow's generally crude handling of Asian sensibilities over the years served to further strengthen an anti-Soviet consensus in the Pacific and encourage a substantial resurgence of US military power and political prestige.

Moscow also was excluded from the region's dramatic "economic miracle." Japan had surpassed the USSR as the world's second ranking economic power, and other non-Communist Asian nations (particularly South Korea and Taiwan) were enjoying rapid economic growth. Soviet anticipation that this dynamism would spread to its own Far Eastern regions had been frustrated by the USSR's closed economic system and its rigid political posture.

NEW APPROACH ARTICULATED

The Gorbachev regime has made a dramatic attempt to alter the political environment for Soviet policy in Asia and to shift regional perceptions in its favor. As elsewhere, the major components of this new approach are the downplaying of the utility of military instruments of power, an emphasis on the peaceful resolution of regional disputes, a de-emphasizing of the role of ideology, and a stepped-up effort to pursue relations with regional states through traditional diplomacy.

In major foreign policy speeches in the Soviet Far East (Vladivostok in July 1986 and Krasnoyarsk in September 1988), Gorbachev articulated his new approach. The heart of his first speech was an appeal to China based on positive initiatives with respect to two of China's three demands for improved relations.[6] Gorbachev announced Soviet plans to withdraw six regiments from Afghanistan and expressed his intention to withdraw "a substantial part" of the estimated 60,000–70,000 Soviet troops in Mongolia.[7] He made a further gesture of conciliation to Beijing, indicating that the navigational channel of the Amur-Ussuri River could serve as the border between China and the USSR, a concession on one aspect of the long-disputed border issue between the two states.[8]

Gorbachev also made a series of proposals at Vladivostok aimed at reducing regional tensions and lowering the general level of military activity.[9] He called for an end to the proliferation of nuclear weapons in Asia and the Pacific; urged negotiations to reduce naval fleets in the Pacific; encouraged a resumption of talks on turning the Indian Ocean into a zone of peace; suggested the establishment of nuclear-free zones in the South Pacific, Korea, and Southeast Asia; called on the United States to give up its base in the Philippines (indicating that, if it were to do so, the USSR would reciprocate at Cam Ranh Bay); and offered to embark on a radical reduction of armed forces in Asia down to limits of reasonable sufficiency.[10]

Two years later, in his speech in Krasnoyarsk, Gorbachev repeated most of these points and expanded on several. He declared that the USSR would not increase nuclear weapons in the Asia-Pacific region and called on the United States and other nuclear powers to make a similar commitment. This unconditional offer went beyond his Vladivostok offer as it did not require a corresponding commitment by the United States. He also made explicit an offer which had been implicit in his speech at Vladivostok, stating that if the United States eliminated its bases in the Philippines, the USSR would give up its naval supply station in Cam Ranh Bay after consultations with Vietnam.[11]

Gorbachev spent considerable time in his speech at Krasnoyarsk on the issue of expanding economic relations between the Soviet Far East and the nations of the Pacific. He called for various measures to energize these relations, including greater autonomy and incentives for regions and enterprises within the USSR, the creation of joint enterprise zones, and the establishment of a regional body in the Far East to coordinate economic contacts. He called for expanding economic cooperation with China and, for the first time, held out the prospect of improved relations with South Korea, stating that the general improvement in the situation in the Korean Peninsula had opened the way for the creation of economic relations between Moscow and Seoul.[12] Subsequent Soviet policy in the region has built on virtually all aspects of these two speeches.

NEW POLICIES IN ASIA

The Opening to China

Since the death of General Secretary Leonid Brezhnev in 1982, and particularly since Gorbachev's speech at Vladivostok in 1986, there has been a steady improvement in Sino-Soviet relations. Border tensions have diminished significantly and barter trade has increased tenfold over the level in 1982—to some $3 billion annually. Soviet experts and technicians are renovating Chinese factories and constructing new ones, and scientific and cultural exchanges have increased dramatically. Polemics have been muted, and the two sides have commented favorably on elements of the other's economic reforms. For its part, Moscow, without fanfare, shut down its clandestine Ba Yi radio station which, for decades, had broadcast disinformation crafted to foment uncertainty and mutiny within the Chinese Peoples' Liberation Army. The Chinese, in turn, have gradually come to the conclusion that the new Soviet leader is serious about domestic reform, the need for an international "breathing space," and the desirability and feasibility of rapprochement with China.

The symbolic and substantive highlight of the Sino-Soviet rapprochement was, of course, Gorbachev's historic visit to China from May 15 to 18, 1989, and particularly his meetings with senior leader Deng Xiaoping, Premier Li Peng, and General Secretary Zhao Ziyang on May 16. These summit meetings officially ended the Sino-Soviet dispute after 30 years of hostility and rancor and marked the first Sino-Soviet summit since Nikita Khrushchev's visit to China in 1959. The joint communique issued at the end of the visit favorably mentioned Gorbachev's "new political thinking" and, for the first time, Chinese media implicitly acknowledged the similarity between Gorbachev's "new thinking" and Deng's concept of a new international order.[13]

The visit and the joint communique also marked a determination to reduce the military confrontation between the two sides with an agreement that measures would be taken to reduce military forces along the border to "a minimum level." Soviet accounts of the talks referred to the creation of a "working negotiating mechanism" to reduce forces on the border although Chinese accounts carried no such endorsement. The first session of talks between teams of Soviet and Chinese experts on reducing military forces along the border was held in Moscow in November 1989. The two sides agreed to work for reductions.[14]

The summit communique also noted progress on border issues by indicating that negotiations on eastern and western sectors of the border would be merged and held at the foreign ministerial level; previously the Chinese had insisted on resolving the more controversial issues in the eastern sector first, and those discussions had been held at a lower level—the deputy foreign minister level. Only the Cambodian issue stood in the way of progress on all fronts as the two sides acknowledged that they "still have differences" despite "all-around and in-depth exchanges."[15]

Soviet Vice President Anatoliy Lukyanov visited Beijing in September 1989, marking the highest level Soviet visit since the Gorbachev-Deng summit and demonstrating that Moscow would not allow the Chinese crackdown on the democracy movement to derail the Sino-Soviet rapprochement.[16]

Background

From the outset of his tenure, Gorbachev had emphasized the importance of improving relations with China. In his speech to the Communist Party plenum that elected him General Secretary in March 1985, he declared that "the USSR would like a serious improvement in relations with the PRC and considers that, given reciprocity, this is fully possible."[17] Three days later, he gave substance to his words by meeting with Chinese Premier Li Peng, the head of the Chinese delegation to the funeral of former General Secretary Chernenko. This was the first meeting of a Soviet General Secretary with a Chinese official in over two decades,[18] and it was followed by a series of symbolic gestures aimed at convincing the Chinese that Moscow was genuine in its desire for better relations.[19]

Gestures on the Border Dispute

Two months after the July 1986 speech in Vladivostok, in which Gorbachev accepted China's position with respect to the Amur River border,[20] China and the USSR announced that they would resume the border talks that had been frozen since the 1979 Soviet invasion of Afghanistan. Talks resumed in February 1987; a joint survey of the Amur River was conducted in the summer of 1987; and an agreement on the use of border water resources was signed in November 1987. Routine meetings to discuss river navigation have been held subsequently, and agreements reached during these sessions have facilitated a significant increase in border trade between the two countries.[21] In August 1989, China confirmed that it had agreed to talks with the USSR on demilitarization of the border—and that a new round of talks on border demarcation would be held at the same time.[22]

The Three Obstacles

In the wake of Gorbachev's expression of willingness to make concessions on the three obstacles (Soviet withdrawal from Afghanistan, Vietnamese withdrawal from Cambodia, and Soviet troop reductions on the border), Moscow agreed to discuss these issues in bilateral meetings with China. Moscow previously had insisted that these issues had nothing to do with the bilateral relationship and should not be included in bilateral consultations. A report on the ninth round of bilateral consultations held in Beijing between Soviet Deputy Foreign Minister Igor Rogachev and Chinese Vice Foreign Minister Qian Qichen in October 1986 included, for the first time, a reference to discussions of "regional issues."[23]

Troop Withdrawals

Moscow, in January 1987, announced its decision to withdraw a division of troops (10,000–12,000) from Mongolia between April and June of that year[24] and, in his speech at the United Nations in December 1988, Gorbachev announced Moscow's intention to make substantial force reductions along the Sino-Soviet border as well. During his visit to Beijing in February 1989, Foreign Minister Shevardnadze elaborated on the offer, stating that the Soviet Union would reduce the numerical strength of its troops in Asia by 200,000 men and that it would withdraw three-fourths of its troops in Mongolia; he indicated that the reductions would be completed in two years and called the plan a "component part of the process of normalizing relations with China."[25] The first contingents of Soviet forces were withdrawn from Mongolia in May 1989,[26] and, in an interview the following month, First Deputy Chief of the General Staff Colonel General Omelichev confirmed additional withdrawals of tanks, artillery, and aircraft.[27] The press spokesman for the Soviet General Staff stated in October 1989 that 23,000 Soviet troops had left Mongolia and that by January 1991, 75 percent of Soviet ground troops would be out.[28]

Cambodia

With the completion of the Soviet troop withdrawal from Afghanistan, the issue of Vietnam's withdrawal from Cambodia became the most intractable of the three obstacles.[29] It was also the most important of the obstacles, however, both to the Chinese and to the nations of Southeast Asia. All considered their security threatened by an expansionist Soviet-backed regime in Hanoi and most supported one or more factions of the Cambodian resistance.[30]

Efforts by Moscow to push Hanoi and Phnom Penh toward a policy of national reconciliation and the withdrawal of Vietnamese troops from Cambodia began to pay off in 1987 with the initiation of talks among the various parties to the dispute. In May 1988, Hanoi announced its intention to withdraw from Cambodia, with its first 50,000 troops scheduled to depart before the end of the year.[31] In early January 1989, Vietnam announced that it would withdraw all its forces from Cambodia by September 1989. China expressed its satisfaction with the decision,[32] but Chinese support for the Khmer Rouge continued to be one of the factors complicating formation of a coalition government in Phnom Penh.[33]

Chinese Response to Soviet Overtures

The first indication that Beijing was preparing for the summit with Gorbachev came in late December 1987, when the Chinese published an interview with the general secretary in their weekly paper *Liaowang*; this was the first interview granted a Soviet leader in a Chinese paper in over two decades. Gorbachev took advantage of the opportunity to stress improvements in bilateral relations and to call for talks at the highest level.[34] The Chinese quickly responded that such talks depended on its preconditions having been met—Vietnamese withdrawal from Cambodia, Soviet troop reductions on the Sino-Soviet border, and Soviet withdrawal from Afghanistan.[35]

By mid-1988, the Soviets were well on their way to meeting these preconditions and, on September 28, 1988, following consultations between Shevardnadze and Chinese Foreign Minister Qian Qichen at the United Nations, the Chinese announced that Qian Qichen would visit Moscow later in the year. He did so, and, in February 1989, Shevardnadze reciprocated with a visit to Beijing. During the latter visit, the two sides made progress in talks on a number of subjects, including the timing of the planned summit. They agreed to set up a group of experts to consider further border troop reductions, agreed to expand economic cooperation, and issued a joint statement on the thorny question of Cambodia. In the statement, Moscow implicitly accepted a deadline of September 1989 for Vietnam's withdrawal from Cambodia—even if a political settlement had not been reached.[36]

In movement toward another Soviet objective, the reintegration of Vietnam into broader regional relations, the Chinese invited Hanoi's First

Deputy Foreign Minister to China in late January 1989. The two countries had not had such direct contact in over 10 years—because of tensions over Cambodia, clashes on their border, and disputed claims to the Spratley Islands in the South China Sea. Soviet commentary attributed the improvement in Chinese-Vietnamese relations to the impact of Moscow's "new political thinking."[37]

Thus far, Beijing's favorable response to Soviet overtures has served its interests well, particularly in view of its own domestic turmoil. It has been able to reduce tensions and create a useful balance to its relations with the West—without making any concessions on political and security matters. In addition, it has been able to start to realize some of the benefits of expanded trade with the USSR.[38] In June 1988, the USSR and China agreed to embark upon joint ventures and to develop direct ties between Soviet territories and Chinese provinces.[39] In 1988, border trade, though still limited, was approximately four times its 1987 level, and a number of cooperative projects were underway.[40] Late in the year, China and Mongolia signed a border agreement that marked a success for Moscow in its efforts to stabilize its southern border.[41]

MODIFIED POLICY TOWARD THE KOREAN PENINSULA

The Soviets have given increased attention to Northeast Asia since Gorbachev came to power and have modified several aspects of their policy. They continue to seek the withdrawal of the 40,000 US troops now stationed in South Korea, but, more importantly, they are determined not to be frozen out of broader political discussion of the Korea question. Moscow has improved relations with both North and South Korea and has encouraged reconciliation between Seoul and Pyongyang. Both countries have responded favorably to Moscow's gestures, for their own reasons.

Strengthened Ties to North Korea

During the mid-1980s, Pyongyang had taken steps to improve relations with the USSR and had adjusted its position on a number of sensitive Sino-Soviet differences such as Afghanistan and Cambodia in Moscow's favor. This shift apparently stemmed from a North Korean perception of its isolation and a resulting decision to seek broader cooperation with communist countries other than China. In 1984, Kim Il-song visited Moscow, marking a major improvement in bilateral relations. His subsequent visit to Moscow in the fall of 1986 resulted in little of substance, but had symbolic value, reinforcing the previous improvement in rhetoric between the two nations. This warming trend was also evident in increased military cooperation. In 1985 and 1986, elements of the Soviet Pacific fleet visited North Korea, and the Soviets began to deliver MIG-23 fighter aircraft to Pyongyang. In return, North Korean naval units visited the Soviet Union,[42] and Korea allowed Soviet reconnaissance aircraft to stage flights for intelligence collection against China.[43]

As it moved to improve relations with the Soviet Union, Pyongyang also indicated a desire to improve its image in the South—an approach strongly endorsed by Moscow. The Soviets gave numerous indications, for example, that they were pressuring Pyongyang to take no actions which would disrupt the Olympic Games in Seoul in the late summer of 1988. They participated in the games, as did most of their allies (Cuba was the major exception), and they suffered no resulting setback in relations with Pyongyang. Soviet diplomats worked in Seoul during the Olympics, thus becoming the first Soviet diplomats to work in South Korea since World War II.

In spite of its low-key reaction to the Olympics, North Korea made clear its concern about increasing contacts between Moscow (and East Europe) and South Korea. Following the establishment of diplomatic relations between South Korea and Hungary in February 1989, Pyongyang downgraded its relations with Hungary and recalled its ambassador.[44] By the end of 1989, Poland and Yugoslavia also had established diplomatic relations with Seoul—without drawing a strong reaction from the North.[45] Moscow has tried to dispel North Korean concerns by giving assurances of its steadfastness. Deputy Foreign Minister Rogachev has stated on several occasions that Moscow's expanding contacts with Seoul do not mean that it is about to officially recognize the South Korean government or establish diplomatic relations.[46] Shevardnadze visited Pyongyang in December 1988 and undoubtedly provided similar reassurances to the North Korean government.[47]

Toward Unification or a Two-State Solution

Moscow has backed North Korean proposals aimed at fostering a dialogue with the South and reducing the US military presence in South Korea. It clearly sees North-South reconciliation as helping its broader efforts to reduce international tensions. In July 1987, North Korea proposed three-party talks with the United States and South Korea to discuss a reduction of foreign military involvement on the Korean Peninsula. Soviet commentary praised the proposal and endorsed Pyongyang's assertion that, while questions regarding unification must be resolved by Koreans alone (as proposed by the South), the resolution of disarmament issues and the easing of tension must include the United States.[48] Moscow subsequently has approved various follow-up proposals by North Korea, including Kim Il-song's call in early 1989 for a summit conference between the two Koreas to discuss problems on the peninsula.[49] In 1989, representatives of the North and South held a series of meetings to prepare for a future meeting of the prime ministers of the two nations.[50] When these talks broke down in mid-1989, the Soviets strongly urged their resumption.[51] Seoul and Pyongyang have also reached agreement to expand economic contacts and develop tourism. Their first joint venture was announced in March 1989.[52]

Moscow has even begun to drop hints about the possibility of a two-state solution to the Korean problem—formerly a prospect it dismissed. In an interview in late 1988, Soviet commentator Aleksandr Bovin gave his personal opinion that there are two independent, sovereign states on the Korean Peninsula and that East and West should move toward "cross recognition."[53] In October 1989, in a move suggesting support for such an approach, Moscow dropped its objections to South Korea's membership in the United Nations.[54]

Improved Relations with South Korea

The changing atmosphere on the Korean Peninsula is due, in large part, to the fact that both Moscow and Beijing are determined to develop links with Seoul's burgeoning economy.[55] South Korea wants more trade with China and the USSR, partially because it fears US protectionism. And, with Korean anti-Americanism threatening the presence of US troops in the South, Seoul wants to reduce the threat of any attack from the North. The conciliatory speech given by South Korean President Roh Tae Woo at the United Nations in September 1988 reflected this shift in South Korean attitudes. In his speech, Roh proposed a conference of North and South Korea, the United States, the USSR, China, and Japan to discuss the situation on the Korean Peninsula.

Trade between the USSR and South Korea has been carried out primarily through such third countries as Japan, and total trade in 1987 amounted to about $160 million or about one-tenth the trade between the ROK and China. Trade in 1988 rose to almost $200 million,[56] and in 1989 to over $500 million.[57] Korean trading firms have opened liaison offices in Moscow, and Korean conglomerates are expanding their manpower in charge of trade with the USSR.[58] The two countries have agreed to undertake joint construction projects in the USSR[59] and have begun a joint venture involving the production and sale of furs and leather.[60] In early 1989 South Korea and the USSR reached their first formal governmental agreement—the opening of direct sea routes between Pusan and Soviet Far East ports[61]—and by late 1989 the two countries were negotiating the opening of direct air routes.[62]

In April 1989, the Soviet Union and South Korea opened trade offices in each other's capitals to facilitate economic contacts—with the caveat that they not undertake consular activities in the absence of governmental relations.[63] By early 1990, however, the two countries had established consular departments in these offices to perform consular functions.[64]

The Soviets have made several gestures designed to facilitate improving relations with South Korea. In addition to approving communist participation in the 1988 Olympics, they have announced their agreement to allow repatriation for the 40,000–60,000 Koreans living on Sakhalin (the survivors and offspring of those Koreans transported there as forced laborers by the Japanese).[65]

In a debate similar to that involving re-establishing relations with Israel, the Soviets have debated establishing diplomatic relations with South Korea. Academic F. Shabshina argued in an *Izvestiya* article in September 1989 that such relations would serve Soviet interests.[66] Deputy Foreign Minister Igor Rogachev responded sharply, stating that this was not Soviet policy.[67]

JAPAN: IMPEDIMENT TO SOVIET PROGRESS

The major void in the pattern of improved Soviet relations in Asia has been Japan, a key country for Moscow because of its geographic location, its close security ties to the United States, and its burgeoning economic strength and influence. The Soviets have wanted to slow the gradual emergence of a US-Chinese-Japanese entente and to erode US-Japanese security ties. They also would like to expand their economic ties to Japan and gain Japanese investment and participation in the economic development of the Soviet Far East.

The issue blocking improved bilateral relations is the continuing claim by Japan to the four islands occupied by the Soviet Union since World War II.[68] Over the years, Soviet diplomacy toward Japan on territorial and economic issues has been heavy handed and has tended to aggravate the differences between them. Rather than working to pull Japan away from US influence by exploiting Japanese-American differences, Moscow appeared almost determined to do the opposite, ranting about "Japanese militarism," warning other Asian states against Japanese "neo-colonialism," and generally treating Tokyo as an implacable adversary.

Under Gorbachev, Moscow has made several tentative efforts to improve the climate of relations. Foreign Minister Shevardnadze visited Japan in early 1986—his first visit abroad as Foreign Minister and the first visit by a Soviet foreign minister to Japan in ten years—and in August 1986, the Soviets agreed to allow Japanese to visit ancestral graves on the islands without obtaining visas.[69] An anticipated visit by Gorbachev has failed to materialize, but, in mid-1988, Gorbachev lent his personal prestige to a new gesture toward Tokyo. In a move designed to placate the protocol-conscious Japanese, he met for three hours on July 22 with former Prime Minister Nakasone, who was visiting Moscow in his capacity as a member of the Japanese Diet.[70] During the visit, Gorbachev stressed Moscow's interest in expanding the dialogue with Japan even in the absence of movement on fundamental issues. In support of this, he announced that Shevardnadze would make another visit to Japan and indicated that a Soviet-Japanese summit was possible. He did not hint at any territorial compromises, however, and he castigated "ultimatum-style approaches and demands" as unacceptable.

On July 27, 1988, Tokyo *Yomiui Shimbun* reported that, at a joint Soviet-Japanese symposium in Tokyo in July, the Soviet side had made a new suggestion that the northern territories be put under the "joint rule" of the two countries. No details of such a plan were provided, but the fact that the Soviet side at this symposium was represented by Yevgeniy Primakov, a close adviser to Gorbachev and now Chairman of the Supreme Soviet's Council of Unions, suggested that Moscow might be toying with the idea of making concessions. In an interview in October, Primakov also stated that, if Japan were willing to compromise, the USSR might also be flexible.[71] During this period, a Japanese newspaper cited comments made the same month in Japan by Aleksandr Bovin, an outspoken *Izvestiya* correspondent, to the effect that there was a dialogue going on within the USSR over the status of the territories.[72]

In December 1988, Soviet Foreign Minister Shevardnadze again visited Japan, and, for the first time, the question of the Northern Territories was officially listed as a part of the agenda. During the visit, the two sides agreed to establish a permanent working group to promote relations and to hold regular meetings at the foreign minister level.[73] During a similar visit in November 1989, Soviet Politburo member Aleksandr Yakovlev hinted at flexibility on the territorial issue without making any specific suggestions.[74] The Soviets appear to fear making any concession to Japan on the Northern Territories before resolving various territorial and border issues with the Chinese; moreover, they would not want to yield the two larger islands because of their role in protecting Soviet strategic submarines in the Sea of Okhotsk.

An article by commentator Aleksey Rogatsnov in the journal *Novoye Vremya* in August 1989 argued that the failure to establish close ties to Japan was one of the weak points in Soviet policy in the Far East. He stated that, because of world progress, it might now be possible for the USSR to relax its principle of not changing World War II boundaries (e.g., to return the islands).

NEW DIRECTIONS IN SOUTHEAST ASIA

Close Ties with Vietnam

Vietnam remains one of the USSR's most important client states. Soviet aid to Vietnam is estimated to exceed $1.2 billion per year with one-third of this thought to be military aid.[75] Soviet policy under Gorbachev has added to already-existing strains between Moscow and Hanoi. East European diplomats in Hanoi and Phnom Penh have reported that Vietnam has been irritated by Soviet pressure on Hanoi to withdraw from Cambodia and seek a compromise settlement. Soviet diplomats have openly complained that much of their $1 billion in aid to Vietnam is wasted by incompetent or corrupt Vietnamese officials. The Vietnamese, for their part, are said to feel that they are being overcharged for often outmoded Soviet technology and that they receive below-market prices for their exports. Finally, a Western diplomat in Hanoi reported that the Vietnamese were irritated by Gorbachev's proposal in September 1988 to trade Soviet access to Cam

Ranh Bay for US naval bases at Clark Air Force and Subic Bay naval base in the Philippines because they consider the Soviet presence at Cam Ranh protection against China.[76]

The Soviets are not likely to abandon Vietnam, and Vietnam's debt of $8 billion to the USSR gives it few options other than staying on good terms with Moscow. There is little doubt, however, that the Soviets would like to reduce the size of their aid package. To this end, they have encouraged better use of Soviet economic aid and the pursuit of economic reform in Vietnam. They also have tried to encourage Vietnam's acceptance back into the world community and, particularly, the Southeast Asian group of nations in order to end Vietnam's isolation and make it eligible for international loans. Finally, the Soviets have decided to reduce their military presence in Vietnam in an effort to enhance their regional image. In January 1990, Soviet Foreign Ministry spokesman Vadim Perfilyev stated that Moscow had withdrawn MIG-23 and TU-16 aircraft from Cam Ranh Bay and expressed the hope that this would "strengthen the climate of trust in the Asia-Pacific region."[77]

Pressure on Vietnam and Cambodia

Soviet efforts to push Hanoi and Phnom Penh to adopt an Afghan-type approach in Cambodia had little success until mid-1987 when Hanoi responded favorably to an Indonesian initiative—the so-called "cocktail party" plan, designed to promote talks between Phnom Penh and the resistance. On August 31, 1987, the Soviet Foreign Ministry, issuing its first statement on Indochina since the end of the Vietnam War, hailed Phnom Penh's adoption of a "reconciliation policy."[78] Several months later Moscow issued a second such statement, this time endorsing Cambodia's agreement to offer Prince Sihanouk a high government post in a new coalition government and to hold talks with all opposition forces except the Khmer Rouge.[79]

In December 1987, Cambodian leader Hun Sen and Prince Sihanouk held their first meeting in Paris, thus putting into action the "cocktail party" plan.[80] The Khmer Rouge refused to participate in or to endorse the talks, but its patron, Beijing, maintained an uncomfortable silence—presumably because it did not want to appear an obstacle to progress. The Soviets strongly endorsed the process.[81]

Moscow issued its third government statement on Indochina in May 1988, this time endorsing Hanoi's plan to withdraw 50,000 troops from Cambodia before the end of 1988.[82] The announcement of Vietnam's withdrawal was made three days before the fourth summit between Gorbachev and President Reagan.[83] In the summer of 1988, Hanoi made yet another concession with respect to the timetable for withdrawal from Cambodia. During his meeting with Gorbachev on July 20, 1988, Vietnamese General Secretary Nguyen Van Linh promised to withdraw the remainder of Vietnam's forces by the "end of 1989" or the "beginning of 1990" in the event of a settlement of the conflict.[84] Previous Vietnamese statements had focused on the possibility of total withdrawal by the end of 1990. The Cambodian government officially agreed to this formulation in January 1989.[85]

Further progress toward a solution to the Cambodian problem was made in 1989. A joint statement was issued during Shevardnadze's visit to China in February agreeing to the withdrawal of Vietnamese forces from Cambodia no later than September 1989. No conditions were attached, another concession on the Soviet side.[86] Once again, the Soviets managed to pull their reluctant clients along. On April 5, 1989, Vietnam, Laos, and Cambodia issued a joint statement indicating that Vietnamese troops would be withdrawn from Cambodia and that foreign state interference and military aid to all sides should end by late September 1989. It called for an international control mechanism to supervise the withdrawal as well as the end to foreign aid.[87]

An international conference on Cambodia convened in Paris in late July 1989.[88] Its objectives were to negotiate a coalition government for Cambodia and to create an international mechanism for monitoring the ongoing Vietnamese withdrawal from Cambodia. On the eve of the conference, the Cambodian National Assembly declared Cambodia's permanent neutrality[89] in a bid for international recognition of the legitimacy of the Hun Sen regime.

The conference failed to achieve either of its tangible objectives. The demands for a comprehensive settlement, made by the Chinese and ASEAN, and Hun Sen's refusal to include the Khmer Rouge in any coalition led to the break down of talks.[90] Moscow tried to put the best possible light on the conference; in a late August news conference, Gerasimov said that a "good foundation had been laid in the search for a settlement."[91] In fact, by gaining an international umbrella for the Cambodian negotiations, the Soviets had helped to spread the responsibility for a settlement and to relieve their own burden. The search for a diplomatic solution gained new impetus in late 1989. Phnom Penh showed flexibility, endorsing an Australian initiative calling for a UN-sponsored transitional period and elections. In January 1990, the deputy foreign ministers of the five permanent members of the United Nations met in Paris to review the status of negotiations.[92] They agreed that the United Nations should play a central role.[93]

Following the Afghan model, Vietnam proceeded with its troop withdrawal in the absence of an agreement on power sharing. The Soviets and Vietnamese claimed that the troops had all been withdrawn by the end of September.[94] In the absence of an international monitoring force, however, the question of possible cheating by Vietnam remained open, and various interested sources (particularly those seeking continuing aid for the Cambodian insurgents) claimed that Vietnamese troops remained in Cambodia.[95]

Moscow may have increased its assistance to the Hun Sen government as the Vietnamese withdrew. According to Asian diplomats and Cambodian rebel leaders, the Soviets increased their deliveries of arms and ammunition—

to twice the 1988 level.[96] Soviet press reporting emphasized that Cambodia was now capable of defending itself.[97] Thus, as in Afghanistan, Moscow continued to provide its vulnerable client with the means to defend itself.

Moscow Seeks Improved Ties to ASEAN

Under Gorbachev, Moscow has embarked on an active campaign to improve relations with the non-communist states of Southeast Asia. Its objectives are to enhance its political image, increase its economic participation in the region's rapid growth, facilitate the political and economic integration of the communist countries of the region into regional affairs (in order to reduce their reliance on Moscow's largesse), and improve the environment for its own broader strategic objectives.

The pursuit of a solution to the problem of Cambodia has been Moscow's primary substantive initiative and its justification for the pursuit of improved bilateral ties with the states of the region, and Moscow has used the issue in its active diplomatic campaign. Its stepped up diplomatic activity included a visit to Indonesia and Thailand by Foreign Minister Shevardnadze in March 1987—the first visit ever by a Soviet Foreign Minister to these nations—and these nations have responded. Indonesian President Suharto visited Moscow in September 1989—the first such visit in 25 years—and the two countries have created a Commission on Trade and Economic Cooperation.[98]

The Soviets also have tried to identify with various ASEAN political positions. During a tour of the region in early 1988, Soviet Deputy Foreign Minister Rogachev expressed support for a number of ASEAN's objectives, including the establishment of a zone of peace and neutrality in the region; he stated this could also apply to the South Pacific and the Korean Peninsula. Rogachev also called for the removal of US military bases in the Philippines (on the eve of US negotiations with Manila about extension of the base agreement), and he reiterated Moscow's call for a mutual reduction of forces in the region.[99]

Thailand

Among the ASEAN states, Thailand has been the particular focus of Soviet attention, probably because of its strong opposition to the Vietnamese presence in Cambodia and because it is a growing economic factor in the region. Moscow has had considerable success in its efforts to improve the tone of Thai-Soviet relations, and bilateral contacts have increased dramatically. The visit to Moscow by Thai Prime Minister Prem Tinsulanon in May 1988 and an exchange of visits by Thai Army Commander-in-Chief Chawalit and Soviet Commander-in-Chief Ivanovskiy in late 1987 were unprecedented.

Prime Minister Prem's visit to Moscow resulted in a joint communique noting the improvement in bilateral relations and citing the establishment of a joint trade commission to help in the expansion of bilateral trade.

The two sides discussed the possibilities of arranging technological transfers and broadening economic cooperation, agreed to maintain periodic consultations, and signed an agreement on scientific and technological cooperation. They noted the need to find peaceful solutions to regional problems and welcomed the signing of the Geneva Accords on Afghanistan which "could create a positive precedent for resolving other regional issues."[100]

In late 1989, in the wake of a visit to Bangkok by Soviet Deputy Foreign Minister Igor Rogachev, the Thai Foreign Ministry was re-evaluating relations with Moscow. Thailand planned to strengthen cultural and economic cooperation with the USSR, East Europe, and Vietnam, previously kept to a minimum because of Soviet backing of the Vietnamese occupation of Cambodia.[101]

The Philippines

Moscow's primary objective in the Philippines is the elimination of the US bases in that country—Clark Air Force Base and the naval station at Subic Bay. The Soviets have had success in their efforts to court the Philippines, recovering from their miscalculation in early 1986, when they badly underestimated the extent of dissatisfaction with the Marcos regime and were unprepared for his ouster. Following the elections in February 1986, the USSR was the first country to herald the Marcos victory in the heavily disputed returns and was seriously embarrassed as a result. Moscow quickly adapted to the government of Cory Aquino, however, and has made a strong effort to improve bilateral relations.

In March 1988, Soviet Deputy Foreign Minister Rogachev visited the Philippines and met with President Aquino. Rogachev probably tried to calm Manila's suspicions that Moscow was meddling in internal Philippine affairs, stating that the USSR was not helping the Communist Party of the Philippines or its armed New Peoples Army. Rogachev also urged Manila not to extend the agreements for US naval bases in the Philippines which run out in 1991. His visit was capped by the signing of a protocol calling for annual consultations between the foreign ministers of the two countries.[102]

In December 1988, Soviet Foreign Minister Shevardnadze visited the Philippines (the first such visit by a Soviet Foreign Minister) and met with President Aquino, laying the groundwork for a visit by the latter to Moscow. The two sides agreed to expand bilateral trade and to encourage cultural exchanges. In a joint statement issued at the end of the visit, they also agreed that all foreign bases in the region are temporary and are preserved only with the clearly expressed consent of the respective parties.[103]

Philippine Foreign Minister Raul Manglapus returned the Shevardnadze visit in July 1989; according to President Aquino, Manglapus was to prepare for her visit in 1990.[104] The joint communique signed at the end of this visit affirmed the two countries' commitment to resolve disputes peacefully, endorsed various Soviet arms control proposals, urged a political settlement in Cambodia, and praised ASEAN's zone of peace proposal.

Moscow and Manila agreed to try to increase Soviet-Philippine trade to an annual level of $200 million.[105]

Despite this improvement in the atmosphere of relations, Manila continues to be cautious in its approach to Moscow and has not accepted any of the economic aid projects which Moscow has proposed. Trade has been erratic since diplomatic relations were established in 1976 and the balance has been in Manila's favor. Trade peaked in 1980 when Philippine exports to the USSR totalled 189 million dollars and imports reached 22 million dollars, so the two countries are basically working to bring their trade level back to this level.

Moscow has had some success in facilitating an improvement in Manila's relations with Hanoi. In November 1988, Philippine Foreign Minister Manglapus visited Vietnam, the first such high-level meeting since the invasion of Cambodia.[106] Subsequent to the visit, Philippine rhetoric with respect to Vietnam became more favorable. Manglapus claimed upon his return that the Vietnamese were resisting suggestions that they provide surplus arms to the New Peoples Army and the Moro National Liberation Front. He also claimed to have obtained a commitment from Vietnam not to interfere in the internal affairs of the Philippines.[107]

OUTLOOK FOR SOVIET POLICY IN ASIA

In the past several years, Gorbachev has provided a comprehensive direction and focus to Soviet policy in Asia that had not been present since the end of World War II. Previous Soviet policies had focused on China, particularly the management of the antagonistic relationship between Moscow and Beijing. Indeed, the rift between the USSR and China contributed to the perception in Asia that the Soviet Union was an "outsider" in the region, essentially a European power trying to manipulate Asian politics against the interests of Beijing. Moscow's preoccupation with the "containment" of China, particularly the massive military buildup on the Sino-Soviet border in the 1960s and 1970s, merely convinced most Asian states that Soviet policies threatened their interests.

Gorbachev has addressed these issues by professing an interest in removing both ideology and militarization from Soviet policy in Asia. In comments that would have been branded ideological heresy several years ago, Gorbachev told Deng in their talks in May 1989 that neither Karl Marx nor Vladimir Lenin had the answers to today's problems for the USSR and China. He said that both Moscow and Beijing had a special responsibility to adapt socialism to new conditions. Two years earlier, in his speech at the 70th anniversary celebrations of the Bolshevik Revolution that was aimed at both China and Moscow's East European neighbors, Gorbachev had stressed the importance of diversity among socialist states and criticized the "arrogance of omniscience."[108] In conceding that there was "no model of socialism to be emulated by everyone," Gorbachev severely compromised the ideological rationale for the Brezhnev Doctrine.

During his visit to China, Gorbachev also revealed some of the details of the military cutbacks for Asia, including 120,000 troops in the Soviet Far East along the border with China, which is part of the general reduction in Soviet forces that he announced at the United Nations in December 1988. The Soviet General Secretary stated that 12 divisions would be withdrawn from the Far East, 11 air force regiments would be disbanded, and 16 battleships would be removed from the Pacific Fleet. The Soviet removal of their SS-20 medium-range missiles from the Soviet Far East, as provided in the INF Treaty, their withdrawal of ground forces from Mongolia, combined with their withdrawal from Afghanistan and their pressure on Vietnam to withdraw from Cambodia have contributed to Moscow's improved image in Asia.

In addressing China's "three obstacles," particularly the Vietnamese military presence in Cambodia, the Soviets have begun the serious overhaul of their security policy toward all of Asia. The relationship with China finally has been normalized, an entree has been developed to the ASEAN states of Southeast Asia, and bilateral relations with the countries of the Southern Pacific have become more stable. The Soviets also have forged a new commercial and diplomatic relationship with South Korea and have exploited Pyongyang's concerns with policies in China to strengthen Soviet relations with North Korea.

Thus, Gorbachev has used traditional diplomatic tactics and the promise of increased economic activity to end Moscow's disadvantaged position as "odd man out" in the Asian quadrilateral. From the Soviet viewpoint, the prospects for improved relations with China are very good, particularly in view of the near-term problems that confront Sino-American relations, and the Soviet "China card" should make it easier to strengthen bilateral relations throughout the region, perhaps even with Japan. The end of the Sino-Soviet rift, for example, will make it more difficult for North Korea to play the USSR against China and removes the rationale for excluding the Soviet Union from diplomatic discussion of the Korean problem. Gorbachev's Asian arms control agenda is popular throughout the region and should allow the Soviets to improve relations with Australia, New Zealand, and many of the ASEAN states.

The major obstacle in Moscow's efforts to become a bridge between Europe and Asia probably will continue to be Japan. It is unlikely that the Soviets will have any success in loosening the security ties between Japan and the United States, and Moscow's continued occupation of the Northern Territories will hamper any progress in Soviet-Japanese relations. Although Soviet Deputy Foreign Minister Igor Rogachev has stated that Moscow is "ready to discuss the whole complex of questions" with Japan, including "issues that could lead to a peace treaty," he warned that Moscow has never said that it was prepared to trade the islands for such a treaty. The Soviets presumably realize that such a compromise would encourage Chinese claims against the USSR and invite closer US monitoring of Soviet nuclear submarines in the Sea of Okhotsk.

Over the long term, Soviet economic problems will prove to be a major constraint on the growth of Soviet influence and presence in Asia. Two-thirds of Soviet territory may be located east of the Ural Mountains, but the region remains underdeveloped and offers little to the advanced industrial states of Asia. Economically, the entire Soviet Union cannot compete with the United States and the key states of West Europe in Asia unless Moscow invites genuine Asian participation in developing the extraordinary oil reserves and hydroelectric potential in the Soviet Far East. Soviet territory east of the Urals remains the main source of Soviet gold, diamonds, and other hard currency-earning minerals that remain largely unexploited. Moscow's efforts to be taken seriously in Asian cooperative ventures in the economic arena will require a difficult political decision in the Kremlin to allow for Asian participation in the economic development of Siberia.

The Soviets presumably realize, however, that their success in Asia over the long term depends in large measure on the stabilization and normalization of relations with China. In order to protect their gains with Beijing, the Soviets have been particularly careful in describing and commenting on the domestic upheaval in China. The Soviet Congress of People's Deputies, which met for the first time in May-June 1989, adopted a statement that did not ascribe responsibility for the violence in Beijing and warned outsiders not to interfere in the outcome of the current struggle for power. Soviet media, moreover, have contrasted Moscow's hands-off approach to the Western reaction to the crackdown which it has described as an attempt to put "pressure" on China. The Kremlin thus is hoping that its restraint in dealing with Chinese developments will enhance Gorbachev's diplomatic successes with Beijing and that its "China card" can be used throughout Asia to strengthen the USSR's position.

The Chinese are themselves increasingly concerned about the impact of Gorbachev's new thinking. They have expressed disapproval of the political revolution sweeping East Europe, blaming Gorbachev for the "disappearance of socialism" there and the resulting "disorder." These events were discussed during a visit to Beijing in December 1989 by a Soviet delegation led by Valentin Folin, Chief of the CPSU Central Committee's International Department.[109] Chinese commentary also has criticized Gorbachev for teaming up with the United States at the expense of its "natural allies," including China.[110] Such new and growing differences, combined with continuing friction over Cambodia, could slow the pace of progress in bilateral relations.

NOTES

1. Donald S. Zagoria, "Soviet-American Rivalry in Asia," in *The Soviet Union and the Third World: The Last Three Decades*, ed. Andrzej Korbonski and Francis Fukuyama (Ithaca and London, Cornell University Press), p. 252.

2. According to Pentagon reports, the Soviet Far Eastern Army grew from 20 divisions to 53 between 1965 and 1986. In addition, Moscow had doubled its

SS-20 missile force east of the Urals and expanded its Pacific Fleet. Moscow's naval presence in the Pacific in 1986 consisted of over 400 ships including at least 115 submarines, 30 of them armed with nuclear missiles (*The New York Times,* August 10, 1986).

3. The Soviets occupied the four islands north of Japan after World War II. These islands, the so-called Northern Territories, consist of two distinct islands (Etorofu and Kunashiri) and a group of smaller islands (the Habomais including Shikotan). The Soviets have included the islands in their security belt, and the two larger islands play a key role in Moscow's anti-submarine warfare capability in the region.

4. Cam Ranh Bay, the former US naval base in Vietnam, fell into communist hands in 1975 with the collapse of South Vietnam. Hanoi agreed to a Soviet presence in 1979, after China attacked northern Vietnam. While many observers believe that US forces in the region could rapidly neutralize the Cam Ranh base in the event of war, there is little doubt that the use of the base has increased Soviet capabilities to project power in the area. The Soviets maintain naval aircraft in Vietnam which conduct reconnaissance, intelligence-collection, and anti-submarine warfare missions in the South China Sea. They also maintain a squadron of MIG-23 Flogger fighter aircraft there. US military reports indicate that 20–25 Soviet Navy vessels, including three or four attack and cruise-missile submarines, routinely operate from the base. (Melvin A. Goodman, "The Soviet Union and the Third World: The Military Dimension," in *The Soviet Union and the Third World: The Last Three Decades,* ed. Andrzej Korbonski and Francis Fukuyama (Ithaca and London, Cornell University Press), p. 52; *The Washington Post,* August 1, 1986; from an interview with Admiral Ronald Hays, Commander-in-Chief of US Pacific Command).

5. The members of ASEAN (The Association of Southeast Asian Nations) are Indonesia, Thailand, the Philippines, Malaysia, Singapore, and Brunei.

6. During the 1980s, the Soviet Union had undertaken a series of initiatives toward China designed to overcome the divisions of the 1960s and 1970s. The Chinese, for a variety of reasons, were not eager to respond favorably and created a flexible formula built around "three obstacles." The Chinese demanded that these obstacles be removed before relations with the USSR could be normalized. The obstacles were the build-up of Soviet forces in Mongolia and elsewhere along the Chinese border, the Soviet military presence in Afghanistan, and the occupation of Cambodia by Soviet-backed Vietnam. Before Gorbachev's speech in Vladivostok, the Soviets had insisted that these issues had no relevance to Sino-Soviet relations and should not be dealt with in a bilateral context.

7. *The Washington Post,* July 30, 1986.

8. This offer was not new, having been made by the Soviets in 1963. But the Chinese had previously refused to accept it unless agreement were reached on other disputed segments of the border as well.

9. Moscow has long sought to reduce US military strength in the region and many of Gorbachev's proposals were aimed specifically at areas where the United States has a military advantage.

10. *Pravda,* July 29, 1986, p. 4.

11. TASS, September 16, 1988.

12. *Ibid.*

13. *Pravda,* May 18, 1989; *Renmin Ribao,* May 18, 1989.

14. TASS, November 27, 1989.

15. *Pravda,* May 18, 1989; *Renmin Ribao,* May 18, 1989.

16. *The New York Times*, September 13, 1989.

17. *Pravda*, March 12, 1985.

18. TASS, March 14, 1985.

19. Moscow ended the jamming of *Beijing Radio's* Russian broadcasts to the USSR in October 1986 and shortly thereafter closed down its clandestine radio broadcasts to China. In August 1987, it named one of its most experienced diplomats, Oleg Troyanovskiy, to the post of Ambassador and reassigned strongly anti-Chinese Mikhail Kapitsa from a policy position as Deputy Foreign Minister to the more academic position of Director of the Institute of Oriental Studies. Gorbachev also removed the Soviet representative at the border talks, Leonid Ilychev, who had long since worn out his welcome in Beijing (*The Washington Post*, November 3, 1986).

20. The USSR and China share a 4,500-mile border guarded by at least a million troops on each side. China claims that it lost more than 600,000 square miles to the Soviets through unequal treaties in the 19th century but is not demanding that all the territory be returned. Open hostilities have broken out several times since the Sino-Soviet split of the 1960s, with the most extensive clashes occurring in 1969.

21. Moscow International Service, April 2, 1989.

22. Hong Kong AFP, August 3, 1989.

23. TASS, October 14, 1986.

24. Daniel Southerland, "Moscow, Beijing Set Border Talks," *The Washington Post*, January 22, 1987.

25. *Moscow International Service*, February 4, 1989.

26. TASS, May 12, 1989.

27. TASS, June 1, 1989.

28. Moscow World Service, October 12, 1989.

29. For further discussion of this issue, see the section "Pressures on Vietnam and Cambodia."

30. The Chinese have backed the Khmer Rouge, the original Communist faction headed by Pol Pot which was responsible for the huge massacres of the mid-1970s. The United States and the ASEAN nations have supported other resistance factions, particularly the grouping headed by Prince Norodom Sihanouk.

31. TASS, May 29, 1988.

32. TASS, January 8, 1989.

33. See the section "Pressures on Vietnam and Cambodia" for further discussion of Cambodia.

34. *Izvestiya*, January 11, 1988 (From interview dated December 27).

35. In a striking gesture reflecting Moscow's desire to move China toward a summit, *Pravda* published a highly laudatory article about senior Chinese leader Deng Xiaoping on August 12, 1988. The article praised Deng for his realism, courage, and pragmatism, and credited him personally with the historic breakthrough of December 1978 that set China on the road to socialist modernization. It recalled Deng's 1986 statement that, while his age precluded much foreign travel, he was willing to go to Moscow to meet with Gorbachev if the USSR would influence Vietnam to withdraw its troops from Cambodia. It welcomed prospects of such a meeting but repeated Moscow's standard assertion that there must be no prior conditions.

36. *Pravda*, February 8, 1989.

37. *Izvestiya*, February 8, 1989, Aleksandr Bovin.

38. During the 1980s trade between the USSR and China has improved rather dramatically. According to *Pravda*, after normalization talks began in 1982, trade expanded, reaching about $2 billion in 1985, eight times the 1981 level. A trade agreement signed between the Soviet Union and China in 1986 envisaged a trade turnover of about $4 billion annually by 1990 (although many observers doubt it will reach that level) (*Pravda*, September 23, 1986, p. 4; *Asiaweek*, August 10, 1986, p. 8). In his interview to *Liaowang*, according to Moscow Radio Peace and Progress in Mandarin on March 3, 1988, Gorbachev said that Soviet-Chinese trade had grown from 490 million rubles in 1983 to 1.8 billion rubles in 1986. He said border trade was also developing rapidly and that over the past five years, such trade had increased 3.4 times.

39. TASS, June 8, 1988.

40. A new bridge was completed in October 1988 spanning the two countries' eastern border, and China was working on a rail link to unite the countries on their western border. More than 750 Chinese laborers had been sent to the Soviet Union on construction contracts, and a Chinese-Soviet joint venture, a photography laboratory, had opened near the eastern end of the border (Nicholas D. Kristof, "For Beijing and Moscow, a Glacial Warming," *The New York Times*, November 11, 1988).

41. *Izvestiya*, December 4, 1988, p. 5.

42. *Krasnaya Zvezda*, July 26, 1986.

43. Goodman, "The Soviet Union and the Third World," p. 54.

44. *Pyongyang Domestic Service*, February 2, 1989.

45. Moscow International Service, December 28, 1989.

46. *Izvestiya*, January 5, 1989, p. 5; *Yonhap*, March 28, 1989.

47. TASS, December 23, 1988.

48. *Pravda*, August 7, 1987, "For Détente on the Korean Peninsula," p. 4.

49. *Krasnaya Zvezda*, January 3, 1989, p. 3.

50. *Izvestiya*, March 4, 1989, p. 6.

51. *Pravda*, July 22, 1989; TASS, September 18, 1989.

52. *Pravda*, February 12, 1989, p. 7; Seoul *Yonhap*, March 9, 1989.

53. Tokyo *Mainichi Shimbun*, October 12, 1988.

54. Seoul *Yonhap*, October 20, 1989.

55. In an article in the Soviet journal *Arguments and Facts* in March 1989, G. Toloraya, a scientific associate at the Institute of the Economics of the World Socialist System, described South Korea's rapid economic growth and its ability to compete with the older industrialized nations. He emphasized the mutual benefits to be gained by trade between Seoul and the socialist countries, arguing that Seoul could export finished goods to the large markets of East Europe in exchange for access to raw materials and the means of production (#11, March 18–24, 1989, p. 4).

56. *The Korea Times*, January 15, 1989, p. 1.

57. Seoul *Yonhap*, January 13, 1990.

58. Tokyo *Sankei Shimbun* in Japanese, September 23, 1988, p. 5.

59. *The Korea Times*, July 29, 1989, p. 5; *The Korea Herald*, December 23, 1988, p. 1.

60. TASS, October 13, 1989.

61. *Yonhap* in English, April 3, 1989.

62. *The Korea Herald*, November 21, 1989.

63. *The Korea Times*, March 25, 1989, p. 2.

64. Seoul *Yonhap*, December 8, 1989; Moscow Domestic Service, January 7, 1990.

65. Seoul *Yonhap*, June 21, 1989.

66. *Izvestiya*, September 1, 1989.

67. *Pravda*, September 6, 1989.

68. The larger two islands play an essential role in the USSR's military position in the Sea of Okhotsk. They have fortified and based a division of troops on the islands. (Edward Neilan, "Japan Awakens to Soviet Military Buildup," *The Washington Times*, January 8, 1987.) In addition, the Soviets continue to believe that any concessions on the islands could weaken their bargaining position on the Sino-Soviet border and open up a Pandora's Box of territorial claims.

69. *The Washington Post*, August 22, 1986, p. 21.

70. *Pravda*, July 23, 1988.

71. Tokyo *Asahi Shimbun*, October 26, 1988.

72. *Nihon Keizai Shimbun*, October 3, 1988.

73. TASS, December 21, 1988.

74. Moscow Television, November 13, 1989.

75. Paul Quinn-Judge, "Moscow Pleased Vietnam Reformers Got Boost in Shuffle," *The Christian Science Monitor*, December 23, 1986, p. 9.

76. Murray Hiebert, "Soviet-Vietnamese Ties Showing Signs of Strain," *The Washington Post*, October 17, 1988.

77. TASS, January 18, 1990.

78. TASS, August 31, 1987.

79. TASS, October 17, 1987.

80. SPK, December 5, 1987.

81. *Pravda*, December 8, 1987.

82. *Pravda*, May 27, 1988.

83. Gary Lee, "Moscow Praises Hanoi's Plan to Reduce Force in Cambodia," *The Washington Post*, May 27, 1988,

84. TASS, July 20, 1988.

85. TASS, January 7, 1989.

86. *Pravda*, February 6, 1989, p. 5.

87. *Pravda*, April 6, 1989, p. 5.

88. The United States, Soviet Union, China, the ASEAN states, Vietnam, and all the Cambodian factions had delegations at the conference.

89. *Pravda*, July 25, 1989.

90. *The Washington Post*, August 23, 1989, p. 29.

91. TASS, August 28, 1989.

92. *Pravda*, January 15, 1990.

93. *The Washington Post*, January 17, 1990.

94. TASS, September 26, 1989.

95. Paul Lewis, "Soviets Said to Double Cambodian Aid," *The New York Times*, October 6, 1989, p. 6.

96. *Ibid.*

97. *Krasnaya Zvezda*, September 21, 1989.

98. *Pravda*, September 13, 1989.

99. Hong Kong AFP, March 25, 1988.

100. *Bangkok Voice of Free Asia* in Thai, May 23, 1988.

101. Bangkok, *The Nation*, December 18, 1989.

102. TASS, March 24, 1988.

103. TASS, December 22, 1988.

104. TASS, April 27, 1989.

105. *Pravda*, July 22, 1989.

106. The Soviets heralded the visit, claiming that it had followed Gorbachev's speech expressing willingness to remove the Soviet base at Cam Ranh Bay if the United States removed its bases in the Philippines (I. Kovalev, "Useful Dialogue," *Izvestiya*, November 29, 1988, p. 5).

107. *Manila Chronicle*, December 3, 1988, p. 3.

108. *The New York Times*, November 5, 1987, p. 1.

109. Hong Kong AFP, January 11, 1990.

110. *Xinhua*, January 9, 1990.

8

SUB-SAHARAN AFRICA

Sub-Saharan Africa ranks lower in Soviet priorities than other Third World areas, in part because it is also a low priority for the West. Nonetheless, Moscow has pursued opportunities to project its power and influence there. Following the collapse of Portuguese colonialism and the fall of Ethiopia's Amharic empire in the 1970s, Moscow's activist policies enabled its client Cuba to become a significant player in the region.[1] The Soviet and Cuban presence yielded numerous dividends during the late 1970s, including access to air and naval facilities in the Atlantic, Red Sea, and Indian Ocean areas; political ties with the leftist regimes that replaced Portuguese administrations and Emperor Haile Selassi's pro-Western regime in Ethiopia; and links with national liberation movements operating against white-ruled Rhodesia and South Africa.

Gorbachev's "new thinking" has produced a significant shift in Soviet policy toward sub-Saharan Africa. The Soviets have modified their support for revolutionary regimes and movements and have pursued policies of accommodation. They participated in the US-brokered, quadripartite negotiations for withdrawal of Cuban and South African troops from Angola and an end to Namibia's struggle for independence; have put pressure on Ethiopia's Mengistu Haile Mariam to negotiate a solution to that country's grinding civil war; have announced plans to withdraw nearly all Soviet military advisers from war-torn Mozambique; and have taken a more flexible approach to South Africa and the African National Congress (ANC). These moves reflect a pragmatic policy tailored to Moscow's economic and strategic priorities, reducing tensions in East-West relations and cooperating with the West in managing regional conflict.[2]

A RECORD OF SUCCESS DURING THE 1970s

Moscow achieved significant gains in sub-Saharan Africa during the 1970s. The fall of the Portuguese empire, with which the United States enjoyed close ties, and the overthrow of Emperor Haile Selassi in Ethiopia, where the United States had been solidly entrenched for years, were a serious setback to Western influence. Although the USSR was not responsible for these events, it capitalized on them and emerged as a key regional actor,

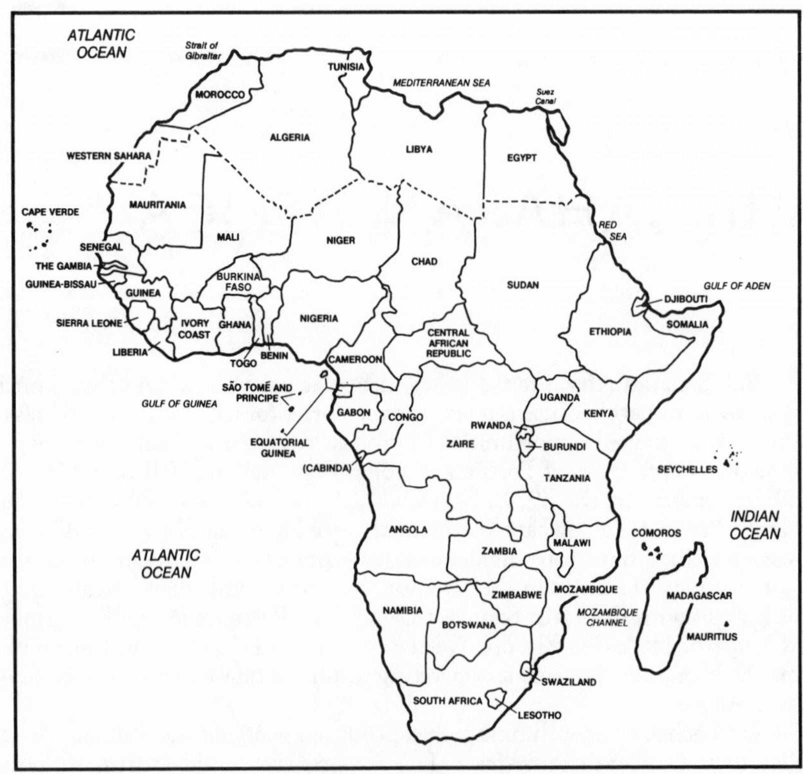

Sub-Saharan Africa (south of the dashed line)

providing security assistance to keep Marxist groups in power in Angola, Mozambique, and Ethiopia—the Movement for the Popular Liberation of Angola (MPLA), the Front for the Liberation of Mozambique (FRELIMO), and Mengistu's leftist Ethiopian regime. The emergence of these new revolutionary governments in turn gave impetus to those groups seeking elimination of white minority rule in Rhodesia and independence for Namibia. In supporting new Marxist regimes and national liberation causes in sub-Saharan Africa, Moscow enhanced its reputation as defender of those seeking independence from colonial rule, undermined the position of the United States and the West—and substantially extended its global reach.[3]

During the 1970s the Soviets and Cubans cooperated in their support for Marxist-Leninist clients. When Fidel Castro, allied with MPLA leader Augustino Neto, sent Cuban troops to Angola in 1975, Moscow provided the essential support, transporting Cuban troops to Angola, extending material aid for the battle and providing extensive military assistance.[4] The

Soviets and Cubans also cooperated in Ethiopia, as Cubans fought under Soviet military leaders in Ethiopia's defense against Somalia's invasion of the disputed Ogaden territory in 1977.[5]

Moscow's success in sub-Saharan Africa was the result of a number of local, regional, and international trends in the late 1960s and early 1970s:

- Marxist-oriented national liberation movements, such as the MPLA and FRELIMO, were fighting to end Portuguese colonialism; these movements were spawned by internal conditions and were not created by the USSR or Cuba.[6]
- Radical nationalism in Africa had expanded as the People's Republic of the Congo (Brazzaville), Somalia, Angola, Guinea-Bissau, São Tomé and Principe, Madagascar, and Benin all declared their adherence to Marxism-Leninism.[7]
- Moscow's ability to project power had increased—especially in terms of its expanding blue water navy and air transport capabilities.
- The United States was not in position to deal with the Portuguese collapse in Angola and Mozambique; US lines of communication were with the Portuguese administration—not with opposition groups in Angola and Mozambique or with other national liberation movements.[8]
- The US defeat in Vietnam had produced disillusionment with Third World interventions—reflected in passage of the Clark Amendment in 1975, prohibiting US military assistance to either side in Angola.

DEEPENING PROBLEMS IN THE 1980s

By the mid-1980s, the USSR faced numerous challenges to its interests in sub-Saharan Africa.[9] First, national communist regimes in Angola, Mozambique, and Ethiopia were engaged in civil wars which had dramatically undermined economic development and produced bureaucratic bottlenecks, black markets, and falling standards of living. Soviet analysts noted that, in these countries, "excessively-grown bureaucratic machinery" had become a "parasitic sponge" on society—underscored by "bureaucratic methods, corruption, bribery, lack of initiative and irresponsibility."[10]

Second, Soviet clients in Southern Africa were turning to market incentives and expanded ties with Western capitalist states in an effort to stimulate economic growth through their own nascent brands of *perestroika*. Angola is a case in point. Angolans, who had known nothing but war since 1961, were living in one of the Third World's most impoverished countries—a "filthy and smelly hovel of crumbling buildings and decaying morals . . . the orphan and amputee capital of the world," as one observer put it, where "money is meaningless."[11] By the mid-1980s, Angola's leaders were trying to resuscitate their economy with decentralized decision-making, more autonomy for local business managers, encouragment of the private sector, the return of land to farmers and shops to entrepreneurs, the tying of prices to market forces and salaries to productivity, and the promotion of foreign investment.

Third, Soviet decision-makers were unhappy with the fact that their clients required extensive military aid just to sustain themselves.[12] Soviet military aid to sub-Saharan Africa rose from $241 million in the decade from 1965–1974 to $3.3 billion in the half decade 1975–1979—and it was not enough.[13] Moscow was spending far more on clients, such as Angola's MPLA, than the United States was providing its Third World allies. This situation produced a much heavier burden of military aid for Moscow than Washington—with the USSR spending about 1.4 percent of its gross national product (GNP) for economic and military to developing countries (including Cuba and Vietnam), compared to less than 0.3 percent of the US GNP. Such was the high cost of defending Moscow's 1970s "successes."[14]

Fourth, Marxist-Leninist ideologies in Southern Africa had not unified the region's diverse ethnic national groups. The Soviets found themselves backing one ethnic national (and Marxist-Leninist) leader of a state opposed by other ethnic national (and often Marxist-Leninist) groups inside the same country. A case in point is Ethiopia, where Eritrean and Tigrean national liberation movements were fighting the Mengistu regime. In Angola, the conflict is between the Ovimbundu-backed UNITA which claimed that the Soviet-backed MPLA represented the interests of whites, mestizos (mulattos), and the Kimbundu people concentrated in the Luanda area.[15]

Moscow was plagued by various other problems in sub-Saharan Africa. In 1983–1984, with their economies in shambles and no end to civil war in sight, Angola and Mozambique independently negotiated cease-fires with South Africa and turned to the West for possible economic assistance.[16] In Rhodesia, Moscow had backed the wrong leader; when Robert Mugabe won the battle, he shunned the USSR until late 1984 when he made his first trip to the Soviet Union.[17] Soviet support for Ethiopia in the Ogaden dispute had reinforced strains in relations with Somalia, which had expelled the Soviets from Berbera in 1970. And, by 1984, the Seychelles, Mauritius, and Madagascar had moderated their previously strong anti-Western and prosocialist rhetoric.[18]

Nor were the Soviets, unlike the Cubans, especially popular in this region. Soviet cultural and racial arrogance, according to some observers, was noticeable in Angola. One Angolan official reported that Soviets arriving in the mid-1970s usually demanded ". . . rooms in the best hotels or well-furnished houses with air conditioning and new stoves and refrigerators, which cost us a lot of our precious foreign exchange—whereas we can put five or six Cubans in a hot one-bedroom apartment with mattresses on the floor and we will never hear a complaint."[19]

All in all the picture was not bright for Moscow when Gorbachev came to power. The costs of defending gains were proving more expensive in economic, political, and social terms than the original costs of helping consolidate pro-Soviet clients during the 1970s. No empires remained to fall and currently strong national liberation movements were of the secessionist variety which Moscow traditionally eschewed. South Africa was very much in control of its home territory, and Pretoria was not a distant colonial ruling regime against which national liberation movements might have more promising prospects as had occurred in the case of Portugal. Moscow was learning just how weak revolutionary regimes in power could be, how destabilizing their effects on East-West relations, and how costly a drain on Soviet resources.

UNTANGLING THE ANGOLA-NAMIBIA KNOT

Moscow's new approach to the Angola-Namibia problem was another dramatic example of "new thinking" in action. Once again the Soviets followed the model established in Afghanistan—withdrawal of military forces (in this case Cuban), pursuit of national reconciliation, and an international mechanism to provide legitimacy. Moscow put pressure on its clients, Angola and Cuba, to negotiate and worked with the United States and South Africa to mediate differences. Soviet pressure on the MPLA also helped produce the remarkable, albeit troubled, June 1989 agreement between Angolan president Jose Eduardo dos Santos and UNITA leader, Jonas Savimbi, for a cease-fire in their 14-year-old civil war.[20] Both former Secretary of State George Shultz and former US Assistant Secretary of State for African Affairs Chester A. Crocker have credited Moscow's performance in resolving this complex dispute.

Before the Soviet policy shift, the Angola-Namibia problem had been complicated by numerous conflicting elements:

- Moscow and Havana backing of the MPLA against South African-supported UNITA forces.
- Soviet, Cuban, and Angolan support for the South West African People's Organization (SWAPO) efforts to liberate Namibia from South Africa.
- South Africa's intrusion into Angolan territory to pursue SWAPO forces, support UNITA, punish Angola for aiding SWAPO, and engage Cuban forces in Angola.
- US assistance to UNITA after the Clark Amendment was abrogated in 1985.
- An unimplemented 1978 UN Security Council Resolution 435 calling for a cease fire, the withdrawal of South African troops from Angola, and elections in Namibia monitored by a mixed civilian-military Transitional Assistance Group (UNTAG).[21]

Much to the credit of both the United States and the Soviet Union, South Africa, Angola, and Cuba signed an historic agreement in Brazzaville, Congo, on December 13, 1988, calling for the withdrawal of all Cuban troops from Angola and independence for Namibia.[22] This settlement was followed by a ceremony at the United Nations on December 22, 1988, during which the three parties signed two accords for implementing the agreements; under the first accord, the South African government agreed to surrender control of Namibia and carry out the UN plan giving independence to the territory. The second accord, signed by Angola and Cuba, provided a timetable for the withdrawal of Havana's 50,000 troops.[23] While major points of disagreement still plagued the Angola-Namibia entanglement, such as the US refusal to suspend military aid to UNITA, the "Brazzaville Protocol" marked a turning point in a long and complicated negotiating process. By November 1989 Cuba had completed withdrawal of half of the 50,000 strong military contingent in Angola, with total withdrawal scheduled for July 1991.[24]

The new Soviet policy consisted of various elements. First, Moscow sought to establish that its military support for Angola was legitimate and conformed with the UN Security Council's Resolution 435. Vladilen Vasev, a high-ranking member of the Soviet Foreign Ministry's African Department, frequently argued that Soviet-backed Cuban troops were in Angola "at the request of a lawful government in full compliance with the UN Charter."[25]

Second, Moscow joined the quadripartite negotiations as an observer with Deputy Foreign Minister Anatoliy Adamishin or another high ranking Soviet official, such as Vasev, present.[26] Adamishin routinely met with his American counterpart, Chester Crocker, typically making optimistic statements about the settlement of the Angolan conflict and vouching for the "good intentions" of Angola and Cuba.[27] As the negotiations proceeded, Adamishin publicly stressed the convergence of Soviet and US views on the complex situation in southern Africa and emphasized that a compatible arrangement on this issue would improve the international atmosphere and reduce US-Soviet tensions in the Third World. In late December 1988, Gorbachev hailed the agreement as an event of "historic significance" made possible by the "changed climate in international relations."[28]

Third, Moscow put pressure on Cuba and Angola to negotiate a settlement. At various times during the process Moscow appeared to urge the Cubans and Angolans to be flexible. A breakthrough probably occurred when the Angolan President, Jose Eduardo dos Santos, visited Gorbachev in late October 1988. Compared to dos Santos' visit in 1986, when the Soviet report of the meetings and Gorbachev's dinner speech for dos Santos affirmed Moscow's "commitment to the obligations under the Treaty of Friendship and Cooperation," Soviet treatment of this visit was cool, and no reference was made to the Treaty.[29]

Soviet Motives for Ending the Angola Conflict

There were a number of compelling reasons for Gorbachev to seek resolution of the sub-Saharan conflict. First, sustaining Angola was requiring increasing Soviet military aid—up from around $600 million in 1984 to $730 million in 1985 and approximately $1 billion by 1987—at a time when Moscow was not receiving payments for its arms shipments.[30] By early 1988

Angola owed the USSR $2.6 billion—a bill created in part by the fall in world market oil prices that diminished Angola's hard currency earnings and ability to repay its debt. Second, moving toward peace in Angola would allow Luanda to proceed with its own *perestroika.* Angola had already demonstrated its interest in qualifying for World Bank and International Monetary Fund (IMF) assistance. It had returned some industries to private ownership, decentralized economic planning, moved back to private farming and made other attempts to move away from the Soviet socialist model of development. In a December 1988 interview Adamishin admitted that he personally did not ". . . think they [southern Africa generally] are going to build socialism in this part of the world."[31]

Third, the Soviets probably lacked confidence in the Angolan military's ability to ever "win" its war against South African-backed UNITA and the South African Defense Force (SADF) inside Angola's borders. The Angolan forces suffered from logistical problems, poor training and low morale as demonstrated in the failed military offensive against UNITA in 1987.[32] Intensified fighting in southern Angola during early 1988, notably the South African-UNITA siege on Cuito Cuanavale from January to March 1988, had escalated the conflict to a higher level, creating direct confrontation of the Soviet-backed Cubans and the South Africans and causing friction between the Soviets and the Cubans. Reports of discord between Angolan and Cuban military troops probably also stimulated Soviet interest in resolving the Angolan problem.[33]

Angola's Motives

Angola's interests in negotiating an end to the war are not difficult to fathom. Defending against South African incursions and UNITA rebels was consuming over half the foreign exchange available for imports by 1987 and, between 1982 and 1985, the defense expenditure more than doubled—from $502 million to $1.2 billion.[34] By 1985, 43 percent of government revenue was spent on defense, a figure which rose to 60 percent of total government income by 1986.[35] In addition, Angola had to meet the operating costs of the thousands of Cuban military personnel stationed in the country.[36] Meanwhile the economy was in ruins, with an estimated 690,000 displaced persons wandering and begging in both urban and rural areas.[37]

One of Angola's problems was how to engage the West while depending on Soviet and Cuban military advisers for its defense needs. A negotiated settlement leading to the withdrawal of Cuban troops and ending South Africa's incursions into Angolan territory would go far, from Luanda's perspective, in easing dependence on the Soviet Union and Cuba, improving Angola's ties with the West, strengthening the possibility of establishing diplomatic relations with the United States, and possibly inducing Washington to reduce its support of UNITA. Angola's contacts with the United States, the only Western country not to recognize the Luanda government, improved in 1984, when the United States brokered the "Lusaka Agreement," which called for South Africa's withdrawal from Angola and Angolan restrictions on SWAPO actions. Angola pursued this agreement against Soviet wishes, and the Cubans were informed of the arrangement apparently only at the last minute—revealing Angola's commitment to its own interests.

The Cuban Perspective

While initially opposed to withdrawing its forces from Angola, Cuba also came around to backing a politically negotiated settlement.[38] Why did Castro make this determination knowing that his departure from Angola might weaken his leverage with Moscow. Castro had used his role as a privileged client whose troops were performing a service for Moscow to strengthen his case for high levels of economic and military aid. There were several reasons for Castro's change of heart.

First, Havana could not miss the central message of Gorbachev's "new political thinking." Soviet belt-tightening meant declining interest in supporting Cuba's military activities, and, without the clear support of the Soviet Union, Cuba faced enormous difficulties in its foreign deployments. Second, Cuba may have hoped its decision would lead to better relations with the United States and open up the possibility of US-Cuban commercial links. This was a major incentive at a time when Moscow's economy was in dire straits. With Angola's capability to support Cuba's military and civilian operations also declining, better relations with the United States were becoming all the more important. Third, popular support for Cuba's war in Angola reportedly was declining. According to General Rafael del Pino Diaz, an Air Force General who defected in 1987, a deepening disillusionment with the war had set in; he estimated that 10,000 Cuban soldiers had been killed, wounded, or were missing in action.[39]

Fourth, Castro probably had decided that Cuba could withdraw from Angola without losing dignity. At the negotiating table, Cuba's diplomats were being treated as equals with those of the United States, and Havana could more directly safeguard its interests.[40] The Cuban military successes in the battle of Cuito Cuanavale from January to March 1988 created an opening for Cuba to withdraw with its dignity preserved. In his 26th of July address to the Cuban people in 1988, Castro exploited this fact, claiming that Cuba's military actions were not designed to gain a military victory but to gain political leverage for an acceptable negotiated settlement.[41]

South Africa's Perspective

The rising human and financial costs of the war during 1987 and 1988 account for South Africa's receptiveness to the Angola-Namibia negotiations. The psychological impact of white war casualties became a major political factor used by the Department of Foreign Affairs to marshal support for negotiations, as more and more parents began to ask why their sons should die for Savimbi.[42] War costs were mounting alarmingly, with the military absorbing around 20 percent of South African imports.[43] These concerns intensified with the battle losses of January–March 1988 as Cuba and Angola confronted the South African Defense Forces in Cuito Cuanavale.

FRESH WINDS IN SOVIET–SOUTH AFRICAN RELATIONS

One of the central themes of "new thinking" in the Third World has been the willingness to expand ties with states formerly treated as pariahs. In sub-Saharan Africa, that state is South Africa. Under Gorbachev, the Soviets have taken a more pragmatic approach to South Africa. They recognize that the government is unlikely to fall as a result of armed struggle alone and have advocated negotiations with South African whites as the best way to end apartheid. In line with this approach, Moscow has urged the African National Congress (ANC) to limit acts of violence and refrain from attacking civilians.[44] They also have told the ANC not to give top billing to socialism in a postapartheid South Africa, reflecting their generally bleak outlook for socialism's prospects in developing countries. Overall, the emphasis under Gorbachev has been to shift the focus in ending apartheid from armed struggle to bringing whites to the bargaining table and finding ways to achieve a political solution.[45]

Soviet spokesmen have left no doubt that they prefer political negotiations over backing black revolution in South Africa since the agreement on Angola and Namibia was reached in December 1988. "In our opinion, we doubt that revolution in South Africa is possible, if you're talking of revolutionaries storming Pretoria," stated Boris A. Asoyan, Deputy Chief of the Department of African countries in the Foreign Ministry and longtime specialist on southern Africa.[46] According to Asoyan, "We support the ANC and we regard it as the main force in contemporary political life in South Africa. But we also believe that there is really no alternative to a peaceful solution." And in March 1989 senior Soviet officials called for political dialogue rather than military action to end apartheid in South Africa. "We would prefer a political settlement and want apartheid to be dealt with by political means," said Yuri Yukalov, head of the Foreign Ministry's Department of African Countries, ". . . any solution through military means will be shortlived."[47]

The Soviets approach to South Africa reflects their linkage of domestic and strategic concerns with Third World politics. Escalating violence in South Africa would impede progress on East-West issues such as arms control and economic cooperation. Moscow does not need another dependent socialist ally, like Cuba or Vietnam. A stable and economically strong South Africa tied to the Western capitalist system may be more beneficial given the *de facto* Soviet–South African connection in marketing gold and diamonds.[48] A weak socialist postapartheid South Africa could disrupt this historic link.

Quadripartite Negotiations and Widening Moscow-Pretoria Contacts

Soviet–South African contacts developed during the quadripartite negotiations on Angola and Namibia. Meetings between Moscow and Pretoria were easy during this period, because the US-mediated discussions were attended by Soviet Foreign Ministry observers, such as Adamishin and Vasev. At one secret meeting, the South Africans reportedly asked the Soviets how they would feel about resuming relations,[49] and during the final rounds of the quadripartite negotiations in December 1988, South African Foreign Minister R. F. (Pik) Botha met with Adamishin in Brazzaville to discuss the monitoring arrangements for the Cuban troop withdrawal and other issues between the two countries.[50] South Africa also invited a Soviet journalist to interview top members of the South African government in late 1988; in return, South African journalists were invited to visit the Soviet Union.[51]

The Impact of Angola-Namibian Settlement on Soviet–South African Relations

The Angola and Namibian settlement undoubtedly has created a more favorable atmosphere for improved Soviet–South African relations. The agreements undercut the image of a "communist onslaught" used by the Botha government to legitimize its aggressive domestic and regional policies.[52] The removal of Soviet-backed Cuban troops and ANC military bases from Angola eased South Africa's security position. The departure of ANC guerrillas from Angola left the ANC with no camps in any country bordering South African–controlled territory. While keeping the pressure on South Africa to dismantle apartheid, Moscow's less rigid approach to Pretoria remained constant throughout 1989. In a gesture to the new de Klerk government, Foreign Minister Shevardnadze observed in November 1989 that it was "not easy" for Pretoria to consent to Namibian independence, and he pointed out that "this very important step" could lead to South Africa rejoining the "international community."[53]

In evaluating the Republic of South Africa at the outset of the 1990s, the Soviets observed that de Klerk's government had opened a new chapter in South Africa's history by:

- Making a delicate attempt to begin a dialogue with the black majority.
- Allowing opponents of apartheid to stage a protest march.
- Releasing one of the leaders of the ANC, Walter Sisulu, and several other political opponents of the existing RSA regime.
- Abolishing the segregational law, in effect since 1953, on the separate use of beaches, parks, and libraries.
- Holding meetings with Archbishop Desmond Tutu, an acknowledged leader of the black community, and with Nelson Mandela, then still serving a life prison sentence.

- Making contact with African heads of state Houphouet-Boigny (Ivory Coast) and Joaquim Chissano (Mozambique) to discuss the problems of ensuring regional security and ending the war in Angola.
- Announcing that the RSA intends to cease armed aggression against countries in the region—underscored by reducing the length of army service for whites by 12 months and closing down various military bases on South African territory.[54]

Yet Moscow has been consistent in stressing that, despite these "liberal" policies, the foundations of the apartheid system and its basic laws remain intact.[55]

The Soviet Union and the African National Congress

While Gorbachev has continued Soviet support for the ANC, a pattern dating back to 1961 when Moscow's training and arming became clear, the new Soviet emphasis on finding political solutions to regional military struggles has reshaped Soviet-ANC relations.[56] Admittedly, the Soviets have not backed completely away from military training for the ANC or completely rejected the possibility of armed struggle. As Adamishin stated in March 1989, the Soviet Union is the only major source of weapons for the ANC and would continue supporting it. "Those who think we are going to stop supplying the ANC with arms to force it into negotiations are engaging in wishful thinking," he said.[57]

Such support, however, has been tempered as Moscow has put pressure on the ANC to modify its approach, limit acts of terror, desist from attacking civilians, and stress the viability of political over military problem-solving. In acknowledging support for the ANC's armed liberation struggle, Soviet spokesmen have stated that Moscow is "not a supporter of armed struggle for national liberation when there exists an opportunity to use peaceful means," and they have indicated that the positive changes associated with the Angola-Namibia settlement suggest that ". . . Apartheid in the Republic of South Africa can also be dismantled by peaceful means. . . ."[58] In stating that the Soviet Union stands for a political settlement of the problems of South Africa, among them the elimination of apartheid, Moscow's diplomats typically indicate that this policy is shared by the ANC.[59]

Soviet pressure has had a clear effect on ANC policies. While a negotiated settlement was never ruled out in ANC policy statements, it was infrequently mentioned during the 1970s. Since Gorbachev came to power, a political settlement is often cited by ANC leaders as a viable objective. The ANC's National Executive Council stated in October 1987, for example, that "We wish to reiterate that the ANC has never been opposed to a negotiated settlement of the South African question."[60] And in a news conference in Moscow in March 1989, ANC President Oliver Tambo noted that the ANC's task is to "intensify its struggle militarily, politically, and diplomatically, in order to hasten the demise of the present regime in South Africa, and to usher in a democratic and nonracist government."[61] The ANC receptiveness to a negotiated settlement was reflected in Walter Sisulu's keynote address at the October 1989 dramatic rally of 70,000 cheering ANC followers—the largest anti-government gathering ever held in South Africa.[62] This shift in emphasis toward a negotiated settlement in both Soviet and ANC policies suggests that Soviet-ANC relations will remain strong as both parties use a combination of militant and peaceful influence to encourage negotiations on the apartheid issue.

The basic change in Soviet and ANC policies toward South Africa applies to the South African Communist Party (SACP), which is allied with the ANC. If anything, the SACP is even more in tune with Gorbachev's "new political thinking" than the ANC. The SACP leadership argues that the best means of attaining change in South Africa is through negotiation and selective violence rather than all-out military action.[63] For the SACP leadership, a Zimbabwe-style settlement seems the best possibility—a point made by SACP members inside the ANC at the time of the Commonwealth Eminent Persons' Group initiative in May 1986.[64] Joe Slovo, the former chief of staff of the ANC's military wing and later Secretary-General of the SACP, stated to South African journalist Allister Sparks that in his judgment "transition in South Africa is going to come through negotiations."[65]

What Has South Africa to Gain?

What has South Africa to gain in moving from talk of a Soviet "total onslaught" to establishment of new relationship with Moscow? To begin with, cooperating with the Soviets (and the United States) would help relieve South Africa's isolation within the international community and expand its access to markets, loans, and diplomatic partners. Political negotiations might help avoid the catastrophic blood bath that some believe is inevitable in South Africa.[66] The abrupt resignation of South African President Peter W. Botha in August 1989 and the subsequent election of Frederik W. de Klerk could pave the way to such negotiations. Botha was forced out of office by cabinet members viewed as more willing to talk with ANC patrons such as Zambian President Kenneth Kaunda.

"NEW THINKING" IN ETHIOPIA

Gorbachev's "new political thinking" has led to a revision of Soviet policy on the Horn of Africa, a change resisted by Ethiopia's Mengistu Haile Mariam until the summer of 1989. Mengistu rejected Moscow's advice to negotiate a political settlement with the Eritrean People's Liberation Front (EPLF) until he had suffered serious military setbacks. Mengistu persisted in his single-minded pursuit of a military victory against the Eritreans, which the Soviets had told him time and again is unwinnable. By the summer of 1989 the civil war had dragged on for 28 years—the longest running war in Africa. It has taken the lives of over 250,000 people, displaced at least another 750,000 and devastated Ethiopia's economy.

In backing Mengistu's Amhara military forces against Eritreans and Tigreans, the Soviets became a counter-insurgency force, contradicting their claim to be the "natural ally" of the Third World and the backer of national liberation movements. The Ethiopian case is especially embarrassing, because Moscow and Havana reportedly had backed the Eritreans, providing arms and technical assistance as early as 1965.[67] With Haile Selassi's overthrow Moscow eventually switched its support to Mengistu, albeit avoiding direct action against the Eritreans. The Marxist-oriented Eritreans, having been bombed for years by Soviet-backed forces of Mengistu have developed a finely-honed hatred of Moscow.[68]

Although Cuba joined the Soviets in helping Mengistu defend against Somalian incursions in the Ogaden in 1977–1978, Havana demonstrated little interest in helping Moscow back Mengistu in his war against Eritreans. From the estimated 12,000 to 15,000 Cuban troops in Ethiopia when the Somalis withdrew in 1978, Cuban forces were down to around 1,500 by 1988, performing security functions for Mengistu in Addis Ababa and in the Dire Dawa-Harar area. Castro's ties with Mengistu are weaker than with the ruling Angola government. Havana's earlier links with the Eritreans help explain Castro's decision not to have his troops participate against Eritrean seccessionists and, ultimately, to withdraw all of them in 1989.

Extensive Soviet military aid ($2 to $4 billion from 1977–1985) and economic assistance have not translated into influence with Mengistu. Mengistu, for example, procrastinated in responding to Soviet pressure to create a Leninist vanguard party in the early 1980s. When the Worker's Party of Ethiopia was finally announced in 1984, it was essentially a continuation of Mengistu's old ruling system in everything but form—and was perhaps even more subject to Mengistu's personal control than its predecessor.[69]

Mengistu's rule remained notoriously despotic. Public resentment was expressed in various ways—young men dodged conscription drives by hiding in relatives homes for long periods of time and foreigners were besieged by local residents seeking jobs abroad. "Chairman Mengistu" jokes expressed such discontent:

> Colonel Mengistu orders a series of postage stamps, all bearing his likeness. Soon after the stamps are put into circulation, postal employees note that they tend to fall off envelopes. Suspecting that the capitalists have short-changed him on the glue, the chairman orders an investigation. . . . After weeks of consumer surveys, the secret police report back: Ethiopians are spitting on the wrong side of the stamp.[70]

Mengistu's despotism has been especially felt by the Ethiopian military. Following an unsuccessful coup attempt in May 1989, Mengistu summarily executed nine generals involved in the affair, reportedly arrested an additional 300–400 officers, almost the entire staff of the Ministry of Defense, and is believed to have killed other generals.[71] Such actions—consistent with Mengistu's machine-gunning of seven political rivals in 1977 and assassination of 22 rival officers in 1976—did not suit Soviet efforts to create a more favorable anti-Stalinist image abroad—or its own move toward democracy as the First Congress of People's Deputies of the USSR began its work in May 1989. These reprisals also deprived the Ethiopian armed forces of at least a fifth of its senior most experienced leaders, with replacements comprised of loyal, but inexperienced individuals.[72] By the summer of 1989 Mengistu remained in power, but in charge of a significantly weakened military force.

A major problem for the Soviets in Ethiopia was that the Eritrean conflict had become internationalized in ways that complicated Moscow's new peace offensive. The Eritreans received support from Saudi Arabia, Sudan, and Somalia; Moscow was seeking improved relations with all of them. Mengistu, for his part, made Ethiopian territory available to John Garang's Sudanese People's Liberation Army (SPLA) as a staging area for his activities in the Sudan.[73] The Sudan, in return, allowed Eritrean and Tigrean rebels to bring weapons and other supplies across its territory into Ethiopia.[74] These complications strengthened Moscow's desire to resolve Ethiopia's conflict.[75]

Moscow's Reaction

The Soviets began to signal their displeasure with the Ethiopian leader's rule in 1987. Moscow urged a politically negotiated settlement to the Eritrean conflict, was cool to Mengistu's requests for increased military support, restricted the flow of arms, tightened up on debt repayment, and urged more effective management of Ethiopia's economy, indicating they would not deliver substantial aid.[76]

Moscow also expressed its discontent with Mengistu's insistence on seeking a military victory in the war with the EPLF and the Tigrean Popular Liberation Front (TPLF). Soviet diplomats told Addis Ababa that they were losing interest in paying for Mengistu's war—a point made to Mengistu himself by Gorbachev during the former's visits to the Soviet capital in 1988 and 1989. Moscow's point was given added urgency by Mengistu's loss of the prized province of Tigre in 1989.[77] Gorbachev told Mengistu in July 1988 that, if the Ethiopian leader wished continued Soviet support, he must make major changes in his agricultural policies, investment priorities, and heavy-handed political rule. Gorbachev reportedly told the Ethiopian delegation that Moscow's involvement in Ethiopia was a product of the Brezhnev period of stagnation, ". . . a period we have broken way from. . . . Our unqualified military and economic commitment cannot continue much further. . . ."[78] Gorbachev urged Mengistu to find a non-military solution to Ethiopia's civil wars and denied Mengistu's request for more military supplies.[79] In an exceptionally frank interview with news correspondents in March 1989, a Soviet diplomat reported that Mengistu had been told that the civil war could not be won militarily, but that

". . . unfortunately no genuine practical steps have been taken in this direction."[80]

Soviet pressures and the attempted military coup of May 1989, appear to have convinced Mengistu to change his strategy. On June 5, 1989, the Ethiopian Parliament announced its endorsement of unconditional peace talks with Eritrean rebels in an effort to end the state's 28-year-long civil war.[81] Diplomats reported that this was the first time Mengistu, who introduced the peace plan, had set no conditions for discussions with the northern insurgents. The Eritrean People's National Liberation Front, for its part, indicated in July 1989 that it too was prepared to enter into peace negotiations.[82]

Movement toward peaceful negotiation of Ethiopia's civil war received added impetus from the United States in 1989. Former US President Jimmy Carter acted as mediator in talks held in Atlanta, Georgia, in September 1989 between Ethiopian government representatives and those of the EPLF.[83] When Ethiopian government officials enthusiastically helped in the search for Representative Mickey Leland (D-Tex.), whose plane crashed in August 1989, the US State Department expressed hope that Ethiopia's "spirit of cooperation" would extend to other issues that had divided the two countries.[84] Like the USSR, the United States had been pressuring Ethiopia to end its 28-year-old civil war in Eritrea and Tigre, improve human rights practices, and conduct major economic reform.

GORBACHEV AND MOZAMBIQUE

The Soviet Union announced in June 1989 that it would withdraw nearly all its military advisers from war-torn Mozambique by the end of 1990.[85] Moscow's withdrawal stems from several factors. Mozambique is of less geostrategic importance than Angola or Ethiopia. Mozambique's President, Joaquim Chissano, has been unable to pay for Soviet-supplied weapons. After a decade of civil war between Chissano's Mozambique Liberation Front, known by its Portuguese acronym FRELIMO, and the South African–backed rebels of the Mozambican Resistance Movement, or Renamo, 600,000 to 700,000 Mozambicans had been killed in a country of 15 million, which had become one of the most destitute in the world. With Maputo unable to service its growing debt, which had reached $3.2 billion by 1987,[86] the Soviets were unprepared to provide further support.

The Cuban connection helps explain Moscow's decision to withdraw its military advisers. Cubans in Mozambique, as in Ethiopia, did not play a major military role. Havana had demonstrated little interest in combat operations in Mozambique, nor did Maputo wish to jeopardize its diplomatic and military initiatives with South Africa and the West by raising the Cuban ante. While the number of Cuban military advisers in Mozambique decreased from an estimated 1,000 in 1981 to between 400 and 600 in late 1987, they nevertheless provided training for security personnel and protection for the President.[87] Although the number of Cuban civilians in

Mozambique ranged from 500–600 by 1987, their presence was declining due to the lack of safety and the country's move toward free market economic programs for which the Cubans were distinctly untrained.[88]

In withdrawing their estimated 700–1,000 military advisers from Mozambique, the Soviets by no means intend to completely abandon what they have gained. A modified military aid program probably will continue—with Moscow providing helicopters, trucks, communications equipment, and light arms instead of heavy weapons and continuing in-country training. Moscow also may continue its internal security assistance, with Mozambicans still going to the USSR and Cuba for military training and technical education.

Moscow's planned withdrawal is probably one important factor behind President Chissano's announcement in late July 1989 of plans to negotiate a peaceful settlement to Mozambique's civil war.[89] The peace process took a step forward in August 1989, when various parties to the conflict gathered in Nairobi, Kenya, to try to work out ways to end the violence—with Kenyan leader Daniel Arap Moi at the center of the talks. The Mozambican government has scrapped orthodox communist ideology, but has yet to solve the problem of power sharing.

IMPEDIMENTS TO SOVIET "NEW THINKING" IN SOUTHERN AFRICA

Several obstacles stand in the way of resolving conflict in sub-Saharan Africa through cooperative political negotiations. First, there are no guarantees that politically negotiated settlements will stay in place once signed. Either the contracting parties or outside groups, perceiving their interests threatened for one reason or another, may act in ways to disrupt the agreement. The Angola-Namibia agreement of December 1988 was nearly derailed in early April 1989 when Angola-based SWAPO guerrillas crossed into Namibia to launch attacks and when South Africa accused UN forces of a pro-SWAPO bias.[90] In January 1990, Cuba announced that it was temporarily suspending its troop withdrawal, charging that the United States was responsible for supporting rebels who had attacked Cuban troops.[91] As the independence plan for Namibia proceeded, a major crisis developed over alleged voter intimidation by South African–led counterinsurgency forces in northern tribal areas, making possible a major showdown between UN forces and Pretoria.[92] As SWAPO fighters join the thousands of Namibian refugees being repatriated, the possibility of open conflict inside Namibia fueled by economic stagnation and social tensions becomes a distinct possibility. The impact of SWAPO leader Sam Nujoma's return in September 1989 remains unclear. And although SWAPO won a majority vote in the November 1989 elections in Namibia, the country remains divided along tribal lines; the dominant Ovambos face ethnic rivalry from other tribes, such as the Hdrero group.[93]

Moscow's control over contending national liberation groups in pursuit of armed struggle remains limited. Moscow's stress on politically negotiated settlements rather than military approaches is not palatable to all members of the ANC, for example, and should Pretoria refuse to pursue peaceful negotiations, such elements may exert more influence on ANC policy. ANC leaders have been calling for a number of steps by Pretoria as a precondition for negotiations, including allowing exiled ANC leaders to return for the start of formal power-sharing negotiations, ending the three-year-old state of emergency, and releasing imprisoned ANC leader Nelson Mandela. Because groups like the ANC and SWAPO are composed of various factions, a troubled peace process is likely.[94]

Other national liberation groups, such as the EPLF and TPLF in Ethiopia or the Sudanese People's Liberation Army (SPLA), will follow their own dictates quite apart from Soviet influence. The EPLF has stated its readiness to engage in peace talks, but given its determined quest for independence and Mengistu's record of intransigence, armed struggle remains a constant threat.

Third, working out political formulas for power sharing between contending Soviet-backed and US-supported adversaries is difficult because Moscow and Washington are likely to continue to provide their clients with the military weapons to force their political agenda. Finally, there is a considerable distance between dos Santos and Savimbi, Mengistu and the EPLF, and Pretoria and the ANC/SACP coalition.[95]

The fact that there are obstacles does not mean that Gorbachev's "new political thinking" in sub-Saharan Africa is doomed to failure. The point rather is that regional conflicts are driven essentially by internal forces over which neither the Soviets nor the United States have complete control. Gorbachev's attempts to manage regional conflict depends not only on Soviet diplomacy but on how regional groups pursue their own agendas.

PROSPECTS

While the path to regional conflict management leads through rocky and perilous terrain, the prospects on balance looked promising at the end of the 1980s. This conclusion is based on the following trends:

- Agreement to a truce in June 1989 by MPLA and UNITA forces after 14 years of civil war, a first step toward national reconciliation.
- Cuba's continuing withdrawal of 50,000 troops from Angola and announced withdrawal of all remaining troops in Ethiopia.
- Pressure by Ethiopian and Sudanese military forces to advance the peace process, marked by the attempted May 1989 coup in Ethiopia and the successful July 1989 military coup in Sudan, followed by Mengistu's heightened efforts to negotiate peace with the EPLF and Sudan's new top military priority of peace negotiations with the SPLA.

- The positive steps toward peaceful negotiation with black South Africans made to date by South African President Frederick W. de Klerk, praised by the USSR as a move in the right direction.[96]
- Pretoria's need to show the rest of the world that it can be a credible partner in an international agreement, such as the Angola-Namibia peace plan, and its need to be free of the costly military involvements in sub-Saharan Africa, policy objectives which the post-Botha government probably will pursue.
- Indications that the United States may admit Angola to the IMF and establish diplomatic relations with Angola, following Angola's June 1989 agreement to open negotiations with US-backed leader Jonas Savimbi.[97]
- Mozambique's July 1989 offer to open peace talks with Renamo rebels, following its 18-month-old amnesty law; while Renamo does not control all guerrilla groups in Mozambique, it directs a large enough number to make its acceptance of peace negotiations a major factor in reducing violence.[98]

These events do not portend the automatic success of Gorbachev's "new thinking" in sub-Saharan Africa. The notoriously weak economies of Angola, Ethiopia, and Mozambique face monumental problems which lie far outside Soviet financial capabilities, and economic strains are likely to generate internal interethnic frictions and political conflicts that can flare up at any moment—as they have within the Soviet Union itself. Sub-Saharan African countries also lack strong political and legal institutions to forge stable state systems of governing and guiding economic growth. As Soviet observers have more than once pointed out, continuing political and economic underdevelopment produces festering conflicts inside these countries and between them, tempting outside governments to deliver weapons that fuel violence and further retard the possibilities for economic growth.[99] One Soviet writer observes ". . . So experience does not confirm the view, which is quite widespread among African revolutionaries, that the seizure of power by progressive forces almost automatically solves the problem of building the new state machinery. . . . Neither does the establishment of a progressive regime automatically bring about political stability."[100]

Still, prospects for peaceful conflict management seemed markedly improving, not least because the superpowers had moved toward more formal cooperative forms of behavior compared to the militant competition during the decade before Gorbachev came to power. With the Soviets seeking to establish "rules of conduct" for superpower behavior in regions like southern Africa and Washington cooperating with Moscow in politically negotiating regional conflicts, regional actors seemed inclined to take similar steps. All in all, Soviet and US downgrading of military policy instruments and backing away from using sub-Saharan Africa as a region to conduct superpower conflict seemed to be having a remarkable effect on leading regional groups to seek alternatives to armed struggle and zero-sum objectives as the decade of the 1980s came to a close.

Among the more interesting developments in sub-Saharan Africa at the end of the decade of the 1980s is the move away from Marxist-Leninist ideology by the region's once socialist-oriented small states. Benin and the archipelago of São Tomé and Principe announced in December 1989 that they would abandon the ideology of Marxism-Leninism.[101] Benin's announcement on December 9 followed weeks of protests by civil servants and students, who had not been paid since October. This southern African version of East European trends does not spell the end of socialism in Africa, however, for as Benin and São Tomé and Principe were departing from Marxism-Leninism, the ruling party of Zimbabwe pledged to create a one-party Marxist-Leninist state.[102]

NOTES

1. This period is covered in a number of well-documented texts, including Joseph G. Whelan and Michael J. Dixon, *The Soviet Union in the Third World: Threat to World Peace?* (New York: Pergamon-Brassey's, 1986), Part IV; David E. Albright, ed., *Communism in Africa* (Bloomington: Indiana University Press, 1980); Daniel S. Papp, *Soviet Policies Toward the Developing Countries During the 1980s: The Dilemmas of Power and Presence* (Maxwell Air Force Base, Alabama: Air University Press, 1986), Ch. 9; and R. Craig Nation and Mark V. Kauppi, *The Soviet Impact in Africa* (Lexington, Mass.: Lexington Books, 1984).

2. Certain continuities continue to drive Soviet policy elsewhere in the region, as in the normal state-to-state relations with "bourgeois nationalist" countries such as Nigeria, Senegal, Kenya, and the Ivory Coast—and low level aid and support given to minor states of "socialist orientation" such as Benin, Madagascar, Guinea-Bissau, Cape Verde, and the Congo. Nor has Moscow changed its behavior in terms of refraining from using one state as a launching pad to destabilize another state or involving themselves in local coups d'etat. See Mark V. Kauppi, "The Soviet Union and the People's Republic of the Congo," Unpublished Paper, Washington, D.C., September 1989. The authors have benefitted from discussion with Professor Kauppi, Defense Intelligence College, regarding continuities in Soviet policy since Gorbachev. This chapter concentrates on the changing aspects of Soviet relations with Angola, Ethiopia, Mozambique, and South Africa, where so much activity has been directed since Gorbachev came to power.

3. In seeking to legitimize their presence in the region, Moscow signed Treaties of Friendship and Cooperation with Somalia (1972; abrogated in 1977), Angola (1976), Mozambique (1977), Ethiopia (1978), and the Congo (1981). These treaties, with the exception of the one with the Congo, helped maintain access to air and naval facilities to project power at a greater distance and round out Moscow's credentials as a global contender with the United States and Western states, and strengthen its claim as defender of weak Marxist regimes against apartheid-governed Africa and Western imperialism.

By keeping regimes such as the MPLA in power, Moscow advanced its own brand of revolutionary warfare on behalf of national revolutionary movements during the 1970s. These movements included, in addition to the MPLA, FRELIMO, and Mengistu's Marxist government, the South-West Africa People's Organization

(SWAPO), struggling for the independence of Namibia, the African National Congress (ANC)'s efforts to end white-rule in South Africa, the Zimbabwe African National Union (ZANU) and the Zimbabwe African People's Union (ZAPU) working against white-ruled Rhodesia, and the Party for the Independence of Guinea-Bissau and Cape Verde (PAIGC). Moscow honed its version of revolutionary warfare in supporting these groups, utilizing propaganda, political mobilization, psychological operations, and other forms of "active measures." See Richard H. Shultz, Jr., *The Soviet Union and Revolutionary Warfare: Principles, Practices, and Regional Comparisons* (Stanford University: Hoover Institution Press, 1988), Introduction and Chapter 5.

4. For Western assessments of Soviet/Cuban intervention in Angola, see Rajan Menon, *Soviet Power and the Third World* (New Haven and London: Yale University Press, 1986), pp. 132–138; Bruce D. Porter, *The USSR in Third World Conflicts: Soviet Arms and Diplomacy in Local Wars 1945–1980* (Cambridge: Cambridge University Press, 1986), pp. 164–170; and Richard J. Payne, *Opportunities and Dangers of Soviet-Cuban Expansion: Toward a Pragmatic U.S. Policy* (Albany: State University of New York Press, 1988), pp. 161–167; and Whelan and Dixon, *The Soviet Union in the Third World: Threat to World Peace?* pp. 236–243.

5. See W. Raymond Duncan, *The Soviet Union and Cuba: Interests and Influence* (New York: Praeger, 1985), Chapter 5.

6. Galia Golan, *The Soviet Union and National Liberation Movements in the Third World* (Boston: Unwin Hyman, 1988), p. 278.

7. Whelan and Dixon, *The Soviet Union in the Third World,* p. 202.

8. Kenneth Maxwell, "The Legacy of Decolonization," Unpublished Paper, Research Institute on International Change, Columbia University, June 1987.

9. On Soviet academic and think-tank analyses of the complexities of sub-Saharan African politics and Moscow's growing awareness of the constraints operating against socialist development during the late Brezhnev years, see Elizabeth Kridl Valkenier, *The Soviet Union and the Third World: An Economic Bind* (New York: Praeger, 1983) and Jerry F. Hough, *The Struggle for the Third World: Soviet Debates and American Options* (Washington, D.C.: The Brookings Institution, 1986).

10. Lev Entin, "African Countries: National Statehood in the Making," *International Affairs* 1 (January 1988), p. 47.

11. *The Wall Street Journal,* September 19, 1988.

12. *Ibid.* Soviet academicians have been stressing the negative aspects of supporting non economically productive Third World socialist countries. "We are told," said one Soviet observer, "that a socialist orientation has advantages. But what are they in light of the fact that many socialist-oriented states are developing more slowly than other newly free states and that people live in dire poverty . . . even starving in some cases?" Alexsel Kiva, "Socialist Orientation: Reality and Illusions." *International Affairs* (July 1988), pp. 76–86. This criticism was aimed at socialist-oriented countries such as Angola and Mozambique. While revolutionary leaders, argued one critic, had no particular difficulty committing themselves to a socialist orientation, "these countries have so far been unable to create a basis, in particular a technological and economic component of it, adequate to the people's democratic state of the Revolution." *Ibid.* While a socialist orientation requires serious class changes and rapid economic progress, stated the Soviet observer, "neither of these changes occurs in the majority of socialist-oriented countries." *Ibid.*

13. See US Arms Control and Disarmament Agency, *World Military Expenditures and Arms Transfers, 1965–1974* (Washington, D.C.: US Arms Control and Disarmament Agency, 1976) and *Ibid.*, 1970–1979 (1982); and *Ibid.*, 1979–1983 (1985).

14. Alex Izyumov and Andrei Kortunov, "The USSR in the Changing World," *International Affairs* 8 (August 1988), pp. 46–56.

15. See Golan, *The Soviet Union and National Liberation Movements in the Third World*, Chaps. 4 and 5.

16. Luanda's negotiations with Pretoria resulted in the February 1984 Lusaka accord, calling for a staged withdrawal of South African troops from southern Angola, in return for which Angola agreed to prevent Namibian insurgents from operating in these areas. Neither the Cubans nor Soviets were consulted. Mozambique announced in December 1983 its attempt to reach a "non-aggression" agreement with South Africa, which led to the famous Nkomati non-aggression agreement in March 1984. Both sides agreed not to allow their territory to be used to prepare acts of violence against the other. Together the Lusaka and Nkomati accords, while not fully implemented, were major setbacks for the Soviets.

17. The decision not to back Mugabe, an avowed Marxist, stemmed from Soviet power politics and competition with the Chinese; since Mugabe's ZANU received Chinese backing, Moscow opted to throw its weight behind the ill-fated Joshua Nkomo, a noncommunist bourgeois nationalist.

18. See Daniel Papp, *Soviet Policy Toward the Developing World During the 1980s: The Dilemmas of Power and Presence*, p. 303.

19. Gerald Bender, "Angola, the Cubans, and American Anxieties," *Foreign Policy* 31 (Summer 1978), p. 10.

20. Also engaged in the effort to reach a cease-fire were more than a dozen African leaders, who held an extraordinary meeting in Zaire at the palatial country estate of Zaire's president, Mobutu Sese Seko. President Kenneth D. Kaunda of Zambia announced the agreement on June 22, 1989. See *The New York Times*, June 23, 1989.

21. *The Washington Post*, December 14, 1988 and December 18, 1988; and Gillian Gunn, "A Guide to the Intricacies of the Angola-Namibia Negotiations," CSIS *Africa Notes* 90 (September 8, 1988), pp. 1–2.

22. *The New York Times*, December 14, 1988; *The Washington Post*, December 14, 1988.

23. *The New York Times*, December 23, 1988.

24. *Moscow Krasnaya Zvezda* in Russian, November 7, 1989, first ed., p. 9 (a January 1990 announcement may have set this deadline back).

25. *Ibid.*

26. Discussion with a high-level US State Department official, June 7, 1989.

27. *Ibid.*; and *The Washington Post*, August 2, 1988.

28. Moscow TASS in English, December 22, 1988; FBIS-SOV, December 23, 1988, p. 37.

29. On the 1986 visit, see TASS, May 6, 1986; on the October 1988 report of the visit, see *Pravda*, October 29, 1988; and Moscow TASS in English, October 28, 1988.

30. *Africa Confidential* 28, No. 6 (March 18, 1987), p. 8; and Gunn, " A Guide to the Intricacies of the Angola-Namibia Negotiations," p. 5.

31. *The Washington Post*, December 15, 1988.

32. Radio Marti, *Quarterly Situation Report, 1st Quarter 1988*, Washington, D.C., p. II–25.

33. Radio Marti, *Quarterly Situation Report*, Third and Fourth Quarter Reports, 1988, p. IV–95.

34. *Africa Confidential* 28, No. 6 (March 18, 1987), p. 8.

35. *Ibid.*

36. *Ibid.*

37. *The Washington Post*, August 14, 1987.

38. At the Third Party Congress of the Communist Party of Cuba (February 4–7, 1986), Castro declared that Cuban troops would not withdraw from Angola, that they would stay there for "10 years, 20 years, 30 years . . . if necessary." Havana International Service, February 8, 1986; FBIS-LAM, February 10, 1986, p. Q 36. And at the Harare summit of the Nonaligned Movement in September 1986, Castro told his audience that Cuban troops might have to stay in Angola until apartheid was overthrown in South Africa, because only that event would guarantee Angola's safety. See Gunn, "A Guide to the Intricacies of the Angola-Namibia Negotiations," p. 4. By late 1987 the Cubans wanted into the negotiations, but were not included in discussions until January 1988. Radio Marti, *Third and Fourth Quarter Situation Reports, 1988*, p. 24.

39. *The Washington Post*, July 1, 1987.

40. Gunn, "A Guide to the Intricacies of the Angola-Namibia Negotiations," p. 4.

41. Havana Domestic Service, July 26, 1986; FBIS-LAM, July 28, 1988, full report.

42. Gunn, "A Guide to the Intricacies of the Angola-Namibia Negotiations," p. 5.

43. *Ibid.*

44. See *The Washington Post*, December 18, 1988.

45. Winrich Kuhne, "A 1988 Update on Soviet Relations with Pretoria, the ANC, and the SACP," *CSIS Africa Notes*, 89 (September 1, 1988), p. 4.

46. *The New York Times*, March 16, 1989.

47. *The New York Times*, March 16, 1989. Yukalov went on to say that "We do not want to emphasize the need to enlarge the armed struggle. South Africa should not be destroyed. It should also be spoken to not only through threats or pounding of fists on the table. There should be dialogue." *Ibid.*

48. See Kurt M. Campbell, "The Soviet–South African Connection," *Africa Report* 31, No. 2 (March-April 1986).

49. See *The Washington Post*, December 18, 1988, for a lengthy discussion of expanding Moscow-Pretoria contacts during 1988. In an interview on December 31, 1988, Yuriy Alekseyevich, head of the USSR Foreign Ministry African Countries Administration, stated that *The Washington Post* depiction of Moscow-Pretoria meetings as "secret" was simply inaccurate reporting. The meetings, he noted, were openly part of the quadripartite negotiations during which the Soviets actively participated as observers. See Moscow *Izvestiya* in Russian, December 31, 1988, p. 6; FBIS-SOV, January 3, 1989, pp. 33–34. Still, that the entire *Washington Post* article on improving Moscow-Pretoria ties was reported in *Izvestiya* indicates Moscow's interest in communicating its view externally.

50. *Ibid.*

51. *Ibid.* The Soviet Union dispatched its first public diplomatic mission to South Africa in April 1989, the first since relations were broken off 33 years before. *The New York Times*, April 27, 1989. The Soviet delegation came to attend a scheduled meeting in Cape Town of the joint commission established to discuss problems arising in the political settlement for Angola-Namibia concluded the previous December. *Ibid.*

52. See Martin Lowenkopf, "If the Cold War is Over in Africa, Will the United States Still Care?," *CSIS Africa Notes*, 98 (May 30, 1989), p. 5.

53. TASS International Service in English and Zulu to South Africa, November 26, 1989, p. 1.

54. *Moscow Izvestiya* in Russian, January 2, 1990, morning ed., p. 3.

55. *Ibid.*

56. On earlier Soviet ties with the ANC, See Golan, *The Soviet Union and National Liberation Movements*, pp. 286–88; also Kurt Campbell, "South Africa: The Soviets Are Not the Problem," *The Washington Post*, September 11, 1985, p. A 15.

57. Johannesburg SAPA in English, March 31, 1989; FBIS-SOV, April 3, 1989, p. 15.

58. See Adamishin's press conference in Harare after he completed a tour of a number of countries in the region. Moscow TASS International Service in Russian, April 1, 1989.

59. See the interview with the Soviet ambassador to Botswana, Viktor Krivda, in March 1989. Johannesburg SAPA in English, March 21, 1989; FBIS-AFR, March 22, 1989, pp. 20–21.

60. Kuhne, "A 1988 Update," p. 5.

61. Moscow in Zulu to Southern Africa, March 10, 1989; FBIS-SOV, March 14, 1989, p. 20.

62. *The Washington Post*, October 30, 1989.

63. *Africa Confidential* 28, No. 8 (April 15, 1987), pp. 6–7.

64. See *Africa Confidential* 27, No. 25.

65. Kuhne, "A 1988 Update," p. 4.

66. *Ibid.*, pp. 7–8. Political negotiations advocated by the USSR have been given favorable attention by some elements within the South African military, the Department of Foreign Affairs, and public interest groups who would rather see dialogue between blacks and whites than a violent conflict. See Kuhne, "A 1988 Update."

67. Golan, *The Soviet Union and National Liberation Movements*, p. 278.

68. *Ibid.*, p. 37. Should the Eritreans win their struggle for independence, they would control the strategic ocean-bordering portions of present-day Ethiopia, leaving Moscow backing a politically divided and economically poor land-locked country.

69. Gerald A. Funk, "Can Ethiopia Survive Both Communism and the Drought," *CSIS Africa Notes* 40 (March 15, 1985), p. 1.

70. *The New York Times*, March 15, 1987.

71. *Ibid.*, May 21, 1989.

72. *The Washington Post*, May 26, 1989.

73. *Swiss Review of World Affairs* 37, No. 10 (January 1988), p. 9.

74. *Ibid.*, p. 9.

75. Discussion with a high-ranking US State Department official, June 21, 1989.

76. *The Washington Post*, April 21, 1989.

77. *Ibid.*

78. *Africa Confidential* 30, No. 4 (February 17, 1989), p. 4.

79. *Ibid.*

80. *The New York Times*, March 30, 1989.

81. *The New York Times*, June 6, 1989.

82. *The Christian Science Monitor*, July 5, 1989.

83. *The Washington Post*, September 3, 1989.

84. *The Washington Post*, August 15, 1989.

85. *The Wall Street Journal*, April 4, 1987. Mozambique had for years been disillusioned with Moscow's inability to provide needed economic aid. As early as 1983 President Samora Machel decided to increase peasant material incentives, loosen tight central control of the economy and seek improved relations with South Africa. See "Mozambique After Machel," *CSIS Africa Notes* 67 (December 19, 1986), p. 2. In late 1984 Mozambique signed the famous Nkomati non-aggression pact with South Africa, an agreement promising an end to South African support for the MNR and economic cooperation between the two countries. Although South Africa failed to live up to the Nkomati agreements, Mozambique and South Africa revived the accords in 1988—with South African businessmen moving into Mozambique to reopen factories and explore other projects. See Johannesburg International Service, May 1, 1989; FBIS-AFR, May 2, 1989. In its positive attitude toward liberalized economic controls, Mozambique encouraged foreign investment and joined the IMF and World Bank, which provided increased, but still insufficient aid.

86. Gunn, "Cuba and Mozambique," *CSIS Africa Notes* 80 (December 28, 1987), p. 7. Even when the Nkomati accords were violated by South Africa, Mozambique refused to play the Cuban card, rather appealing for help from Washington.

87. *Ibid.*; and US Department of State, *Soviet and East European Aid to the Third World, 1981*, February 1983, p. 14.

88. *Ibid.*, p. 8.

89. *The New York Times*, August 1, 1989.

90. *The Washington Post*, April 29, 1989.

91. *The New York Times*, January 26, 1990.

92. *The Washington Post*, June 19, 1989.

93. *The Washington Post*, November 15, 1989.

94. Peter Sidler, "Namibia: Waiting for SWAPO," *Swiss Review of World Affairs* 38, No. 12 (March 1989), pp. 8–9.

95. In the case of dos Santos and Savimbi, for example, dos Santos has talked of "the integration" of officials and supporters of Savimbi's UNITA into the single ruling MPLA party, while Savimbi has said that ". . . we have rejected that. No one will be integrated." *The Washington Post*, July 10, 1989.

96. *The New York Times*, July 9, 1989.

97. *The Washington Post*, July 10, 1989.

98. *Ibid.*, June 24, 1989.

99. Andrei Kozyrev and Andrei Shumikhin, "East and West in the Third World," *International Affairs* 3 (March 1989), pp. 67 ff; and Entin, "African Countries: National Statehood in the Making," pp. 46–47.

100. Entin, "African Countries: National Statehood in the Making," pp. 43–46.

101. *The New York Times*, December 27, 1989.

102. *The Washington Post*, December 23, 1989.

9

LATIN AMERICA

Latin America has played an important role in Soviet-Third World relations since the early 1960s. Fidel Castro's challenge to US regional domination and his claims to a leadership role in the Third World generated considerable Soviet enthusiasm about Latin America—in spite of the region's relatively low priority on the Soviet foreign policy agenda. Following Cuba's 1959 Revolution, Moscow pursued a range of policies designed to capitalize on Castro's assets and strengthen its own global position vis-à-vis the United States. These included cooperative intervention with Cuba in distant conflicts in Angola, Ethiopia, and Nicaragua and the pursuit of closer diplomatic and trade relations with industrializing giants such as Mexico, Argentina, and Brazil.

In Latin America, as elsewhere, Gorbachev's "new thinking" has produced a redefinition of Soviet interests and policies with an emphasis on peaceful resolution of regional conflict and international cooperation to reduce tension. Gorbachev's policies have included

- A diplomatic blitz to strengthen political and trade ties with large industrializing states, such as Argentina, Brazil, Mexico, and Uruguay.
- Putting pressure on Cuba to withdraw from Angola while reinforcing the importance of ties to Cuba. During his visit to Havana in April 1989, Gorbachev categorically opposed the export of revolution and signed a Treaty of Friendship and Cooperation that highlighted Moscow's new thinking and contained no mention of military assistance to Cuba.[1]
- Encouraging Cuba to pursue cooperation with the United States as reflected in Castro's June–July 1989 court martial and execution of four top military officers for drug trafficking—an issue long straining Cuban-US relations.[2]
- Communicating a strong desire to cooperate jointly with the United States in negotiating a solution to the Central American conflict.[3]
- Offering to stop military aid to Nicaragua's Sandinistas if the United States stopped its support of the anti-Sandinista contras and claiming to have halted such aid unilaterally in January 1989.

Latin America

- Strongly endorsing the February 1989 regional peace plan adopted by the Central American presidents to resolve the Nicaraguan conflict.[4]
- Reducing economic aid to Cuba and Nicaragua.

Moscow's energetic and cooperative approach in Latin America is consistent with Gorbachev's new global perspective and his perception that Soviet security and economic development can best be promoted by reducing tension and stimulating East-West detente. This is not to imply that Moscow is abandoning old clients, such as Havana and Managua. Nor has Moscow completely ceased efforts to undercut US influence and support leftist causes. But Gorbachev has moved to redefine the Soviet image, accentuating policies designed to overcome anti-Soviet perceptions, build reliable relations with industrializing states, and improve the climate for cooperation with the United States.

THE LATIN AMERICAN SETTING

Soviet policy in Latin America can be addressed most easily by establishing three distinct regions of interest: (1) Cuba and the Caribbean Basin, (2) Mexico and Central America, and (3) South America—from Colombia and Venezuela in northern South America to Chile and Argentina at the continent's southern tip.

Moscow's traditional interest in the first zone—Cuba and the Caribbean Basin—is easy enough to understand. Its strategic significance lies in its importance as a sea lane through which passes about 55 percent of imported petroleum to the United States and approximately 45 percent of US seaborne trade.[5] The region includes Fidel Castro's Cuba, a Soviet client whose foreign policy pursuits have advanced the Soviet superpower competition with the United States in the Western Hemisphere and southern Africa. Before Castro's 1959 Revolution, Moscow gave little attention to the region because of its fatalistic belief that geography placed the region under US dominance as explicitly stated in the Monroe Doctrine. When Castro repulsed the April 1961 US-backed Bay of Pigs invasion and declared Cuba a Marxist-Leninist state in December 1961, however, Soviet attention to Cuba and the rest of Latin America increased sharply. Opportunities offered by leftists movements throughout the Caribbean during the 1970s—in Guyana, Jamaica, Puerto Rico, and Trinidad—were not lost on Soviet policy makers. Grenada's leftist revolution, led by Maurice Bishop's New Jewel Movement in 1979, especially attracted Soviet interest.

The second zone, Central America and Mexico, also has offered unique opportunities to the USSR. Like Cuba and the Caribbean, it lies in the US "strategic backyard"—but, more importantly, it is geographically contiguous to the United States and includes the Panama Canal with its continuing, albeit declining, role in US trade. Leftist regimes and movements—such as Nicaragua's Sandinistas and El Salvador's Farabundo Marti National Liberation Movement (FMLN)—seriously divided US policy-makers and public opinion and diverted US attention and resources during the 1970s and 1980s, thereby advancing Soviet interests. Mexico is the only Third World state sharing a common border with the United States, in this case a hard-to-protect 2,000-mile-long zone over which pass illegal immigrants from Mexico and Central America and a thriving drug trade. Mexico's location, deeply rooted opposition to US pressure, potential political instability, and increasing significance as a Latin American actor have made it a key target of opportunity for Moscow.

The third zone, South America, has attracted Soviet attention because of its growing industrial and manufacturing strength as well as its natural resources. Important regional states—such as Argentina and Brazil—play key roles in regional and global politics; Soviet diplomatic contacts with them help Moscow legitimize its claim to political equality with the United States in Latin American affairs. This area also contains important newly industrializing Third World countries (NICs). Traditionally, Moscow has focused on South American commercial and trade opportunities, seeking Argentine grain and Brazilian food products in exchange for Soviet exports of heavy equipment.

SOVIET POLICY TOWARD LATIN AMERICA BEFORE GORBACHEV: SUCCESSES AND FAILURES

Moscow's policy toward Latin America in the period before Gorbachev was similar to its policies throughout the Third World. It sought to undercut US power, competing more effectively in Washington's strategic backyard and striving for political equality with Washington through an expanded presence and role. Its efforts included backing Cuba and radical nationalist regimes and movements in the Caribbean Basin, widening diplomatic ties, cultivating trade relations with Latin America's large industrializing states, and maintaining contacts with local communist parties. In addition, the Soviets pursued their long-range ideological goals by supporting leftist causes—as in relations with Havana, ties to Nicaragua's Sandinistas, support for Grenada's New Jewel Movement (from 1979 to 1983), and links to regional pro-Soviet communist parties.

Soviet Successes Before Gorbachev

Moscow's Latin American record included a number of successes by the time Gorbachev assumed power. The Soviet Union had emerged as a more significant regional player in Latin American affairs than it had been during the late 1950s and early 1960s—demonstrated by its expanding diplomatic ties, widened commercial contacts, scholarship programs, and technical assistance projects. From the US perspective, the USSR had become a major—and threatening—actor in regional politics by the late 1960s. Moscow's close relations with Cuba and Nicaragua created considerable US concern about the "Communist Threat" in the Western Hemisphere and produced a variety of policies aimed at combatting the "threat"—from President John F. Kennedy's Alliance for Progress in 1961 to support for the anti-Sandinista contras during the middle 1980s. If Soviet "success" is defined as an expanded regional presence and an undercutting of US power and influence, Moscow's policies in Latin America had been successful.[6]

Soviet Setbacks and Constraints

A balanced picture of Soviet activities in Latin America before Gorbachev must also include setbacks and constraints. US intervention in Grenada in October 1983 ended a promising experiment in leftist revolution and loss of a fledgling Caribbean Basin client, just as a military coup in Chile ten years earlier had ended Salvador Allende's rule as the first elected Marxist president in Latin America. Soviet economic limitations, meanwhile, severely constrained Moscow's capabilities to finance "other Cubas," as vividly demonstrated by Nicaragua's huge economic problems. Neither Cuba nor Nicaragua provided an attractive model of economic development; Cuba's economy was in decline despite Moscow's $4–5 billion in annual aid. Other limits to Soviet power included

- Latin America's debt crisis and need for economic aid, which Moscow could not supply.[7]
- Balance of trade deficits with Latin America, owing to lack of attraction of Soviet goods and insignificant Latin American arms purchases from the USSR.[8]
- Latin America's nationalism and resistance to great power intervention, be it US or Soviet; anti-Americanism in Latin America does not equal pro-Soviet sentiments, and even Cuba resists Soviet pressure.
- Factionalism that prohibits unified party behavior (as in El Salvador's Farabundo Marti National Liberation Front—FMLN).[9]

GORBACHEV'S "NEW THINKING" IN LATIN AMERICA

Gorbachev's "new thinking" soon became apparent in Latin America. While the new Soviet leader did not immediately cut back aid to established leftist clients like Cuba and Nicaragua or stop competing for influence with the United States, Gorbachev did make it clear that he was going to redefine the nature of Soviet–Latin American ties. As in other Third World arenas, he emphasized less ideological and more pragmatic regional policies—improved state-to-state relations, nonmilitary forms of competition, political settlement of regional conflicts, and the downgrading of support for national liberation movements. Gorbachev offered to stop military aid to Nicaragua's Sandinistas if the United States would stop its support for the contras, stated that such military aid had been halted in January 1989, and gave full support for the Contadora and Costa Rican peace proposals for a diplomatic negotiation of Central America's conflicts. Gorbachev's Latin American posture demonstrates the new Soviet assumption that global interdependence, the pursuit of a balance of interests between East and West, and the creation of an international security system cannot coexist with Soviet support for national liberation struggles and class conflict.[10]

Gorbachev's efforts to redefine the nature of the Soviet presence was reflected in various policy initiatives. Moscow began to lean on Cuba to work for a peaceful settlement of the conflict in Angola, expressed support for the Contadora and Costa Rican peace processes, and sought closer ties to Brazil and Mexico. Moscow continued, however, to provide rhetorical support to anti-US sentiments in Costa Rica, Honduras, Mexico, and Panama, and continued "active measures" as a form of peaceful competition.

As elsewhere in the Third World Gorbachev energized state-to-state relations, sending out one diplomatic mission after another. Soviet visits that had averaged around 13 per year from 1976 to 1984 jumped to approximately 20 per year after 1985. Gorbachev sent an especially high-level delegation to Cuba's Third Party Congress in February 1986, headed by the then number two man in the Politburo, Yegor Ligachev.[11] Soviet Foreign Minister Shevardnadze visited Mexico in October 1986, the first visit by a Soviet foreign minister to a Latin American country other than Cuba.[12] Shortly thereafter, Deputy Foreign Minister Viktor Komplektov—one of eight Deputy Foreign Ministers under Shevardnadze in the Ministry of Foreign Affairs—visited Brazil, Uruguay, and Mexico. Boris Yeltsin, at the time a key Politburo member, led a four-person delegation trip to Nicaragua in March 1987: Carlos Nunez of Nicaragua's National Directorate described this as the most important Soviet visit to date—not surprising as Yeltsin reaffirmed Soviet support for Managua.[13] Foreign Minister Shevardnadze returned to Latin America in the fall of 1987, meeting with top officials in Brazil, Argentina, Uruguay, and Cuba.[14] These trips were topped off by Gorbachev's historic visit to Cuba in April 1989.

In meeting after meeting Shevardnadze and his colleagues repeated the themes of "new thinking," stressing the need to remove the nuclear threat, establish zones of peace and cooperation, and reduce military spending. They called for universal and total disarmament with international verification. They denounced the export of revolution and the use of force as well as the use of international terrorism in all its forms. And they called for diversification of trade and the development of cooperation in all spheres.

Soviet diplomats tailored Gorbachev's "new political thinking" to the Latin American agenda—the debt issue, creation of a new international economic order to benefit the developing countries, and support for Latin American solutions to regional conflicts, particularly in Central America. While Moscow cannot afford the aid needed by Latin America, they can package and publicize the aid they can afford. They offered to reduce Peru's debts, for example, by agreeing to purchase Peruvian goods, and they have signed a number of cultural exchange and economic cooperation agreements, notably in Brazil, Uruguay, and Argentina.[15] Besides providing economic benefits, agreements like these allow Latin American governments to demonstrate their independence from the United States.

Visiting Latin American delegations have received the red carpet treatment from Soviet officials eager to strengthen bilateral ties. When President Sanguinetti of Uruguay visited Moscow in March 1988, for example, Gorbachev argued that the USSR was not the cause of Central America's conflict, that it had no military-political aims regarding the region, and that it firmly backed the Contadora and Arias peace processes. As to his own view of international relations, Gorbachev stated that:

> The world has changed and is changing in such a way that the need for an improvement in the international climate is becoming ever more pressing. The peoples do not want to accept tension, the arms race, and economic adversities. It is the task of politicians to detect these sentiments and reflect them in appropriate actions. . . . One should not reduce world politics to Soviet-U.S. relations, however important.[16]

DOMINANT TRENDS AFFECTING GORBACHEV'S LATIN AMERICAN POLICY

Gorbachev's emergence as Soviet leader coincided with the development of trends in Latin America that were favorable to reinvigorated Soviet–Latin American ties. First, military governments in Peru, Argentina, Brazil, and Uruguay had been replaced by new civilian democracies during the early to mid-1980s. These new governments were more receptive to closer state-to-state relations with the USSR, improved relations with Cuba, and political openings for legal communist parties—with their ties to student organizations, peasant groups, and trade unions.

Second, Gorbachev has benefited from rising tides of anti-US nationalism. The Soviets have tailored their rhetoric to specific national situations, backing Panama's strongman, Manuel Noriega, when he was accused of drug trafficking by US officials, predicting the US invasion of Panama, emphasizing Honduran concerns about the large US military presence, and playing up US support for the Nicaraguan contras. The Soviets also have given increasing attention to Mexico, not least because Mexican nationalism consistently evokes anti-US sentiments. Shevardnadze's discussions with high-ranking Mexican officials in 1986, for example, played to Mexican and Latin American grievances with the United States.[17]

Third, Central and Latin America peace proposals for regional conflict have provided opportunities for the Soviets to weigh in with their own new emphasis on peaceful resolution of regional conflicts. The more cooperative Soviet-US relationship emerging during 1987–1988—based on arms control negotiations and the formula worked out for a settlement of the Angolan controversy—established a foundation for regional talks on Central America. By early 1989—following Gorbachev's previous indications at a White House luncheon in late 1987 that Moscow wished to "work together" to diminish the flow of arms to the region—both Moscow and Washington were engaged in efforts to reduce tensions in Central America. In March 1989, Soviet Ambassador Yuri Dubinin communicated to the US State Department his positive reaction to the February 1989 meeting of five Central American presidents in El Salvador.[18] Aides to Secretary of State James Baker, meanwhile, indicated in early 1989 their desire to revitalize talks on Central American with the Soviets, taking advantage of the April 1989 Gorbachev visit to Cuba.[19]

Fourth, Latin American perceptions of the USSR have shifted since Gorbachev came to power. Trips to the USSR by Latin American leaders to meet with top Soviet leaders demonstrate regional interest in the processes of change in the USSR and in Moscow's renewed interest in Latin America. Soviet talk of interdependence and East-West detente are received far more favorably by Latin American leaders than was rhetoric dealing with Cold War conflict, wars of national liberation, and class struggle.

Fifth, the issues that provided Moscow with opportunities before 1985 remain extant. These include Latin America's rising external debt, North-South development priorities, Liberation Theology, and "Dependista" arguments over how best to achieve economic development. Cuba and Nicaragua remain in great need of Soviet military and economic help, insuring Moscow's continued presence in these countries, and leftist insurgencies—still supported by Cuba and Nicaragua—continue to flourish in Central and South America, diverting US attention from regions more geographically important to the Soviets.

SOVIET-CUBAN RELATIONS

Gorbachev's April 1989 visit to Havana demonstrated Cuba's continuing value to Moscow. The Soviet-Cuban Treaty of Friendship and Cooperation, the first such treaty initialed by Gorbachev and the first between the USSR and Cuba indicated that Moscow would continue its support for Cuba despite the strain in Soviet-Cuban relations and Moscow's efforts to reduce East-West tensions.[20] At the same time, the treaty was limited in scope and gave Castro no security guarantees. Rather it emphasized the new Soviet foreign policy agenda.

The Soviet-Cuban relationship is one of converging interests, with Moscow and Havana seeking to maximize the benefits and minimize the costs of dealing with each other. They advance their compatible goals through cooperation, but strains result when their goals are not the same. Frictions have resulted from Moscow's displeasure with Havana's stagnant economic growth and mismanagement, Castro's discontent with levels of Soviet economic aid, Moscow's global East-West concerns compared to Cuba's regional North-South focus, and Castro's discontent with Soviet caution and restraint during the US intervention in Grenada in 1983.[21]

Soviet-Cuban Cooperation Since Gorbachev

Soon after coming to power, Gorbachev set about improving Moscow's deteriorating relationship with Havana. In May 1985 a high-level Soviet delegation arrived in Havana, led by Politburo member Mikhail Solomentsev, to commemorate the 25th anniversary of the establishment of diplomatic relations between the two countries.[22] In October, Soviet Foreign Minister

Shevardnadze visited Cuba, bringing "warm wishes" from Gorbachev.[23] The 3rd Congress of the Communist Party of Cuba in February 1986 attracted an extremely high-ranking Soviet team, headed by Yegor Ligachev, then number two man in the Politburo. This warming trend continued with Castro's attendance at the 27th Congress of the Communist Party of the Soviet Union in February-March 1986, his first visit to Moscow in over two years. During his speech to the Congress, Castro paid tribute to Gorbachev's "brilliant and valiant main report"—a sharp improvement in Castro's mood compared to his attitude less than a year before.[24]

Since the two 1986 party congresses, Gorbachev and Castro have stressed their determination to pursue cooperative relations. Castro has enjoyed basking in the red-carpet treatment he has received from Gorbachev. During the festivities marking the 70th anniversary of the October Revolution held in Moscow in November 1987, Castro was given a place of honor at Lenin's Tomb to view the USSR's 70th Anniversary Parade. Upon his return to Cuba, Castro announced that his recent Moscow journey had been his "happiest trip to the Soviet Union."[25] Indeed, Castro went to extremes in Havana to tell the Cuban people just how popular he was in the USSR; Gorbachev treated him, said Castro, "with a deference, interest, and a friendliness that might be described as exceptional."[26]

Gorbachev's April 1989 visit accentuated the strength of Soviet-Cuban ties, with Moscow and Havana downplaying frictions. In his lengthy introduction of Gorbachev to Cuba's National Assembly of the People's Government, Castro said that people were "imagining" Cuban discord with the Soviet Union, praised the newly signed Treaty of Friendship as an indicator of great Cuban-Soviet cooperation and highlighted the value of Moscow's generous aid.[27] Gorbachev, for his part, noted the "immense moral impact" of Cuba's Revolution on world opinion and Soviet pride in standing with Cuba through years of common struggle. He stated that the USSR "cherishes its friendship with socialist Cuba" and is prepared ". . . to continue developing Soviet-Cuban relations."[28] While making clear his discontent with Cuba's sagging economic conditions, Gorbachev did nothing to indicate that the Soviets were going to "cut their losses" in Cuba.

Gorbachev's treatment of Castro strongly suggests that "new thinking" does not require a down-grading of relations with Cuba. Despite Gorbachev's East-West foreign policy priorities, detente and arms control with the United States, new approaches to regional conflict, and *perestroika* at home, Gorbachev appears prepared to nurture his Cuban ally. The Soviet investment in Cuba is too deep to allow for abandonment or a sharp decline in support. Castro for his part, has continued to back Gorbachev's regional peace efforts in Central America and agreed to the Soviet-backed 1988 peace settlement in Angola. Soviet-Cuban cooperation was accentuated during the Shevardnadze-Castro meetings of October 4–5, 1989, which Castro described as "profound, positive and with full identity of views."[29] The TASS version of the communique described the meetings in Havana as

Cuba in its regional setting

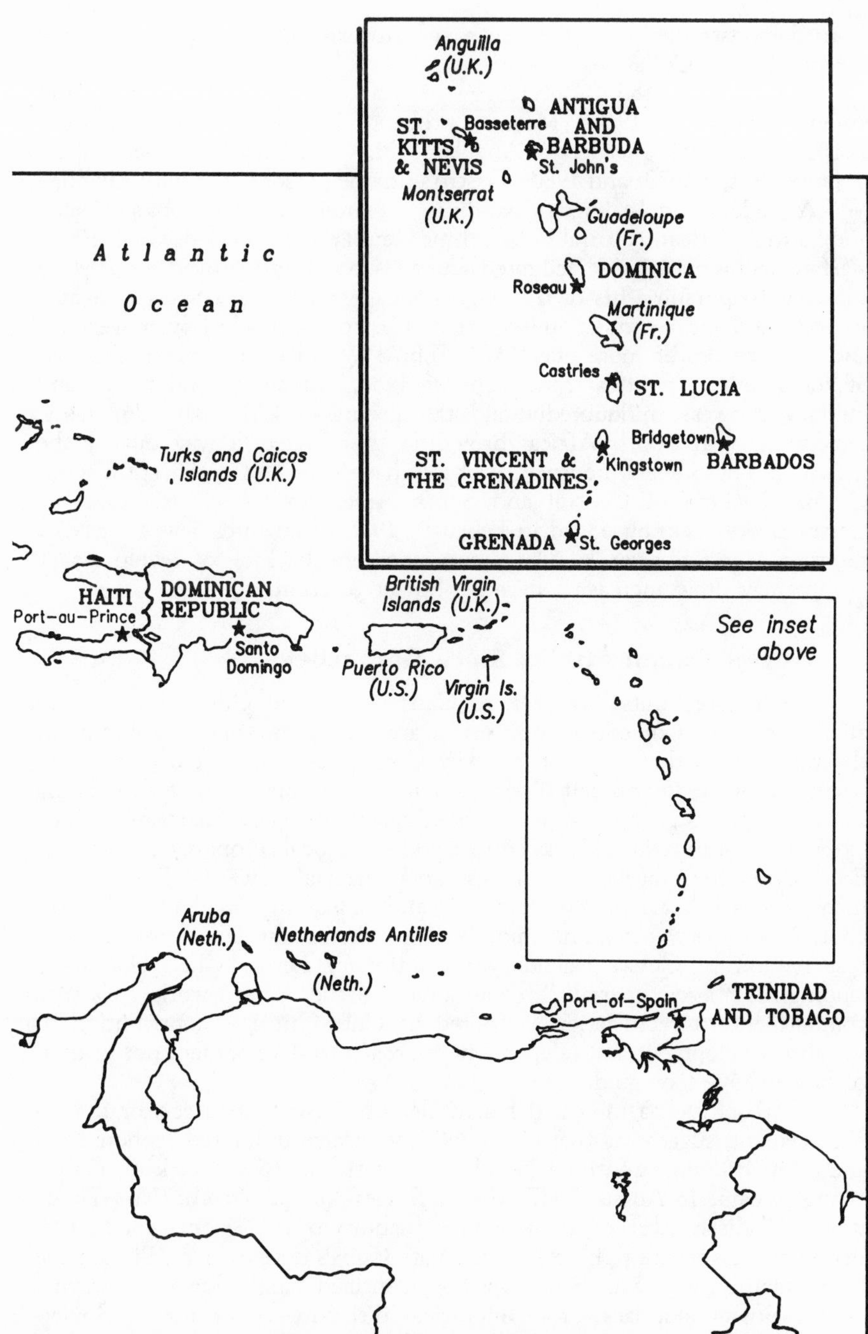

Anguilla (U.K.)
ANTIGUA AND BARBUDA
ST. KITTS & NEVIS
Basseterre
St. John's
Montserrat (U.K.)
Guadeloupe (Fr.)
DOMINICA
Roseau
Martinique (Fr.)
Castries
ST. LUCIA
Bridgetown
BARBADOS
ST. VINCENT & THE GRENADINES
Kingstown
GRENADA
St. Georges
Atlantic Ocean
Turks and Caicos Islands (U.K.)
HAITI
Port-au-Prince
DOMINICAN REPUBLIC
Santo Domingo
British Virgin Islands (U.K.)
Puerto Rico (U.S.)
Virgin Is. (U.S.)
See inset above
Aruba (Neth.)
Netherlands Antilles (Neth.)
Port-of-Spain
TRINIDAD AND TOBAGO

again demonstrating ". . . the depth and sincerity of the relations uniting the Soviet and Cuban peoples."[30]

Having witnessed the overthrow of previously supported Third World leaders during the 1960s, Moscow probably greatly appreciates Castro's assistance in keeping leaders of Angola's MPLA and Nicaragua's Sandinistas in power in the 1970s and 1980s. Castro's unique personal ties with Luanda's MPLA leaders and Managua's Sandinistas combined with Cuba's African and Latin American cultural links, ethnic identity and knowledge of guerrilla warfare techniques have facilitated Cuba's success and proved an asset to Moscow. In pursuing his own foreign policy agenda with respect to armed struggle and local conflict intervention, Castro has made Soviet weapons and military power more effective in Third World civil wars. In the case of the Angolan political settlement of 1988, Cuban ground forces and military prowess undoubtedly laid the groundwork for the diplomatic settlement with South Africa, providing the Soviets a way out of the situation. The Soviets, however, probably have been less enthusiastic about Castro's backing of Central and South American leftist insurgents—as Castro openly acknowledged in February 1988 in an interview with NBC reporter Maria Shriver.[31] Cuba's more energetic backing of revolutionary groups may draw increasing negative Soviet reaction.[32]

Soviet-Cuban Strains Since Gorbachev

There are limits, however, to Castro's value to Gorbachev. Despite all the indicators of cooperation and warm relations, there are strains in the relationship that will not go away. Castro's economic reform program begun in mid-1986 and called *rectification* takes an approach to stimulating economic productivity that is at odds with Gorbachev's *perestroika*. The latter emphasizes reduced Party control and more local autonomy in economic decision-making, market incentives, and material rewards. Rectification incorporates criteria previously tried—and failed: increased central party control, austerity, discipline, moral rather than material incentives, and resurrection of Cuba's legendary revolutionary hero, "Che" Guevara—lauding his "heroic guerrilla" revolutionary virtue of hard work.[33] Castro's commitment to rectification is touted as Cuba's unique contribution to socialist development, an independent approach to development not in need of Soviet advice or guidance.[34]

Gorbachev has indicated his displeasure with Cuba's economic mismanagement, suggesting that Cuba will not receive unlimited economic aid should its economy continue to fail. Perhaps the sharpest attack on Cuba's economy came in August 1987, when a Soviet *Novoye Vremya* (*New Times*) writer, Vladislav Chirkov, discussed the inability of the Council for Mutual Economic Assistance (CEMA) to stimulate Cuba's development. Placing the blame mainly on the Cubans, Chirkov identified Cuba's low productivity, wasted Soviet aid, lack of technological discipline, poor use of Soviet-trained specialists, and huge defense burden as key impediments to Cuban progress.[35] Chirkov's remarks prompted an outraged counter-attack by Carlos

TABLE 9.1 Distribution of Trade and Partner Concentration (in percentage)

Category	*1980*	*1981*	*1982*	*1983*	*1984*	*1985*	*1986*	*1987*
Total trade	100.0	100.0	100.0	100.0	100.0	100.0	100.0	100.0
Socialist trade	74.5	78.1	86.8	86.6	86.4	86.3	86.2	88.3
Market economies trade	25.5	21.9	13.2	13.4	13.6	13.7	13.8	11.7

Sources: Comite Estatal de Estadisticas, Havana, Cuba, *Anuario Estadistico,* 1986, and *Quarterly Economic Report* (QER) December 1987. Banco Nacional de Cuba, Havana, Cuba, *Informe Economico,* June 1988.

TABLE 9.2 Cuban-Soviet Trade Turnover (in billion of pesos and rubles)

	AEC[a]	Granma	*SFTH*[b]
1983	8.1	n/a	6.1
1984	8.7	8.1[c]	7.2
1985	9.8	close to 9.0[d]	8.0
1986	9.2	more than 8.0[e]	7.6
1987	n/a	more than 8.5[f]	7.5

[a]Comite Estatal de Estadisticas, Havana, Cuba, *Anuario Estadistico de Cuba*
[b]*Soviet Foreign Trade Handbook* (Moscow), by year
[c]*Granma,* Havana, Cuba, 25 March 1986
[d]*Granma,* Havana, Cuba, 25 March 1986
[e]*Granma,* Havana, Cuba, 31 May 1986
[f]*Granma,* Havana, Cuba, 19 January 1987

Rafael Rodriguez, a Cuban Politburo member personally close to Castro, who strongly defended Cuba's economic performance given the serious constraints under which it operated.[36]

There are indications that Soviet economic support for Cuba may be declining. Cuban trade with the Soviet Union and CEMA has increased from 74.5 percent of total trade in 1980 to 88.3 percent in 1987—a growing dependency indicated in Table 9.1. But Soviet exports to Cuba have been decreasing. This decline in Soviet-Cuban trade, reflected in Table 9.2, is not a healthy indicator for Havana, especially when Cuba has been unable to increase trade with the developed capitalist countries.

Moscow also has begun to reduce its support in other key economic sectors. The Soviet sugar subsidy remains an essential aspect of aid to Cuba, but the USSR has lowered its sugar subsidy—from 45 cents per pound in 1985 to 38 cents in 1986.[37] Soviet oil exports to Cuba have continuously declined since 1984, as mirrored in Table 9.3. Soviet oil deliveries dropped from 7 million tons in 1986 to 6.7 million tons in 1987—at a time when Cuba requires about 9–12 million tons of oil per year.[38] This decline in oil deliveries has forced oil rationing in Cuba, and Castro has consistently urged his countrymen to produce more with less and to save oil, energy, cement, and other raw material.[39]

To add insult to injury the Cubans are paying more than the world market price for oil—because the precipitous decline in world market prices occurred after they agreed on a price with the Soviets.[40] The relatively

TABLE 9.3 Value of Soviet Crude Oil and Oil Products Exported to Cuba (in million of pesos and rubles)

	Cuban Value	*Soviet Value*
1983	1,050.8	1,184.4
1984	1,291.7	1,324.7
1985	1,580.7	1,258.9
1986	n/a	1,216.8
1987	n/a	1,177.2

Sources: Cuban values: Comite Estatal de Estadisticas, Havana, Cuba, *Anuario Estadistico de Cuba;* Soviet values: *Soviet Foreign Trade Handbook* (Moscow).

high price paid for Soviet oil also makes less attractive Cuba's previous arrangement of selling unused Soviet oil on the open market for hard currency used in turn for purchases from the West. Cuba's debt to Western creditors had increased to approximately $6.4 billion by 1989—as Castro's Revolution turned 30—putting further pressure on Cuba's economy.[41]

Gorbachev's policies of *perestroika* and *glasnost* may pose subtle challenges to Castro, one reason why these terms are not widely used in Cuba.[42] Gorbachev's revolution has generated enthusiasm among many sophisticated mid-level Cuban officials and the population at large.[43] Havana's inhabitants seem fascinated with events in the USSR, and *Novedades de Moscu,* a Soviet weekly in Spanish, tends to sell out rapidly. No Cuban publication can boast similar popularity.[44] Senior Cuban officials, according to some reports, seem uncomfortable with Gorbachev's reforms, and as tens of thousands of Cubans studying or working in the USSR return to Cuba, they bring home the latest reform ideas from the USSR.

Castro, meanwhile, has continued to scorn the Soviet model of reform.[45] He publicly has said that Cuba will take a "wait and see" attitude toward Gorbachev's restructuring.[46] Privately, Cuban officials have expressed even sharper language. "We can't understand why they are taking their revolution backwards," one Foreign Ministry official has stated.[47] Castro's December 5, 1988, speech marking the 32nd anniversary of the "Granma" landing and the 30th anniversary of the FAR, made only passing mention of appreciation of Soviet aid. Castro staunchly defended socialism and Marxism-Leninism and declared, "We, Cubans, could even say with satisfaction, that we have not made many mistakes others have made. We have made mistakes and we must rectify according to our own mistakes. We must not rectify according to someone else's mistakes. . . . Some of our errors were based on imitating the experiences of other socialist countries."[48] The Soviets did not receive Castro's criticism gracefully;[49] one Soviet diplomat commented that Cuba would have to adapt its centralized system to deal directly with the USSR's more independent factories and agencies.[50] This situation has already begun to generate serious strains between Cuba and the Soviet Union, and even some members of CEMA, for example, Hungary, also have been creating similar strains with Cuba as they move toward market-based economies.

Cuba's anti-American sentiments continue to drive Cuban policy although Castro has adapted somewhat to the new Soviet approach. There have been signs of improvement in Cuban-US relations, with both Havana and Washington softening their positions on an immigration agreement, uses of chartered flights between the two countries, and Cuba's releasing of about 30 political prisoners.[51] Indeed, in an interview with Venezuelan journalist Nelson Bucaranda in Caracas, Venezuela, during Castro's attendance at the inauguration of President Carlos Andres Perez in February 1989, Castro said that improvement in US-Cuban relations would be a smart move for the Bush Administration—providing the US President with a place in history.[52] Still, Castro focuses on bitter memories of the past. Castro stated in a news interview with NBC's Maria Shriver in February 1988 that ". . . we are left with the honor of being one of the few adversaries of the United States."[53] Shriver queried, "That's an honor?" Castro: "Of course it is an honor, because for such a small country as Cuba to have such a gigantic country as the United States live so obsessed with this small island . . . is an honor for us."[54]

During Gorbachev's visit to Cuba in April 1989 there were indications of the different approaches of the two leaders. On the eve of Gorbachev's visit, Cuban Deputy Foreign Minister Raul Roa had restated Cuba's belief that it had a "right" to support revolutionary movements in the region because the United States continued to provide support for counterrevolutionaries, specifically the Nicaraguan contras.[55] Gorbachev took issue with this policy, however, stressing Moscow's opposition to the export of revolution. In addition to calling for an end to outside military aid to Latin America, Gorbachev implicitly played down Cuba's importance as Moscow's privileged ally by accentuating relations with what he called the "giants of the region," such as Argentina and Brazil.[56]

The Soviet-Cuban Friendship Treaty signed in April 1989 emphasized Gorbachev's new thinking and, unlike other Soviet Friendship Treaties, contained no references to military cooperation between the Soviet Union and Cuba and no mention of consultation by signatory powers if attacked or under direct threat.[57] Although he paid homage to Gorbachev and the Friendship Treaty—which helped demonstrate Cuba's continuing value to the USSR—Castro made clear his differences with Moscow during the Gorbachev visit. Castro:

- Took a distinctly anti-imperialist stance in his public addresses, saying that ". . . we do not know for certain, we do not have proof that the imperialists have assimilated that new international mentality, and we have more than enough reason to distrust them."[58]
- Delivered a blistering attack on the United States during his introductory remarks for Gorbachev's presentation to the National Assembly of the People's Government, leading the senior US diplomat in Havana, John J. Taylor, to walk out in protest, not staying for Gorbachev's speech.[59]

- Publicly analyzed the USSR's errors and problems in economic and socialist development, including those of the Stalin era.[60]
- Left little doubt that he did not intend to follow Gorbachev's conciliatory approach to the United States or his model for domestic economic and political change.[61]
- Interrupted a question to Gorbachev during a news interview to assert that Cuba was not a "colony" of the Soviet Union.[62]

Castro certainly recognizes that Soviet economic assistance is likely to continue to decline. Cuba's debt to the USSR is going up annually, reaching around $15–22 billion in 1989. Soviet aid is approximately $4–5 billion annually, but Cuba's needs have been rising and Moscow has not increased its aid. Soviet aid therefore is declining in terms of Cuba's relative requirements. Castro probably also heard the expressions of Soviet discontent in the new 1989 Congress of People's Deputies in the USSR regarding large-scale aid to countries like Cuba and Vietnam, when the Soviet economy is experiencing rapid deterioration.[63] These pressures may push Castro to establish a more favorable atmosphere for cooperative relations with Cuba's natural trading partner, the United States.

Such pressure may account for the extraordinary events of June–July 1989: the military shake-up, political purge, trial and execution of high-ranking Cuban military officers accused of international drug trafficking.[64] Castro's attack on Cuban drug-trafficking, which the United States had criticized for years, could open the door to Soviet-American-Cuban cooperation in fighting drugs—clearing the path for a new international role by Cuba and, down the line, normalization of US-Cuban relations. In July 1989, suggesting this trend, it became public knowledge that senior Cuban officials, following up statements by Castro, had offered to work with the United States in curbing a surge of drug-smuggling flights over Cuban territory.[65]

Castro's sense of concern about the direction of Soviet-Cuban relations and the future of the USSR itself appeared clearly in his July 26, 1989, anniversary speech. "We are living in a time of great economic problems," he said, and " . . there are difficulties in the socialist movement. We cannot say with certainty that the supplies that have been arriving with clockwork punctuality from the socialist camp for thirty years will keep arriving with the same certainty."[66] In a defiant assertion of his revolutionary purity and moral authority compared to the USSR, he stated that "Cuba stands firm, Cuba is valiant, Cuba is heroic, Cuba neither surrenders nor sells out."[67] As if to point to the USSR as a sinking ship, Castro declared that even if the USSR "disintegrated," "Cuba and the Cuban Revolution would continue to struggle and to resist."[68]

The profound economic and political events sweeping East Europe in late 1989 intensified Castro's public resistance to such reforms even if it meant distancing himself from his allies. In his first public comment on the state of East-West relations after the Soviet-US summit meeting in early December 1989, Castro stated that "if destiny assigns us the role of one day being among the last defenders of socialism; in a world in which the Yankee empire was able to make a reality of Hitler's dreams of dominating the world, we would know how to defend this bastion until the last drop of blood."[69] Although Castro did not criticize Gorbachev or any East European leader by name, he complained about the "impossibility" of building socialism when others are ". . . slandering socialism, destroying its values, discrediting the party, demoralizing the vanguard, relinquishing its leadership role, eliminating social discipline, and sowing chaos and anarchy everywhere."[70] East European transformation, coupled with Soviet *perestroika* and *glasnost*, undoubtedly give Castro cause for concern about his own political future—as well as the negative economic consequences produced by East Europe's turn toward market economies, loss of unity within CEMA, and reduced tensions between the United States and this part of the world.

Moscow and Havana also have diverged on the offensive launched by the FMLN in early November 1989. The Soviets have made clear their strong rejection of the insurgents' violent tactics and have profusely denied any Soviet support for the escalated FMLN conflict.[71] When a light plane carrying two dozen Soviet-made antiaircraft missiles crashed in eastern El Salvador in November 1989—with documentation indicating the plane had taken off from Managua—the Soviets apparently upbraided Cuba and Nicaragua for their involvement in the El Salvador war.[72] Cuba appears to have sent the consignment of arms destined for FMLN rebels, using Nicaraguan territory with the complicity of Nicaraguan army and party officials who may not have informed the nine members of Nicaragua's National Directorate.[73] Whereas the FMLN violent path favors Castro's brand of "proletariat internationalism," it greatly endangers Soviet-US detente and Gorbachev's new thinking.

SOVIET RELATIONS WITH NICARAGUA

Gorbachev's new thinking, did not lead to immediate changes in Soviet policy toward Nicaragua. By 1988–1989, however, the improved climate of Soviet-US relations had created the possibility for a cooperative approach to this Central American conflict. Nicaragua has been included in the talks on Third World regional issues between Secretary of State James Baker and Soviet Foreign Minister Shevardnadze, and a letter to President Bush in May 1989 from Gorbachev stated that Moscow had ceased sending weapons directly to Nicaragua since January 1, 1989.[74] Moscow's approach to the Nicaraguan problem appears to parallel its emphasis on negotiating political solutions *a la* Afghanistan, Angola, Namibia, Ethiopia, and Mozambique.

Soviet ties with Nicaragua are in many ways similar to its relations with Cuba. Soviet economic aid includes most of Managua's oil supplies and considerable technical assistance. Until 1989 Moscow supplied Managua's

TABLE 9.4 Soviet–East European Economic and Military Assistance to Nicaragua (in millions of U.S. dollars)

	1982	*1983*	*1984*	*1985*	*1986*
Economic assistance[a]	180	275	325	450	585
Military deliveries	160	260	320	300	590
from the U.S.S.R.	150	250	300	250	550
from Eastern Europe	10	10	20	50	40

[a]Includes economic assistance from Cuba

Source: U.S. Department of State, *Soviet-Bloc Assistance to Cuba and Nicaragua* (Washington, DC: U.S. Department of State, 1987), p. 1.

Sandinistas with high levels of military weapons and supplies—an estimated $2.3 billion worth between 1980 and 1988.[75] Nicaragua could not have prevailed against the US-backed contras or created the largest and most powerful armed force in Central America without this assistance. Table 9.4 illustrates the high levels of total Soviet, East European, and Cuban military and economic aid propping up Nicaragua's government during the 1980s. Approximately 250 Soviet advisers have monitored this aid.

Cuba has played an even bigger role in advising Sandinista leaders, helping manage Nicaragua's military and security systems, extending educational and technical assistance, and defending Sandinista interests in the socialist community. Since helping the Sandinistas during their battle for power, including providing weapons during the final offensive against Somoza, Cuba has increased its personnel in Nicaragua.[76] By 1985 about 2,500 Cubans worked in the Ministries of Defense and Interior, operating at all levels of the armed forces and security services. Cuban military personnel help train Sandinista military, fly Nicaraguan helicopters, and perform counterinsurgency combat operations.[77] In addition, Havana has provided Sandinista leaders with a model for consolidating power—a large army, government bureaucracy, cadres within party cells or block committees, and a security apparatus involving roughly 400,000 people out of a total population of about three million.[78]

Like Cuba, Nicaragua does not provide an attractive model of socialist development. As a result of extraordinary military spending and ineffective economic management, Nicaragua's economy declined by 9 percent during 1988, reached an astounding 23,000 percent annual inflation rate, experienced a 96 percent drop in purchasing power, and lost 9,700 jobs because of the government's austerity program; Hurricane Joan caused a further $840 million in damages. By 1989, Nicaragua's citizens, particularly its educated and skilled workers, were fleeing the country in droves. Since 1979 about one-third of Nicaragua's 33,000 college-educated professionals have left the country.[79]

The Soviets are unlikely to increase aid to the Sandinista government or to back it in any future conflict with the United States. Gorbachev has carefully avoided actions that might precipitate direct US intervention.[80]

The Soviets have refrained from introducing offensive MIG-23 fighter planes into Nicaragua—as requested by Ortega; and Soviet bloc arms shipments declined by about 20 percent during 1989.[81]

Gorbachev has indicated that, despite substantial Soviet economic and military aid, Managua will have to make whatever accommodations are necessary to exist in the US sphere of interest. On the economic front, Moscow has insisted that its aid is limited to protecting the economy from total collapse, leaving the tasks of economic development essentially up to the Sandinistas. While the Sandinistas blame the US-backed contra war for its economic shambles, some Soviet political analysts blame the mess on Sandinista inefficiency and mismanagement. One Soviet official in Managua stated that, "they seem unable to decide whether they want a market economy or a planned economy."[82]

In an interview with foreign correspondents in November 1988, Moscow's new ambassador to Nicaragua, Valeriy Nikolayenko, emphasized Gorbachev's approach. Stressing that Moscow had "nothing to hide in Nicaragua," Nikolayenko stated that Moscow had no intention of placing a military base in Nicaragua and would continue current levels of Soviet aid (around $750 million for 1988). He said that Moscow did not have as much to give as it would like, but was "morally behind Nicaragua with our whole heart."[83]

Soviet Foreign Minister Shevardnadze used his first visit to Nicaragua in early October 1989 to launch a broad peace initiative in Central America that envisioned a widened political role for the USSR and a diminished role for the United States as the dominant actor in the region. Shevardnadze proposed that the USSR and the United States jointly guarantee peace and security in Central America, in part by presiding over deep cuts in arms stockpiles and armed forces throughout the region.[84] Shevardnadze also extended an invitation to open diplomatic relations with El Salvador and Honduras, the United States' two closest allies in Central America, and affirmed the Soviet embargo on arms shipments to Nicaragua. Shevardnadze's proposal was similar to offers made by Gorbachev in 1987 and 1988 to cut arms deliveries to Nicaragua if the United States would take similar actions in Honduras and El Salvador. In addition, Moscow strongly backed the Central American presidents summit meeting of February 1989, which passed resolutions calling for voluntary demobilization and repatriation of the Nicaraguan Resistance and their relatives to Nicaragua or third countries within a 90-day period, coupled with Nicaragua's declaration to hold national elections before February 25, 1990.[85]

Gorbachev's "new political thinking" appeared to be having an effect on Nicaragua's approach to the United States by the late 1980s. When combined with the Bush Administration's commitment to a peace process in Central America, an ending of Reagan-era support for the contras, and Central American leaders' efforts to negotiate a political settlement to Nicaraguan turmoil, Soviet implicit pressure pushed the Sandinistas to announce elections in February 1990 and to move toward peaceful resolution of their internal conflict.[86]

GORBACHEV'S LATIN AMERICAN POLICY ON BALANCE

Gorbachev's approach in Latin America reflects the same elements present in other Third World regions. Moscow continues to compete with the United States, supporting leftist causes though in a more cautious and restrained manner. The Soviets continue their support for Cuba and Nicaragua as well as for leftist groups through party-to-party ties and active measures. Soviet aid to Cuba has remained at approximately $4–5 billion annually and Soviet oil supplies to Nicaragua continue to flow. Soviet Latin American analysts still maintain that the central cause of underdevelopment lies in the region's economic and political dependency on the United States, and Soviet rhetorical support for anti-American sentiment continues.[87]

Gorbachev's commitment to stable coexistence, the reduction of East-West tensions, and the political settlement of regional disputes is redefining the nature of Moscow's Latin American policy, however. Support for wars of national liberation in places like El Salvador and Guatemala has been downgraded. The pursuit of actions that identify Moscow with leftist insurgents or associate Moscow with Havana's support of guerrilla causes would undermine Gorbachev's more important interests.

Gorbachev's new emphasis on the political settlement of regional disputes has been reflected in his approach to Cuba and the Central American conflict. In July 1988, Cuba, in response to Soviet pressure, announced that it had agreed to start bringing home Havana's estimated 50,000 troops from Angola in a politically arranged settlement with Angola, South Africa, and the United States. Castro's speech at the 26th of July 1988 celebrations in Santiago de Cuba faulted Soviet tactics in the Angolan War and asserted Cuba's independence from Soviet control, suggesting Castro's unhappiness with Soviet pressure.[88] Castro argued that 15,000 Cuban reinforcements had averted a disaster in the southeastern Angolan town of Cuito Cuanavale and won a major victory against the anti-government guerrillas of Jonas Savimbi, backed by South Africa. Many observers consider this victory the turning point that produced the successful negotiations on Angola. This event fortified Castro's argument that Cuba was leaving Angola with its opponents on the defensive and that Cuba had achieved what it set out to do in the first place—in spite of Soviet pressure.[89]

Gorbachev has communicated Soviet interest in a peaceful political settlement of Central America's conflict. Toward this end the Soviet leader pledged to President Ronald Reagan in their December 1987 summit meeting a halt in "all military aid" to Nicaragua's government if the United States ended its support for the contras, and in his May 1989 letter to President Bush went so far as to say that Moscow had stopped weapons transfers to Nicaragua.[90] In addition, Gorbachev reiterated his support for a political settlement of the Central American conflict during his Malta summit meeting with President Bush, while Foreign Secretary Shevardnadze continued to stress that Moscow had ceased its arms shipments to Nicaragua.

And the Soviets have pressed for international supervision of Central America's conflict by such organizations as the United Nations and Organization of American States. Even before the US invasion of Panama in December 1989, Moscow was expressing deepening concern about escalated tensions in the region—notably in El Salvador.[91]

Moscow applauded the 1989 Central American presidents' summit, citing Central America's leaders as "creating favorable possibilities for an acceleration of the process of national reconciliation in Nicaragua and normalization of the situation in the region as a whole."[92] Gorbachev's team used the political momentum created by the Central American presidents' summit to argue that normalization of relations between Washington and Havana and Washington and Managua would be in the US national interests as it would stimulate conditions for greater regional stability.[93]

Moscow's support for peaceful political solutions in Central America may lead to increased pressure on Cuba, Managua, and Washington to craft a Central American version of national reconciliation and regional stability. Indeed, in his visit to Nicaragua in October 1989, the first by any top ranking Soviet official, Soviet Foreign Minister Eduard Shevardnadze proposed that the United States and USSR jointly guarantee peace and security in Central America and called for a "permanent mechanism" to cut armed forces and weapons supplies to the region to the minimum necessary for self-defense.[94]

Gorbachev's new approach has helped alter the political environment in Latin America as elsewhere. Soviet policies toward Cuba and Nicaragua make it clear that new revolutionary regimes will be on their own economically in terms of generating a viable economic order. To be sure, Gorbachev has extended enormously high levels of military aid to guarantee the survivability of the Sandinistas. He has not, however, provided needed food supplies to upgrade living conditions in Nicaragua, has not extended badly needed levels of economic aid, nor provided technical assistance on the scale required for sustained economic growth. Moscow's new leader has firmly impressed on would-be revolutionaries that they can expect little in the way of economic assistance from the USSR, whose own priority is economic rebirth inside the USSR.

While the US invasion of Panama to oust General Manuel Noriega from power and install that country's democratically elected government produced sharp Soviet criticism in December 1989, Moscow made it clear that the US action would not undermine its efforts to improve relations with Washington. Following the January 1990 voluntary surrender by General Noriega to the American troops surrounding the Papal Nunciature where Panama's dictator had sought refuge, Moscow continued its criticism of Washington for regarding the countries of Latin America as ". . . its backyard . . . imposing its orders on them by fire and sword."[95] But compared to Moscow's characterization of the 1983 US intervention in Grenada—when US action was described in hostile terminology—Soviet treatment of the Panama invasion was restrained. In October 1983, for example, Moscow "condemned" US intervention in Grenada; in December 1989 the Soviets "urged" the US administration to ". . . stop its intervention against sovereign Panama."[96] Havana, in sharp contrast, offered to "give their own blood and their own life, if necessary, for the just cause of the Panamanian people."[97]

NOTES

1. See Moscow TASS in English, April 5, 1989; Foreign Broadcast Information Service's *Daily Report: Latin America* (Washington, DC—hereafter FBIS-LAM), April 5, 1989, pp. 49–50.

2. On the arrest of General Arnaldo Ochoa Sanchez and eight others, see *The Washington Post,* June 17, 1989. Subsequent issues of *The Washington Post* covered the trial and execution of Ochoa and others.

3. See Ambassador Dubinin's call at the US State Department to present a Soviet Foreign Ministry statement on the meeting of the five Central American presidents—backing their peace efforts. *The Washington Post,* March 3, 1989.

4. See Gorbachev's letter to President Bush in which the Soviet leader stated that Moscow had ceased weapons transfers to Managua. See *The Washington Post,* May 16, 1989. On Soviet support for the Central American peace plan endorsed by the five Central American presidents, and strongly backed by Soviet Ambassador to the United States, Yuri Dubinin, see *The Washington Post,* March 3, 1989.

5. US Department of State and Department of Defense, *The Soviet-Cuban Connection in Central America and the Caribbean,* March 1985, p. 3.

6. Latin America's geographic location undoubtedly has reinforced US perceptions of threatening Soviet penetration—more so than in far away Africa and the Middle East. Civil wars close to a great power's borders—as in Central America next to the United States—have been a traditional security factor in post–World War II international politics. In this respect Central America has been to the United States what Afghanistan has been to the USSR.

7. Cole Blasier, *The Giant's Rival: The USSR and Latin America* (Pittsburgh: University of Pittsburgh Press, 1987), p. 64.

8. For background reading on this point, see *ibid.,* Chapter 3.

9. On the cultural and political roots to Latin American factionalism, see John P. Gillin, "Some Signposts for Policy," in Adams, *et al., Social Change in Latin America Today* Ch. 1; also Francisco Jose Moreno and Barbara Mitrani, *Conflict and Violence in Latin American Politics* (New York: Thomas Y. Crowell Company, Inc., 1971).

10. On Soviet perceptions of national liberation movements since Khrushchev, see Galia Golan, "Moscow and Third World National Liberation Movements," *Journal of International Affairs* 90, No. 2 (Winter/Spring 1987), pp. 303–323.

11. For coverage of Cuba's Third Party Congress, see daily entries for February 3–12, 1986, in FBIS-LAM and *Daily Report: Soviet Union* (Washington, D.C.—hereafter FBIS-SOV).

12. Coverage of these trips may be found in FBIS-SOV and FBIS-LAM, October 1986.

13. See FBIS-LAM and FBIS-SOV, March 1987.

14. FBIS-LAM, FBIS-SOV, September-October 1987.

15. *Ibid.*

16. Moscow *Pravda* in Russian, March 23, 1988, FBIS-SOV, March 23, 1988, p. 52.

17. See FBIS-SOV, October 1986.

18. *The Washington Post,* March 3, 1989.

19. *Ibid.*

20. For coverage of the visit, see FBIS-LAM, April 4–7, 1989.

21. See W. Raymond Duncan, *The Soviet Union and Cuba: Interests and Influence* (New York: Praeger, 1985), Ch. 6.

22. See FBIS-LAM, May 1985.

23. FBIS-SOV, October 1985.

24. FBIS-LAM, February 27, 1986.

25. United States Information Agency, Radio Marti Program, *Cuba-Quarterly Situation Report* Fourth Quarter, 1988, Washington, D.C., p. II–1.

26. Radio Marti Program, Fourth Quarter Situation Report, 1988.

27. Castro's speech to a special session of the National Assembly of the People's Government to introduce General Secretary Mikhail Gorbachev, Havana Cubavision in Spanish, April 5, 1989; FBIS-LAM, April 5, 1989, pp. 3–7.

28. Gorbachev's speech to deputies of the National Assembly, Moscow TASS in Russian, April 5, 1989; FBIS-SOV, April 5, 1989, pp. 42–48.

29. *Granma Weekly Review,* October 15, 1989, p. 9.

30. FBIS-SOV, October 6, 1989, p. 35.

31. Castro Interview with NBC Reporter Shriver, Havana Television Service in Spanish, February 28, 1988, FBIS-LAM, March 3, 1988.

32. The Soviet Union probably is aware in some detail of Castro's clandestine activities in Central and South America, given Soviet close connections with Cuba's intelligence services. See Leon Goure, "Soviet-Cuban Military Relations," in Irving Louis Horowitz, ed., *Cuban Communism* (New Brunswick and Oxford: Transaction Books, 1988), Ch. 32.

33. See Cuba-Quarterly Situation Reports for 1988, Radio Marti Program.

34. Castro's rectification comes at a time when Cuba's sagging economy, mismanagement, absenteeism, food lines, black market, and distinct lack of consumer goods hardly make it a model of socialist efficiency. Among Cuba's economic difficulties are widespread unemployment and growing alienation among Cuba's youth and an acute housing shortage, which government officials have tried to solve through construction microbrigades incorporating unemployed youth. Julia Preston, "Even Castro Has Problems With His Children," *The Washington Post National Weekly Edition,* January 30-February 5, 1989, p. 18. A high-ranking Cuban defector, Major Florentino Azpillaga, officer in Cuba's Direccion General de Intelligencia (DGI), reported in 1987 that Cuba's housing shortage affects both ordinary workers and government officials. Major Azpillaga reported corruption, privilege, waste, and even opposition to Fidel Castro's centralized control—other facets of Cuba's economic difficulties. *Third Quarterly Situation Report,* Radio Marti Program, pp. 1–2.

35. "An Uphill Task," *New Times,* No. 33 (August 1987), pp. 16–17.

36. See *New Times,* No. 41 (October 19, 1987), pp. 16–17.

37. *The New York Times,* March 16, 1988.

38. *Fourth Quarterly Report,* 1988, Radio Marti Program, pp. II, 3–12.

39. *Fourth Quarterly Report,* 1988, pp. II, 3–12.

40. *Fourth Quarterly Report,* 1988, pp. II-7.

41. *Cuban Bank Report,* Havana, January 1988.

42. Jorge Casteneda, "Glasnost in Havana," *Los Angeles Times,* December 16, 1987, pp. II–13.

43. Casteneda, "Glasnost in Havana."

44. Casteneda, "Glasnost in Havana."

45. *The New York Times*, January 11, 1989.

46. *The Washington Post*, January 1, 1989.

47. *The Washington Post*, January 1, 1989.

48. Havana International Service, December 5, 1988, FBIS-LAM, December 12, 1988, p. 3.

49. *The New York Times*, January 11, 1988.

50. *Ibid.*

51. *The New York Times*, October 4, 1987.

52. Castro Interview with Bucaranda in Caracas, Venezuela, February 10, 1989, in FBIS-LAM, February 17, 1989, pp. 1–14.

53. Shriver Interview, Havana Television Service in Spanish, February 28, 1988, in FBIS-LAM, March 3, 1988, p. 13.

54. *Ibid.*, p. 13.

55. *The Washington Post*, April 4, 1989.

56. See Gorbachev's speech to deputies of the National Assembly, previously cited.

57. See Text of Soviet-Cuban Treaty of Friendship, previously cited.

58. Castro's remarks introducing Gorbachev to the National Assembly, previously cited, p. 3.

59. *The Washington Post*, April 5, 1989.

60. See Castro's remarks introducing Gorbachev to the National Assembly.

61. See *The Washington Post*, April 5, 1989.

62. *Ibid.*

63. In an interview with Nikolay Shmelev, economist and USSR People's Deputy in June 1989, Shmelev stated: "Why should we pay 400 percent of the world price for Cuban sugar? Just 100 percent is enough and the same applies, for instance, to Cuban nickel, for which we pay 1,000 percent." Turin *La Stampa* in Italian, June 20, 1989, p. 10; in FBIS-SOV, July 6, 1989, p. 3. Another Soviet economist, B. Sergeyev, argued that "A majority of the recipients of Soviet aid are experiencing serious economic difficulties. . . . Thus every ruble that is granted in aid is dearer for us. . . . It is necessary to abandon hidden forms of subsidization in foreign economic relations. . . ." See Moscow *Argumenty i Fakty* in Russian, No. 27, July 8–14, 1989, p. 2; FBIS-SOV, July 19, 1989, pp. 10–11.

64. In the worst shake-up of the Revolution, four high-ranking officers were sentenced to death by firing squad, including a Cuban war hero, General Arnaloo Ochoa Sanchez. See coverage in *The Washington Post* and *The New York Times*, June 17, 1989 ff.

65. *The Washington Post*, July 19, 1989.

66. Translation by The Cuban-American Foundation, Washington, DC, July 26, 1989.

67. *Ibid.*

68. *Ibid.*

69. FBIS-LAM, December 8, 1989, p. 5.

70. *Ibid.*

71. Moscow TASS in English, November 15, 1989.

72. *Paris Le Monde*, November 30, 1989, p. 4.

73. *Ibid.*

74. On discussion of Nicaragua by Secretary of State Baker and Soviet Foreign Minister Shevardnadze, see *The Washington Post*, March 3, 1989. On President

Bush's pressuring Gorbachev to cease weapons transfers to Nicaragua, see the report on his letter to Gorbachev regarding this issue *The Washington Post*, March 31, 1989. Gorbachev's letter to Bush, indicating that Moscow had ceased sending weapons to Nicaragua is discussed in *The Washington Post*, May 16, 1989.

75. *Soviet Military Power* (Washington, DC: Department of Defense, 1988), p. 29.

76. U.S. Departments of State and Defense, *The Sandinista Military Build-Up: An Update*, October 1987, p. 16.

77. *Ibid.*

78. *The Washington Post*, July 24, 1988.

79. *The Christian Science Monitor*, January 23, 1989.

80. U.S. Department of Defense. *Soviet Military Power: An Assessment of the Threat 1988* (Washington, DC: U.S. Government Printing Office, 1989), p. 29.

81. *The Washington Post*, October 5, 1989.

82. *The Washington Post*, July 24, 1988.

83. *The Washington Post*, November 6, 1988.

84. *The Washington Post*, October 5 and 6, 1989, and FBIS-SOV, October 4–6, 1989.

85. Central American Presidents' News Conference, San Salvador Domestic Service, February 15, 1989, FBIS-LAM, February 16, 1989.

86. See *The Washington Post*, July 19, 1989.

87. Voytek Zubek, "Soviet 'New Thinking' and the Central American Crisis," *Journal of InterAmerican Studies and World Affairs* 29, No. 3 (Fall 1987), pp. 87–106.

88. See Castro's 26th of July 1988 speech, FBIS-LAM, July 28, 1988.

89. Castro's 26th of July 1988 speech, FBIS-LAM, July 28, 1988.

90. *The Washington Times*, December 16, 1987.

91. See TASS interview with Shevardnadze after the Malta Summit, TASS International Service in English, December 8, 1989.

92. Moscow TASS International Service in Russian, February 21, 1989.

93. *Pravda* in Russian, February 22, 1989, second edition, p. 4. Interview with V. V. Volskiy, Director of USSR Academy of Sciences, Latin American Institute.

94. *The Washington Post*, October 5, 1989.

95. TASS International Service in Russian, January 4, 1990.

96. FBIS-SOV, December 21, 1983, p. 32. See also FBIS-SOV, selected October 1983 coverage of the Grenada intervention.

97. See FBIS-AFR, December 26, 1989, p. 16.

PART FOUR

Prospects for the Future

10

CONCLUSIONS

This study will not end debate over the nature and significance of Gorbachev's policy toward the Third World. Many observers will continue to argue that Gorbachev's new thinking is tactical, that he is simply pursuing traditional Soviet objectives through more flexible policies. They will contend that, when the Soviets have strengthened their economic base, they will return to a more aggressive policy of military growth and expansionism.

We believe, however, that while Moscow's policies remain rooted in its ongoing and essential need to secure its basic national interests (physical security, economic viability, political legitimacy), new thinking represents a dramatic reorientation of Soviet strategy and objectives, generated by a shift in fundamental perceptions and assumptions. Under Gorbachev, the Soviets have redefined the components of Soviet national interest and reordered their priorities.

The change in Soviet perceptions and assumptions has generated a host of new policies and a new Soviet political lexicon (*glasnost*, *perestroika*, democratization, deideologization, interdependence, mutual security, balance of interests). In pursuit of traditional national interests, Gorbachev has sought arms control agreements and reduced military competition with the West (in order to reduce military expenditures and recapture resources for investment in the USSR's economic infrastructure). To create an environment conducive to reduced competition, he has emphasized the deideologization of Soviet foreign policy, argued that security for one can only be gained by ensuring the security of all, and stressed the need to balance the interests of all parties.

New thinking has produced radical changes within the Soviet Union itself, in East Europe, in East-West relations, in the arms control agenda, and in the Third World. The ramifications and implications of the Soviet revolution remain uncertain as does the future of Gorbachev himself. It is clear, however, that Gorbachev and new thinking have permanently altered the international environment.

This chapter will try to draw conclusions about the impact of new thinking on the Third World. It will address the significance of Gorbachev's new assumptions and objectives as well as the nature of the policies currently being pursued by Moscow in the Third World. It will assess the successes and failures of Moscow's policies to date and examine the continuing opportunities and impediments to those policies. Finally, it will project several alternate scenarios, focusing on the prospects for the continuation of new thinking.

SOVIET GOALS AND ASSUMPTIONS

Economic restructuring and growth have replaced the drive to achieve military parity (or superiority) with the United States as the primary goal of Soviet policy. This fundamental shift occurred because the leadership had come to believe that Soviet national interests were no longer being served by "old thinking." Rather, they recognized that those interests were being threatened by a deteriorating economy and an inability to participate and compete successfully in the international economic community. This new perception of reality invalidated previous assumptions about the Soviet political and economic system.

Gorbachev's reformulation of the USSR's Third World agenda is not his own creation. It draws on progressive Soviet academic thought of the past 30 years that cautioned against an overzealous approach to the exceedingly complex Third World setting. Gorbachev's predecessors (Brezhnev and Andropov) already had endorsed many of these views. What is new, however, is that this revisionist thinking has now become policy.

Moscow's Third World policies reflect revised assumptions about the Soviet role in developing countries. In looking at what had happened to the USSR as a result of its Third World expansionism of the 1970s, Gorbachev and his advisers concluded that Moscow's aggressive military policies had undermined its fundamental security interests, stimulated the formation of rival coalitions organized to combat Soviet expansionism, and unleashed an economically detrimental and unwinnable arms race with the United States. Soviet expansionism in the Third World, they concluded, was based on a flawed perception of the USSR's state interests. A more pragmatic and deideologized approach to the Third World was required—something more in line with Soviet economic capabilities and reform objectives and less geared to notions of class struggle and military competition with the West.[1]

In adopting new thinking, the Soviets demonstrated a capacity to learn from the past. Their perception that the costs of their Third World empire outweighed the benefits included recognition that:

- Local conflicts are not easily resolved militarily.
- Soviet military intervention spawns a countervailing US military response.
- Anti-communist coalitions will resist perceived Soviet threats, requiring spiraling military expenditures that are incompatible with reforming the Soviet economic system and stimulating higher productivity at home.

- Efforts to exploit regional conflicts entangle the Soviets in local and regional turmoil and poison the atmosphere for stable East-West relations.
- Soviet policy in Third World settings cannot be separated from East-West relations, given the interdependent nature of the global economic and political system.
- Third World clients are not easily manipulated; they are driven by their own perceived interests that are often at odds with Soviet interests.
- Local and regional obstacles block the transition to progressive socialism. These include traditional cultures, ethnic conflict, underdeveloped economies, and competing local and regional rivalries.
- Third World economic development is heavily dependent on international economic institutions dominated by Western capitalist states and requires creative thinking, adaptability, and flexibility in the use of competitive market and price mechanisms.

These and other lessons from the past now permeate Gorbachev's Third World policies.

SOVIET POLICIES IN THE THIRD WORLD

The terms "retrenchment" and "retreat" have been used to describe Gorbachev's new approach to the Third World, and they have some validity. The Soviets clearly have decided that the costs of maintaining their besieged Third World empire have been too high in political, economic, and military terms. They have withdrawn their own military forces where they were engaged (Afghanistan) and put pressure on their clients (Cuba and Vietnam) to do the same. They have announced dramatic reductions in their military forces worldwide and in their military budget, and they have expressed a willingness to reduce their force projection capabilities. They are withdrawing from Cam Ranh Bay, and in January 1990 Shevardnadze told a US congressional delegation that the Soviet Union planned to withdraw all its military forces stationed in other countries.[2] They have put their clients on notice that they are no longer willing or able to foot the bill for inefficiency, mismanagement, and overextension. Finally, they have indicated that they are no longer interested in supporting communist revolution or insurgency throughout the world, both because they cannot afford it and because such support undermines their broader strategic objectives. Thus, a strong case can be made that Moscow has undertaken a broad retreat from *military* engagement in the Third World.

The Soviets have not, however, made a similar political or economic retreat from involvement in the Third World. On the contrary, their political and diplomatic initiatives with respect to Third World issues have been numerous and creative. Their efforts to engage Third World countries in cooperative economic arrangements have been energetic and persistent.

They have made it clear that they will not abandon their key Third World clients (Afghanistan, Cuba, Cambodia), and they have continued to pursue an aggressive arms sale policy as part of their overall attempt to earn hard currency and remain a relevant international actor.

Rather than retreating from the Third World, Gorbachev has tried to *redefine* the Soviet presence. He has sought to maintain established positions at lower cost and with reduced risks—and in the context of a restructured relationship with the United States and the West. In contrast to previous periods, when Soviet decision-makers believed Third World matters could be pursued apart from East-West relations and internal domestic activities, three factors—domestic reform and restructuring, East-West relations, and Third World diplomacy—are now closely interconnected in Soviet policy.

Gorbachev has reordered the priority of traditional policy instruments. Weapons transfers, security assistance, economic aid, trade, diplomacy, propaganda, and active measures are all still used by the Soviets, but the emphasis has shifted. Diplomacy and the politics of cooperation, for example, have replaced military intervention and security assistance as the preferred options in regional conflict situations. A more aggressive political and commercial approach to developed Third World countries has superseded support for national liberation movements. This approach contrasts with the Soviets' previous proclivity to try to capitalize on regional conflict situations to advance their own position and undermine that of the United States. Instead of manipulating regional conflicts to achieve a Soviet presence, the Soviets are now trying to reduce conflict and resolve tensions.

Afghanistan provides the model of the new Soviet approach to regional conflict resolution. The withdrawal of Soviet military forces from Afghanistan coupled with a campaign to form a coalition government acceptable to all sides to the conflict (national reconciliation) was the heart of the policy. Moscow had to put pressure on Kabul to acquiesce, and it did so effectively. The Soviets also began to talk to other parties to the conflict (e.g., the mujahedin) as they tried to negotiate a coalition government. Moscow wanted the United Nations (or another international body) to participate and to provide a mediating service, a monitoring force, and legitimacy to the process. Finally, dialogue and cooperation with the United States were pursued, both to help insure the success of the venture and to create a better overall environment for superpower negotiations.

This pattern has been replicated elsewhere in the Third World, notably in Cambodia and Angola. In those cases, it was the forces of Vietnam and Cuba which had to be withdrawn, and Moscow had to put pressure on Hanoi and Havana as well as Phnom Penh and Luanda in order to achieve its objectives. In Southeast Asia, the Soviets had the cooperation of the ASEAN states and China in creating an international conference to discuss a settlement. In Southwest Africa, they signed on to the quadripartite talks involving the United States and South Africa. Moscow was not a primary participant in either of these proceedings, but there is no doubt that its decision to cooperate and the pressure it put on its clients to acquiesce were crucial to the progress made in both cases.

Other regional conflict situations do not fit quite so neatly into the Afghan model, but the basic elements discussed above are employed by Moscow where appropriate. In the Middle East, the Soviets support an international conference to resolve the Arab-Israeli conflict. They have encouraged the PLO in its move toward moderation and have put pressure on Syria to be more forthcoming. They have upgraded their dialogue with Israel and expanded formal contacts, and they have urged an approach which takes into account the interests of both sides of the conflict.

In Africa, Moscow has encouraged Mengistu to pursue a negotiated settlement to the Ethiopian civil war and even publicly endorsed the Ethiopian talks with the Eritrean insurgents sponsored by former President Jimmy Carter in Atlanta in 1989. Moscow has urged the ANC to pursue a political approach in South Africa, and has opened a dialogue with Pretoria.

Gorbachev has not reduced Soviet economic involvement in the Third World although the emphasis of policy has changed. The Soviets are no longer pushing socialist models of development, arguing instead that Third World states must achieve economic efficiency and making it clear that Soviet clients will be increasingly on their own in pursuing economic development. The Soviets have intensified efforts to expand commercial relations with the more industrialized Third World states.

The Soviets have continued to provide economic assistance to their Third World friends. Soviet credit extensions in 1988 rose dramatically, largely as the result of long-term credit extended to India for its nuclear power plants and aid to Afghanistan and Nicaragua. This fact suggests that Moscow continues, to the extent possible, to sustain its economic commitment both to crucial Third World allies such as India and to its beleaguered clients. At the same time, it is aggressively pursuing infusions of capital from economically strong Third World states such as South Korea and Kuwait as it seeks to broaden its own economic base.

The Soviets also have continued their policy of selling arms to Third World states, even when such sales appear to undermine their broader agenda. Delivery of the SA-5 anti-missile system and MIG-29 fighter planes to Libya and the reported delivery of MIG-29s to Cuba in late 1989 drew a strong negative reaction from the United States. Similarly, continuing East Bloc military assistance to Nicaragua has created tension in Soviet-American relations in spite of Soviet assurances that the USSR itself has stopped direct deliveries. Soviet arms deliveries to Afghanistan and Cambodia increased after the withdrawal of Soviet and Vietnamese troops. And Moscow has indicated that it will sell arms to Iran even though this will create problems in its relations with both Iraq and Saudi Arabia. The Soviets presumably are reluctant to relinquish their share of the world arms market because these sales still earn considerable hard currency, because such sales remain their most successful means of improving bilateral relations with Third World states, and because they do not want to risk losing their relevance and credibility in the Third World.

Moscow's continuing effort to sell sophisticated weapons and commercial aircraft was graphically demonstrated at the Paris Air Show in June 1989.[3] There the Soviets displayed their SU-27 long-range interceptor, SU-25 close air support aircraft, and, for the first time in the West, displayed their MI-28 attack helicopter.[4] A solid hard currency earner, the MIG-29 fighter aircraft showed up in Third World inventories before being distributed in Eastern Europe.

In competing with the West for arms sales to Third World countries, Moscow will probably increase its efforts to sell sophisticated weapons, making commercially aggressive offers in this arena where it enjoys less lead time in making actual weapons transfers compared to the United States. Although the Soviet Union registered a substantial decrease in its share of Third World arms transfer agreements during 1987–1988—falling from 50.3 percent in 1987 to 33.4 percent in 1988 ($19.4 billion in 1987 to $9.9 billion in 1988), throughout the 1980s the Soviets sustained a consistently high level of arms transfers to the Third World.[5]

Gorbachev has infused his policies with a new political energy and attention to diplomacy not at work in previous eras. The General Secretary—using the skill and expertise of professionals at research institutes and newly appointed staff members familiar with Western Europe and the United States—has launched remarkable efforts in diplomacy: (1) energetically pursuing politically negotiated national reconciliation agreements in Afghanistan, Angola, Cambodia, Ethiopia, and Nicaragua; (2) participating constructively in efforts to mediate regional conflicts (the Iran-Iraq war, the Lebanese quagmire, and the Arab-Israeli conflict); (3) pursuing innovative policies with previously black-listed countries, such as Israel, South Korea, and South Africa; (4) sending high-level teams to expand political and economic ties to Latin America's industrializing giants, such as Mexico, Argentina, and Brazil; and (5) encouraging Soviet academics and institutes to engage in greater cooperation with Western counterparts through joint research projects, seminars, symposiums, and conferences.

The new diplomatic look consists of:

- *Flexibility.* Moscow has urged old clients, such as Cuba, Vietnam, and the PLO to pursue new openings in relations with regional adversaries. It has changed course when old policies failed to reflect regional trends—as in its shift from a positive to a neutral approach with respect to Panama's fraudulent elections in 1989 when it became clear the Organization of American States (OAS) was critical of Panama's notorious strong man, General Manuel Noriega.
- *Sophisticated attention to the complexities of negotiation.* This has been well demonstrated by First Deputy Foreign Minister Vorontsov as he pursued a solution in Afghanistan, by Deputy Foreign Minister Anatoliy Adamishin in his work with the quadripartite negotiations

on Angola/Namibia; and by numerous Soviet officials in their support for a peaceful settlement in Cambodia, resolution of the Iran-Iraq and Arab-Israeli conflicts, and a cease-fire in Lebanon.

- *Comprehensive orchestration of multiple instruments of policy.* Moscow has skillfully combined diplomatic negotiations in regional conflicts, calls for national reconciliation in such countries as Afghanistan, Angola, Ethiopia, and Nicaragua; promotion of academic forums; invitations to foreign journalists; greater concentration on the use of the United Nations to enhance Moscow's position with respect to regional conflicts and national reconciliation; and working for closer cooperation with the United States in managing regional conflict.
- *Energized diplomacy.* Moscow has sent a steady stream of high-level delegations to Third World countries since Gorbachev's assumption of power as General Secretary. Both Gorbachev and Foreign Minister Shevardnadze have traveled extensively, with Gorbachev making dramatic visits to Cuba in April 1989 and China in May 1989.
- *New style of Soviet ambassadors.* Soviet ambassadors to important posts now tend to be experts in their fields. Valeriy Nikolayenko, appointed Ambassador to Nicaragua in November 1988, brought *glasnost* to Nicaragua; he speaks fluent Spanish and English, conducts his diplomacy with less secrecy, and quickly made open and clear that the USSR had no intention of placing a military base in Nicaragua or anywhere else in Central America.

SUCCESSES TO DATE

Gorbachev's "new political thinking" has produced a number of Soviet foreign policy successes—all keyed to maintaining its support for and position with old clients but at lower cost and risk and under conditions that permit improved relations with the West. These include:

- Afghanistan: Moscow has negotiated its military withdrawal from Afghanistan and started the process of national reconciliation there without abandoning support for the PDPA regime of Najibullah. Thus the Soviets have altered their image as an "interventionist" power, an enemy of Islam, and a perpetrator of Communist expanionism in the Third World—without suffering the widely predicted "Vietnam-type" setback.
- Angola: Moscow played an important role in the quadripartite negotiations leading to the withdrawal of Cuban troops from Angola, independence for Namibia, and the opening for national reconciliation between the Angola's MPLA and UNITA. Moscow successfully pressed Luanda and Havana to settle with South Africa during this process of negotiation.

- Cambodia: The Soviets stimulated the search for a more stable Southeast Asia and for better relations with China by pressing Vietnam and Cambodia to accept Vietnamese withdrawal from Cambodia and to adopt a policy of national reconciliation.
- Middle East: The Soviets have helped shift the regional political balance in favor of the moderates, assisting PLO leader Yasir Arafat to pursue a course of negotiation and contributing to the acceptance of Egypt back into the Arab world.
- Iran-Iraq: Moscow maneuvered skillfully during the war and has been accepted as a postwar mediator by both countries.
- Ethiopia: The Soviets have urged Ethiopia's Mengistu Haile Mariam to settle his long-standing conflict with the Tigrean and Eritrean national liberation movements peacefully rather than with force.
- Holding the line on aid to clients such as Cuba and Vietnam: The Soviets have stabilized aid to Cuba since 1985. Given Cuba's rising needs, it could be argued that Soviet assistance, relative to its client's requirements, has declined.
- Reducing the economic burden placed on it by poor clients, e.g., Angola, Ethiopia, Mozambique, and Nicaragua: Moscow has encouraged political stability through national reconciliation and the encouragement of trade ties with the West.
- Setting up diplomatic initiatives leading to new relations with major regional actors, such as Israel, Saudi Arabia, South Korea, and South Africa, thus widening diplomatic options in regional settings.
- Improving Moscow's image in the West and United States by joining in cooperative problem-solving, thereby becoming a more credible actor in the international system.
- Reducing East-West and East-East tensions (Sino-Soviet) thereby creating an atmosphere conducive to reductions in Soviet defense spending, reallocation of capital investment to the civilian sector, and access to Western trade and technology.

The success of Soviet policy with respect to its beleaguered clients has been surprising—probably even to Moscow. The Soviets decided to cut their losses in these areas, to pull their own and their clients' military forces out and to seek compromise solutions. They almost certainly expected the Kabul regime to fall and may not have been particularly optimistic about the regime in Cambodia. These regimes remain in power, albeit tenuously, as does the MPLA in Angola. These governments have improved their international legitimacy, are looking to the West for help in economic reconstruction and, in some cases, may be stronger than they were in the early 1980s.

Angola is a case in point; the negotiated settlement with South Africa reduced the security threat to the Luanda regime. The PDPA has held on in Afghanistan, and the onus for continued conflict appears to be increasingly borne by the US-backed mujahedin. In Central America, the US-backed contras have become weaker and, in Cambodia, the Soviet-Vietnamese backed regime of Hun Sen is beginning to emerge as a viable and acceptable option in the eyes of the international community.

By changing the character of its own behavior in the Third World, Moscow also has altered the regional environment and affected US behavior. The United States has become more willing to deal with some communist groups, such as the MPLA. In Afghanistan, the United States faces a more complicated situation because it is supporting an anti-regime insurgency that is itself divided and increasingly appears ineffective. New thinking has pushed the United States toward political negotiations in regional settings, often in a forum urged by Moscow.

IMPEDIMENTS TO "NEW THINKING" IN THIRD WORLD SETTINGS

There remain major impediments to the continued success of new thinking. There are dramatic forces at work inside the USSR itself as well in the Third World, where turbulent political and social settings, interethnic rivalries, infighting among country leaders, religious rivalries, interstate conflict and developmental strains so often lead to violent forms of problem-solving. As in the past, a Soviet presence is no guarantee to long-term regional influence in Third World settings, where internal forces so quickly produce unexpected events.

A major limit to Soviet influence in the Third World is the USSR's own internal economic and political problems. Moscow's monumental domestic difficulties severely limit its ability to provide the assistance sought by Third World countries so desperately in need of both material support and workable models of development. The months and years ahead inside the Soviet Union will find Gorbachev and/or his successors with extremely difficult and complex situations. The food situation is likely to grow worse, the economy will weaken before it improves, inflation may increase and unemployment rise to extremely serious levels. The lack of a reforming majority in the Soviet government will make matters worse, as will the lack of a clear blueprint for fundamental reform of the economy. Ethnic and national tensions within the USSR will put severe pressure on Moscow and further undermine the prospects of economic progress.

As internal economic and political pressures mount, Gorbachev will face rising demands for greater popular control over foreign economic aid programs and may meet increasing resistance to servicing external client needs. The dilemma arises from the fact that the USSR has its own pressing demands that must be met if it is to achieve economic growth and safeguard internal stability during a period of rising popular discontent; why should the USSR give aid to the Third World when it is itself in such economic distress? Public questions to this effect already have surfaced in the Soviet Union.

The fora for expressing displeasure with Soviet foreign economic aid programs have been academic journals and the new Soviet Congress of People's Deputies. In June 1989 a prominent economist, Nikolay Shmelyov, told the Congress of People's Deputies that it was imperative to launch immediate measures to bring down the budget deficit; among these measures he included a drastic reduction of aid to Cuba and other Latin American countries.[6] In July 1989, Shmelyov indicated that one of the ways to reduce the budget is to "stop overpaying allies such as Cuba for raw materials such as sugar."[7] And in July 1989, Soviet economist B. Sergeyev wrote in the Soviet journal, *Argumenty i Fakty* (Arguments and Facts) that:

> . . . every ruble granted in aid is dearer for us [than for the US]. . . . In forming a new mechanism of cooperation with developing countries, it . . . should take the following form: —aid programs, their purposes, and the specific recipients should be examined and approved by the Supreme Soviet, taking into account capabilities, necessity, and specific results; —it is necessary to abandon hidden forms of subsidization in foreign economic relations and to differentiate strictly between aid and commercial activity.[8]

In December 1989 the same journal printed a response to a question concerning the difficulties to the Soviet economy created by foreign economic assistance—in this case, to India. In a less than enthusiastic explanation, the commentator stated that the USSR receives interest of only 2.5 percent, less than that charged by the United States, and that India repays in consumer products.

As the USSR is beset by uneasiness and uncertainty over the future of reforms, Gorbachev will have to struggle against those opposed to change. In a process of experimenting with free market forces in what remains a controlled economy, opponents of reform are likely to exploit popular dissatisfaction with declining living standards, unemployment, and rising prices; such criticism will make further substantive change—such as price deregulation and removal of subsidies—difficult. Gorbachev's Third World economic relations, already under popular attack in some quarters, could suffer even more from Soviet hardliners, who, in seeking to undermine Gorbachev, could further delay economic progress and force the country into increased political turmoil.

The image of a Soviet Union in economic decline has not been lost on Moscow's Third World clients. Fidel Castro, whose communist Cuba receives over fifty percent of all Soviet aid extended to communist and non-communist Third World countries, is acutely aware of Gorbachev's difficulties. In a pointed reference to Moscow's declining economic and political power, Castro voiced his deep concern that Cuba faced a bleak future of potential decline in Soviet aid so critical for Cuba's survival. In his July 26, 1989, Moncada Anniversary Speech, Castro stated:

> . . . We are living in a time of great economic problems in the world, above all the Third World, of great debts, of great economic crises for this world.

> We are living at a special juncture within the world revolutionary movement. Let's not be squeamish; we must call a spade a spade. There are difficulties in the world revolutionary movement. There are difficulties in the socialist movement. We cannot even say with certainty that the supplies that have been arriving with clockwork punctuality from the socialist camp for thirty years will keep arriving with the same certainty.[9]

And in a reference to Gorbachev's internal problems, Castro said:

> . . . The problems of the Soviet Union are something of extreme concern to all Third World countries, to former colonies, to all those people who do not want to be colonized again; because in the USSR they found their fundamental and firmest ally.[10]

Finally, Castro noted:

> . . . if we were to wake up either tomorrow or any other day to the news that a great civil conflict had arisen in the USSR, or even if we were to wake up to the news that the USSR had disintegrated, which naturally we hope will never happen, even under those circumstances, Cuba and the Cuban Revolution would continue to struggle and to resist.[11]

Fidel Castro's pessimistic observations illustrate how Moscow's Third World clients view the USSR at the outset of the 1990s. In contrast to the 1970s, when the Soviet Union seemed determined to assist Third World countries along socialist paths of development and appeared capable of doing so, the image of the 1990s is of a USSR in turmoil—less able to assist socialist Third World countries and groping for its own type of market system. Change in Third World perceptions of the USSR in turn has led some of these countries to change policies. Syria has moved to improve relations with Egypt and South Yemen with North Yemen as they adjust to Moscow's declining commitment to their interests. Mozambique began to shift away from the USSR and its allies, reducing the number of Soviet-bloc military advisers and seeking closer ties to Western countries, including the United States and Great Britain. In its draft program outlining development directions, announced in July 1989, Mozambique's ruling party eliminated or toned down all references to Marxism-Leninism as its guiding ideology.[12]

Regional and Local Obstacles to Influence

Beyond the issue of Soviet capabilities in assisting its socialist clients, another range of impediments center on the application of Gorbachev's new thinking to local and regional Third World settings. Local and regional pressures may cause regional conflicts to flare up or explode despite Soviet efforts to help contain them politically. Soviet efforts to move the Middle East negotiating process forward have helped strengthen moderate Arab forces; as frustration with lack of movement toward a solution builds, however, this situation easily could disintegrate.

In addition there are no guarantees that politically negotiated settlements will stay in place after they are signed. Either the contracting parties or outside parties, perceiving their interests threatened for one reason or another, may act in ways to disrupt the agreement. The Angola-Namibia agreement of December 1988, was nearly derailed, for example, in early April 1989 when Angola-based SWAPO guerrillas crossed into Namibia to launch attacks and when South Africa accused UN forces of a pro-SWAPO bias in the agreement reached on getting the Namibia peace plan back on schedule after the incursions.[13] Another aspect of negotiated agreement break-downs in the independence plan for Namibia is the crisis over alleged voter intimidation by South African–led counterinsurgency forces in northern tribal areas. A major showdown between UN forces and Pretoria in terms of controlling the election process opened up the possibility that Cuban troops might remain in Angola.[14]

Moscow's control over national liberation groups remains limited. The PLO and its contending factions will determine their own future course of action. Soviet stress on moderation is not palatable for all members of the African National Congress, and should Pretoria not open more avenues for peaceful negotiations, such elements may exert more persuasive influence on ANC policy.

There are limits to the concessions the USSR will grant or be able to grant in its pursuit of political settlements to regional conflicts. While Moscow has expressed support for national reconciliation, it also has provided the support necessary for its clients to sustain themselves in power. At some point, the Soviets may have to make a choice between a client and the implementation of new thinking.

Soviet-American cooperation in regional conflict management also faces numerous obstacles. There are opponents to such cooperation in both the USSR and US who will exert influence in future negotiations—through the executive and congressional branches of government in the United States and in the USSR's new Soviet Congress of People's Deputies. Other impediments range from the complexities of agreeing to rules of behavior in the Third World under superpower competitive conditions, to problems of misperception and miscommunication, to complications arising from intelligence activities (such as the alleged KGB activity in the US State Department in the Felix Bloch case during the summer of 1989).

Actions of third parties (Israel and the PLO in the Middle East, Cuba in Latin America, China or Vietnam in Southeast Asia) further complicate the process of conflict management. Israel's refusal to negotiate with the PLO, Cuba's export of revolution in Central America, and Ethiopia's response to insurgent pressures are all variables uncontrolled by either Moscow or Washington. Because regional conflicts stem from their own internal forces and are reinforced by other regional actors (as in Iraq's sudden entry into the Lebanese situation in 1989) managing such conflicts through superpower cooperation is only one part of the peace equation.

ALTERNATE FUTURE SCENARIOS

There are numerous potential scenarios for Soviet policy toward the Third World in the decade of the 1990s and a multitude of variations within each. We will address several broad possibilities. The first is for a continuation of Moscow's current policy approach; this assumes the Soviets will persist in their redefinition of their presence in the Third World, trying to retain their positions but at reduced cost and risk. Given this assumption, Moscow would continue to assist its key strategically located clients, such as Cuba, Vietnam, Syria, Angola, and Ethiopia, but will gradually seek to lower the level of such aid and push these countries toward peaceful resolution of the internal and regional problems that are draining their resources.

Where regional conflict prevails—as in Central America, South Asia, the Middle East, sub-Saharan Africa, and Southeast Asia—Soviet leaders will seek cooperation with the United States in negotiating political solutions and working toward peaceful forms of conflict management. They will continue to emphasize diplomacy, using the United Nations and other forms of international cooperative behavior. Such activity will remain a key element of Soviet foreign policy, both because it promises some solutions and because it is so closely connected to East-West cooperation and sought-after Western aid, trade, and technology.

At the same time Gorbachev or his successors will continue trying to expand commercial relations with the industrialized Third World, including sales of sophisticated weapons systems, while building bridges at the political and cultural levels. These efforts will be made difficult by the lack of attractive Soviet goods to market in the Third World, but Moscow will explore various avenues, including joint ventures and barter arrangements.

A second scenario derives from the prospect of a Soviet Union in such political and economic turmoil that its leaders decide it can no longer afford to support its allies and cut its aid back sharply. Should those Soviet economists who are voicing their opinions in the new Soviet Congress of People's Deputies become more influential or should their views find broader acceptance, a sharp Soviet decline in the annual $4–5 billion sent by Moscow to Cuba and the approximately $2 billion sent to Vietnam could occur. Such action could result from mounting Soviet unemployment, shortages of food and consumer goods, social tensions, labor strikes, and interethnic conflicts—factors that would encourage greater concentration on domestic problems and less on turbulent Third World affairs where benefits to Soviet policy are less discernible to People's Congress deputies. Indeed, under deteriorating economic conditions and even greater need for cooperation with the United States and the West, Gorbachev or his successors might reason that giving up positions and presence in far-flung locations, such as Cuba and Vietnam, is worth the gains in cooperative relations with the West.

Another prospect with similar results could occur if there were a rejection by Third World states of their connections with the Soviet Union. As Marxist-Leninist models fail to deliver even the minimum in decent standards of living and life in the Soviet Union itself is seen to be barely above that in the underdeveloped Third World, Third World socialist regimes could abandon their Marxist-Leninist experiments and move more sharply toward the Western world. Angola, Mozambique, and Ethiopia seem already to have embarked, in varying degrees, on such a path. Castro's July 1989 speech suggests that Havana would be the last hold out of socialist models of change. In noting the many difficulties besetting the socialist world—in the USSR, Poland, Hungary, and other East European countries—Castro stated, "Cuba stands firm, Cuba is valiant, Cuba is heroic, Cuba neither surrenders nor sells out."[15]

The third, and probably least likely, scenario addressed here entails a reversal of current Soviet policy trends and a return to the approach of the Brezhnev era. Such a shift presumes the replacement of Gorbachev by those who believe current policies have undermined the Marxist-Leninist underpinnings of the Soviet state and have dangerously weakened Moscow's legitimacy and credibility (both domestically and internationally).

A return to an emphasis on military strength (parity if not superiority with the United States), a determination to reimpose Soviet control over Eastern Europe, and an effort to again expand the USSR's presence and role in the Third World would require enormous repression and put tremendous pressure on the Soviet Union's economic and political structure. The difficulty of putting the genie back in the bottle (as in China) and the derivative costs of such an undertaking make it highly unlikely that the USSR would have the political and economic capability to simultaneously pursue costly Third World venture.

Soviet–Third World relations in the 1990s seem most likely to consist of a blend of the first two scenarios discussed above. Gorbachev and/or his successors will try to maintain established positions while being pressed by internal critics who believe domestic priorities should take precedence over unhappy clients who want more aid.

The question of Gorbachev's survival in power is certainly relevant, given his obvious predilections and his demonstrated political capabilities. Questions of his success in improving the standard of living in the USSR (unlikely for the foreseeable future) and in containing and channeling the political forces that have been unleashed are also relevant. But Gorbachev's foreign policies, particularly in the Third World, may have such wide support that they would survive his replacement. In this respect the differences in the Soviet public's perception of Gorbachev's domestic and foreign policy are striking. A visitor to the Soviet Union in June 1989—Moscow, Leningrad, and Soviet Central Asia—was struck by the public's distinctly uncertain, at times, bleak, view of Gorbachev's internal reforms, offset by its optimistic opinions of his international behavior. Delighted with Gorbachev's reception in Western Europe and progress in Soviet-US relations, Soviet citizens expressed their joy over the withdrawal from Afghanistan and general satisfaction with the reduction in Moscow's commitment to far-off lands.[16]

NOTES

1. See Vyacheslav Dashishev, *Literaturnaya Gazeta,* May 18, 1988.

2. *The Washington Post,* January 19, 1990.

3. Soviet efforts to attain high sales in commercial air and aerospace industry is covered in *Aviation Weekly and Space Technology,* June 5, 1989.

4. *Aviation Weekly and Space Technology,* July 3, 1989, pp. 34 and 43; June 19, 1989, pp. 28 ff.; and June 26, 1989, pp. 44.

5. Richard F. Grimmett, *Trends in Conventional Arms Transfers to the Third World by Major Supplier, 1981–1988* (Washington, D.C.: Congressional Research Service, July 31, 1989), p. 3.

6. *The Washington Post,* June 9, 1989.

7. *The Washington Times,* July 4, 1989; see also Turin *La Stampa* in Italian, June 20, 1989, p. 10; FBIS-SOV, July 6, 1989, p. 3.

8. Moscow *Argumenty i Fakty* in Russian, No. 27, July 8–14, 1989, p. 2; FBIS-SOV, July 19, 1989.

9. See Castro's July 26, 1989 speech, Camaguey, Cuba, FBIS-LAM, July 27, 1989.

10. *Ibid.*

11. *Ibid.*

12. *The Washington Post,* July 30, 1989.

13. *The Washington Post,* April 29, 1989.

14. *The Washington Post,* June 19, 1989.

15. Castro's 26th of July speech, 1989, FBIS-LAM, July 27, 1989.

16. In reflecting on Gorbachev's foreign policy, a teacher in Alma Ata stated in June 1989 that for him *perestroika* in foreign policy meant Soviet willingness to compromise, in which he took pride for Soviet sophistication. Interview by author in Alma Ata, Kazakhstan, USSR, June 23, 1989.

APPENDIXES

APPENDIX A

Arms Transfer Agreements with the Third World, by Supplier (in millions of constant 1988 U.S. dollars)

	1981	*1982*	*1983*	*1984*	*1985*	*1986*	*1987*	*1988*
Non-Communist								
Of which:								
United States	8,175	12,685	9,655	7,473	5,391	4,195	5,757	9,222
France	2,207	8,003	1,957	7,001	1,665	1,655	3,190	3,050
United Kingdom	1,856	1,678	547	826	10,088	897	549	1,000
West Germany	2,194	1,231	664	577	197	502	704	70
Italy	493	1,412	1,363	780	1,424	598	135	250
All Other	8,424	4,225	7,199	3,416	4,556	4,985	1,926	2,500
Total non-Communist	23,349	29,235	21,385	20,074	23,321	12,831	12,261	16,092
Communist								
Of which:								
U.S.S.R.	17,718	25,592	7,921	24,081	16,867	17,325	19,387	9,920
China	3,907	1,944	967	430	1,544	1,911	4,774	1,850
All Other	6,295	2,752	3,203	1,945	4,009	4,227	2,144	1,860
Total Communist	27,921	30,287	12,091	26,456	22,421	23,463	26,305	13,630
GRAND TOTAL	51,269	59,522	33,476	46,530	45,742	36,294	38,566	29,722

Source: Richard F. Grimmett, *Trends in Conventional Arms Transfers to the Third World by Major Supplier, 1981–1988,* Congressional Research Service Report for Congress, July 31, 1989.

APPENDIX B

Arms Transfer Agreements with the Third World, by Supplier, 1981–1988 (expressed as a percent of grand total, by year)

	1981	*1982*	*1983*	*1984*	*1985*	*1986*	*1987*	*1988*
Non-Communist								
Of which:								
United States	15.95%	21.31%	28.84%	16.06%	11.79%	11.56%	14.93%	31.03%
France	4.30%	13.45%	5.85%	15.05%	3.64%	4.56%	8.27%	10.26%
United Kingdom	3.62%	2.82%	1.64%	1.77%	22.05%	2.47%	1.42%	3.36%
West Germany	4.28%	2.07%	1.98%	1.24%	.43%	1.38%	1.83%	.24%
Italy	.96%	2.37%	4.07%	1.68%	3.11%	1.65%	.35%	.84%
All Other	16.43%	7.10%	21.50%	7.34%	9.96%	13.74%	4.99%	8.41%
Total non-Communist	45.54%	49.12%	63.88%	43.14%	50.98%	35.35%	31.79%	54.14%
(Major West European)*	13.17%	20.71%	13.54%	19.74%	29.24%	10.06%	11.87%	14.70%
Communist								
Of which:								
U.S.S.R.	34.56%	43.00%	23.66%	51.75%	36.88%	47.74%	50.27%	33.38%
China	7.62%	3.27%	2.89%	.92%	3.38%	5.26%	12.38%	6.22%
All Other	12.28%	4.62%	9.57%	4.18%	8.76%	11.65%	5.56%	6.26%
Total Communist	54.46%	50.88%	36.12%	56.86%	49.02%	64.65%	68.21%	45.86%
GRAND TOTAL	100.00%	100.00%	100.00%	100.00%	100.00%	100.00%	100.00%	100.00%

*Major West European category includes France, United Kingdom, West Germany, Italy.

Source: Richard F. Grimmett, *Trends in Conventional Arms Transfers to the Third World by Major Supplier, 1981–1988,* Congressional Research Service Report for Congress, July 31, 1989.

APPENDIX C

Regional Arms Transfer Agreements, by Supplier, 1981–1988 (in millions of current U.S. dollars)

	East Asia/Pacific		*Near East/So. Asia*		*Latin America*		*Africa (Sub-Saharan)*	
	1981–84	*1985–88*	*1981–84*	*1985–88*	*1981–84*	*1985–88*	*1981–84*	*1985–88*
Non-Communist								
Of which:								
United States	5,583	6,136	24,372	15,579	1,293	1,434	454	484
France	230	240	14,630	7,160	850	1,220	490	570
United Kingdom	550	530	2,420	10,570	200	230	850	260
West Germany	820	840	2,110	470	490	10	390	70
Italy	160	130	2,210	1,660	360	220	670	230
All Other	3,690	680	12,340	10,060	1,930	1,170	1,220	1,300
Total non-Communist	11,033	8,556	58,082	45,499	5,123	4,284	4,074	2,914
(Major West European)*	1,760	1,740	21,370	19,860	1,900	1,680	2,400	1,130
Communist								
Of which:								
U.S.S.R.	7,100	11,470	39,590	31,980	6,910	8,260	9,340	8,570
China	270	550	5,340	8,980	0	0	220	120
All Other	290	270	10,280	8,880	350	1,530	670	870
Total Communist	7,660	12,290	55,210	49,840	7,260	9,790	10,230	9,560
GRAND TOTAL	18,693	20,846	113,292	95,339	12,383	14,074	14,304	12,474

*Major West European category includes France, United Kingdom, West Germany, Italy.

Source: Richard F. Grimmett, *Trends in Conventional Arms Transfers to the Third World by Major Supplier, 1981–1988,* Congressional Research Service Report for Congress, July 31, 1989.

APPENDIX D

Percentage of Each Supplier's Agreements Value by Region, 1981–1988

	East Asia/Pacific		*Near East/So. Asia*		*Latin America*		*Africa (Sub-Saharan)*		*TOTAL*	*TOTAL*
	1981–84	*1985–88*	*1981–84*	*1985–88*	*1981–84*	*1985–88*	*1981–84*	*1985–88*	*1981–84*	*1985–88*
Non-Communist										
Of which:										
United States	17.61%	25.96%	76.88%	65.92%	4.08%	6.07%	1.43%	2.05%	100.00%	100.00%
France	1.42%	2.61%	90.31%	77.91%	5.25%	13.28%	3.02%	6.20%	100.00%	100.00%
United Kingdom	13.68%	4.57%	60.20%	91.20%	4.98%	1.98%	21.14%	2.24%	100.00%	100.00%
West Germany	21.52%	60.43%	55.38%	93.81%	12.86%	.72%	10.24%	5.04%	100.00%	100.00%
Italy	4.71%	5.80%	65.00%	74.11%	10.59%	9.82%	19.71%	10.27%	100.00%	100.00%
All Other	19.24%	5.15%	64.34%	76.15%	10.06%	8.86%	6.36%	9.84%	100.00%	100.00%
Total non-Communist	14.09%	13.97%	74.17%	74.28%	6.54%	6.99%	5.20%	4.76%	100.00%	100.00%
(Major West European)*	6.42%	7.13%	77.91%	81.36%	6.93%	6.88%	8.75%	4.63%	100.00%	100.00%
Communist										
Of which:										
U.S.S.R.	11.28%	19.03%	62.90%	53.05%	10.98%	13.70%	14.84%	14.22%	100.00%	100.00%
China	4.63%	5.70%	91.60%	93.06%	.00%	.00%	3.77%	1.24%	100.00%	100.00%
All Other	2.50%	2.34%	88.70%	76.88%	3.02%	13.25%	5.78%	7.53%	100.00%	100.00%
Total Communist	9.53%	15.08%	68.70%	61.17%	9.03%	12.02%	12.73%	11.73%	100.00%	100.00%
GRAND TOTAL	11.78%	14.60%	71.40%	66.80%	7.80%	9.86%	9.01%	8.74%	100.00%	100.00%

*Major West European category includes France, United Kingdom, West Germany, Italy.

Source: Richard F. Grimmett, *Trends in Conventional Arms Transfers to the Third World by Major Supplier, 1981–1988,* Congressional Research Service Report for Congress, July 31, 1989.

APPENDIX E
Arms Deliveries to the Third World, by Supplier (in millions of constant dollars)

	1981	*1982*	*1983*	*1984*	*1985*	*1986*	*1987*	*1988*
Non-Communist								
Of which:								
United States	7,760	9,759	10,994	6,338	5,911	6,533	7,577	4,865
France	5,127	4,563	4,391	4,592	5,531	4,515	1,657	630
United Kingdom	3,258	1,931	1,584	1,346	854	950	1,605	280
West Germany	1,506	592	1,433	2,782	624	256	570	190
Italy	1,480	1,268	1,421	1,323	1,084	534	249	240
All Other	3,998	5,722	16,191	6,029	3,527	2,605	3,418	2,530
Total non-Communist	23,128	23,834	36,014	22,410	17,532	15,393	15,075	8,735
Communist								
Of which:								
U.S.S.R.	18,782	19,326	19,080	18,211	14,786	15,991	19,573	18,710
China	519	1,509	1,829	2,307	734	1,324	2,392	3,070
All Other	2,985	3,634	2,749	3,778	3,965	2,882	2,910	2,480
Total Communist	22,287	24,469	23,658	24,296	19,485	20,196	24,876	24,260
GRAND TOTAL	45,415	48,303	59,672	46,706	37,018	35,589	39,950	32,995

Source: Richard F. Grimmett, *Trends in Conventional Arms Transfers to the Third World by Major Supplier, 1981–1988,* Congressional Research Service Report for Congress, July 31, 1989.

APPENDIX F
Arms Transfer Agreements with Cuba, 1981–1988, Suppliers Compared
(in millions of current U.S. dollars)

	1981–1984	*1985–1988*	*1981–1988*
SUPPLIER:			
Soviet Union	5,770	6,050	11,820
China	0	0	0
All Other Communist	120	1,350	1,470
Total Communist	5,890	7,400	13,290
European Non-Communist	5	0	5
United States	0	0	0
All Other Non-Communist	5	0	5
Total Non-Communist	10	0	10
GRAND TOTAL	5,900	7,400	13,300

Source: Richard F. Grimmett, *Trends in Conventional Arms Transfers to the Third World by Major Supplier, 1981–1988,* Congressional Research Service Report for Congress, July 31, 1989.

APPENDIX G

Arms Deliveries to Cuba, 1981–1988, Suppliers Compared (in millions of current U.S. dollars)

	1981–1984	*1985–1988*	*1981–1988*
SUPPLIER:			
Soviet Union	5,770	6,050	11,820
China	0	0	0
All Other Communist	120	1,380	1,500
Total Communist	5,890	7,430	13,320
European Non-Communist	5	0	5
United States	0	0	0
All Other Non-Communist	5	0	5
Total Non-Communist	10	0	10
GRAND TOTAL	5,900	7,430	13,330

Source: Richard F. Grimmett, *Trends in Conventional Arms Transfers to the Third World by Major Supplier, 1981–1988,* Congressional Research Service Report for Congress, July 31, 1989.

SELECTED BIBLIOGRAPHY

Books

Allison, Roy. *The Soviet Union and the Strategy of Non-Alignment in the Third World.* Cambridge: Cambridge University Press, 1989.

Blasier, Cole. *The Giant's Rival: The USSR and Latin America.* Pittsburgh: University of Pittsburgh Press, 1987.

Golan, Galia. *The Soviet Union and National Liberation Movements in the Third World.* Boston: Unwin Hyman, 1988.

Gorbachev, Mikhail. *Perestroika: New Thinking for Our Country and the World.* New York: Harper and Row, 1987.

Hough, Jerry F. *The Struggle for the Third World: Soviet Debates and American Options.* Washington, DC: The Brookings Institution, 1986.

Katz, Mark. *Gorbachev's Military Policy in the Third World.* New York: Praeger Publishers, 1989.

Kolodziej, Edward A., and Kanet, Roger E., eds. *The Limits of Soviet Power in the Developing World.* London: The Macmillan Press, 1989.

Korbonski, Andrzej, and Fukuyama, Francis, eds. *The Soviet Union and the Third World: The Last Three Decades.* Ithaca and London: Cornell University Press, 1987.

Larkin, Bruce D. *Vital Interests: The Soviet Issue in U.S. Central American Policy.* Boulder/London: Lynne Rienner Publishers, 1988.

Lynch, Allen. *The Soviet Study of International Relations.* Cambridge: Cambridge University Press, 1989.

Maxwell, Kenneth, and Clark, Susan L. *Soviet Dilemmas in Latin America: Pragmatism or Ideology?* New York: Council on Foreign Relations, 1989.

McGregor, Charles. *The Sino-Vietnamese Relationship and the Soviet Union.* Adelphi Papers, 232 (Autumn 1988).

Menon, Rajan. *Soviet Power and the Third World.* New Haven: Yale University Press, 1986.

Mujal-Leon, Eusebio, ed. *The USSR and Latin America: A Developing Relationship.* Boston: Unwin Hyman, 1989.

Papp, Daniel S. *Soviet Policies Toward the Developing Countries During the 1980s.* Maxwell Air Force Base, Alabama: Air University Press, 1986.

Payne, Richard J. *Opportunities and Dangers of Soviet-Cuban Expansionism: Toward a Pragmatic U.S. Policy.* Albany: State University of New York Press, 1988.

Pike, Douglas. *Vietnam and the Soviet Union: Anatomy of an Alliance.* Boulder, CO: Westview Press, 1987.

Rubinstein, Alvin Z. *Moscow's Third World Strategy*. Princeton: Princeton University Press, 1988.

Saivetz, Carol R., ed. *The Soviet Union in the Third World*. Boulder, CO: Westview Press, 1989.

Shulman, Marshall D. *East-West Tensions in the Third World*. New York: W.W. Norton Co., 1986.

Shultz, Richard. *The Soviet Union and Revolutionary Warfare: Principles, Practices, and Regional Comparisons*. Stanford: Hoover Institution Press, 1988.

Staar, Richard F. *1989 Yearbook on International Communist Affairs*. Stanford: Hoover Institution Press, 1989.

Valkenier, Elizabeth Kridl. *The Soviet Union and the Third World: An Economic Bind*. New York: Praeger Special Studies, 1983.

Whelan, Joseph G. and Dixon, Michael J. *The Soviet Union in the Third World: Threat to World Peace?* Washington, DC: Pergamon-Brassey's, 1989.

Journal Articles

Adams, Jan S. "Change and Continuity in Soviet Central American Policy." *Problems of Communism* (March-June 1989), pp. 112–120.

Albright, David E. "The USSR and the Third World in the 1980s." *Problems of Communism* (March-June 1989), pp. 50–70.

Breslauer, George. "Ideology and Learning in Soviet-Third World Policy." *World Politics* (April 1987), pp. 429–448.

______. "Soviet Third World Policy," *World Politics* 39, No. 3 (April 1987), pp. 429–448.

Daley, Tad. "Afghanistan and Gorbachev's Global Foreign Policy." *Asian Survey* 29, No. 5 (May 1989), pp. 496–513.

Fukuyama, Francis. "Gorbachev and the New Soviet Agenda in the Third World." *RAND Corporation Report*, June 1989.

Golan, Galia. "Gorbachev's Middle East Strategy," *Foreign Affairs* (Fall 1987), pp. 41–57.

Gunn, Gillian. "A Guide to the Intricacies of the Angola-Namibia Negotiations." *CSIS Africa Notes*, September 8, 1988.

Kaplan, Robert D. "The Loneliest War." *The Atlantic Monthly*, July 1988.

Kuhne, Winrich. "A 1988 Update on Soviet Relations with Pretoria, the ANC, and the SACP." *CSIS Africa Notes*, September 1, 1988.

Lowenkopf, Martin. "If the Cold War is Over in Africa, Will the United States Still Care?" *CSIS Africa Notes*, May 30, 1989.

MacFarlane, S. Neil. "The Soviet Union and Southern African Security." *Problems of Communism* (March-June 1989), pp. 72–89.

Primakov, Y. "USSR Policy on Regional Conflicts." *International Affairs*, June 1988.

Snyder, Jack. "The Gorbachev Revolution: A Waning of Soviet Expansionism?" *International Security* (Winter 1987–88), pp. 93–131.

Valkenier, Elizabeth. "New Soviet Thinking About the Third World," *World Policy Journal* (Fall 1987), pp. 651–674.

Government Documents

Central Intelligence Agency. Directorate of Intelligence. *Handbook of Economic Statistics*, September 1989.

Grimmett, Richard F. "Trends in Conventional Arms Transfers to the Third World by Major Supplier, 1981–1988," *Congressional Research Service: The Library of Congress* 89-434 F, July 31, 1989.

U.S. Arms Control and Disarmament Agency, *World Military Expenditures and Arms Transfers 1988*, June 1989.

U.S. Government Printing Office. *Foreign Broadcast Information Service (FBIS)*, daily, by region.

U.S. Government Printing Office. *Joint Publications Research Service (JPRS)*. Translations of foreign periodic literature.

U.S. Information Agency. Radio Marti Program. *Cuba-Quarterly Situation Reports.*

INDEX